MW00983497

Sages, Saints, and Seers

A Breviary of Spiritual Masters

RICHARD H. SCHMIDT
ILLUSTRATED BY DEAN MOSHER

Morehouse Publishing
NEW YORK

Books by Richard H. Schmidt

Glorious Companions: Five Centuries of Anglican Spirituality
(Wm. B. Eerdmans, 2002)

Praises, Prayers & Curses: Conversations with the Psalms
(Forward Movement, 2005)

Life Lessons from Alpha to Omega
(Seabury Books, 2005)

A Gracious Rain: A Devotional Commentary on the Prayers of the Church Year
(Church Publishing, 2008)

God Seekers: Twenty Centuries of Christian Spiritualities
(Wm. B. Eerdmans, 2008)

Copyright © 2015 by Richard H. Schmidt
Illustrations copyright © Dean Mosher

Unless otherwise noted, the Scripture quotations contained herein are from the New Revised Standard Version Bible, copyright © 1989 by the Division of Christian Education of the National Council of Churches of Christ in the U.S.A. Used by permission. All rights reserved.

Morehouse Publishing, 19 East 34th Street, New York, NY 10016

Morehouse Publishing is an imprint of Church Publishing Incorporated.
www.churchpublishing.org

Cover design by Laurie Klein Westhafer

Library of Congress Cataloging-in-Publication Data

Schmidt, Richard H., 1944–
    Sages, saints, and seers : a breviary of spiritual masters / Richard H. Schmidt ; illustrated by Dean Mosher.
        pages cm
    ISBN 978-0-8192-2926-7 (pbk.) — ISBN 978-0-8192-2927-4 (ebook)
    1. Religious leaders—Biography.   I. Title.
BL72.S355   2015
200.92'2—dc23
[B]
                                                                2014047423

Printed in the United States of America

Contents

Introduction

When I was a young boy, my father said to me, "It's important to learn all you can, and the most important thing you will learn is how little you know about anything. Think of what you know as the air inside a balloon. As you learn more, the balloon expands to contain your new knowledge. As it expands, it comes in contact with more and more of what's outside it, things you do not know. So the more you know, the more you know how little you know."

Such has been my experience. My growing awareness of the diversity of spiritual traditions around the world has confirmed what my father told me many years ago. Like many young people, I once thought I knew a lot, including what was true and untrue, what was right and wrong. That was a long time ago. While I still have convictions about such things, as I have lived and learned from other people, I have come to appreciate the wisdom of understandings different from my own and become aware of things I do not and probably cannot understand. I now see life not as a problem to be solved or a question to be answered, but as a mystery to be embraced. This is especially true where ultimate things are concerned, like the nature of human life, how it should be lived, to whom or what human beings are accountable, and how that is discerned.

Throughout human history, thoughtful people have wrestled with such mysteries. The mysteries do not exist apart from the people wrestling with them and the best way to approach them is through the lives of such people. This book is therefore not about ideas and practices, but about people who embraced ideas and practices. The book's subtitle calls these people "spiritual masters." But what do the words "spiritual" and "spirituality" mean? And how are they related to "religion" and "theology"? We need some definitions.

Spirituality

I chose the title for this book, but the publisher chose the subtitle. In using the term "spiritual" in the subtitle, the publisher stepped into a region of heavy fog, but it's hard to think of another word to take its place.

I have written elsewhere and at some length about spirituality. So have a gazillion other people. Spirituality has been a hot topic in the Western world for several decades now. Bookstores devote entire aisles to it, but the titles available there are so diverse that they seem to have little in common. I've seen books on the spirituality of baseball, of sex, of the cinema, and of whole grain diets. One observer has said the term suggests "do-it-yourself" salvation and another that it "seems to be synonymous with any way of making yourself feel better." Spirituality means whatever anyone wants it to mean. It is grounded in nothing, yet people like me continue to use the term as if its meaning were clear and everyone knows what we're talking about.

The word "spirituality" derives from the Latin *spiritus*, a translation of the Greek *pneuma*, which itself is a translation of the Hebrew *ruach*. All three words refer to moving air, like breathing or the wind, suggesting an unseen power or vitality originating outside oneself. In an earlier book I wrote, "When I use the word spirituality, I refer to the search for what is truly important, valuable, and beautiful and to our relationship to it." But I later came to see that like the word "spirituality" itself, my definition lacked a focus. What of a man who thinks of his car as truly important, valuable, and beautiful? Would we call that man spiritual? I think not. So I decided a definition of spirituality should include a reference to God. But then what of Buddhism, an ancient and thriving tradition which surely everyone would regard as spiritual but where God does not figure in? I'm still trying to get a grip on the words "spiritual" and "spirituality." So at this moment (and probably until this afternoon at least), I would define spirituality as one's relationship to an unseen Other experienced as mysterious, tremendous, and alluring (those adjectives were suggested by Rudolf Otto's 1917 classic, *The Idea of the Holy* where he discusses the *numinous* as *mysterium, tremendens, et fascinans*).

The phrase "unseen Other" takes us beyond ourselves, in the direction of what the word "God" refers to, but without requiring belief in a personal deity. Virtually every culture in human history has acknowledged, often without question, the reality of an unseen Other. The one place out of step with this broad consensus of human cultures is modern, secular western Europe and those influenced by western European thought of the past three centuries. It is as if many Westerners have become deaf to a voice everyone else hears. Only among them is it fashionable or even conceivable to deny the unseen Other. This has created an empty (and many would say God-shaped) hole in the hearts of many Westerners. We know we have lost something mysterious, tremendous, and alluring; we are looking for a lost love but don't know where to find it. This explains the popularity of books on spirituality in Western culture today.

This book is about people who were not or are not deaf to the unseen Other. Most come from cultures far removed in time or place from modern Western culture; some are modern Westerners out of step with the reductionist secular culture around them but in step with everyone else. The subjects of these brief biographies represent a huge diversity in thought and practice, but they are all "spiritual masters" because they seek a relationship with the unseen Other.

Religion and Theology

Spirituality may be all the rage these days, but religion and theology are not. Whereas spirituality sounds exciting and new, the word "religion" can suggest rigid institutional structures promulgating narrow, outdated teachings, and "theology" is often seen as an arid, esoteric exercise for the intellectually inclined but having nothing to do with anyone else.

There is something to this. The long list of petty, self-serving, even cruel injustices committed over the centuries in the name of religion should give anyone pause—the lone seeker after spirituality seems so much more authentic and benign. And theologians like to debate arcane questions using a vocabulary all their own, thereby excluding others from their conversations (assuming others are interested in them).

But none of this is surprising. Other institutions—governments, universities, corporations—also engage in petty, self-serving, and cruel acts, and scholars in other fields—medicine, economics, the law—also address one another in their own jargon, which others find off-putting. As a human activity, religion is subject to all the temptations of any other human activity. Its foibles and failures are not a commentary on the validity of what it seeks to do, but on the fallibility of those who undertake to do it.

Like spirituality, the word "religion" is hard to define. It has something to do with spirituality, that is, with the unseen Other. But is religion an impediment to people searching for the Other or an aid to them? It is sometimes one and sometimes the other. Yes, religion can get bogged down in arguments over authority, doctrine, liturgy, and morality, but it does so because such things are important. Moreover, those pondering such questions are almost never the first to do so. Healthy religion guides the spiritual seeker away from dangerous curves and ditches beside the road by introducing her to the wisdom of those who have traveled that road before. When people learn something important, they create structures designed to spare those who follow them from making the same mistakes they made. Those structures comprise the religions of the world.

I have often used the example of someone walking along the beach. The beach-walker observes waves breaking, smells the salty air, and dips his toes in the surf. His knowledge of the ocean is accurate but extremely limited. He can do very little with what he knows. If the beach-walker desires a fuller knowledge of the ocean—and perhaps to sail across it—he would do well to consult with sailors, fishermen, oceanographers, cartographers, meteorologists, and others, to learn from those who have experienced the ocean before him. A treasury of knowledge pertaining to the spiritual quest is available in churches, synagogues, mosques, and temples. The wise spiritual seeker will avail himself of that knowledge.

Theology is one of the means religions use to guide spiritual seekers. It is the attempt to make sense of spiritual experience but should not be confused with spiritual experience itself any more than a map of the United States should be confused with the experience of driving from New England to California. But someone undertaking such a drive would be foolish not to consult a map, which is based on the experiences and knowledge of many others. Theological teachings, creeds, catechisms, and the like are similarly useful to anyone seeking to nurture a relationship with the unseen Other. Not surprisingly, most of the spiritual masters in this book were key thinkers in their respective religious traditions.

Do All Spiritual Traditions Say the Same Thing?

In studying the world's spiritual traditions, I have noted some things which recur from one tradition to another.

The first is mysticism. Here is another word that begs definition. To many people, the word "mysticism" and the related words "mystic" and "mystical" suggest something arcane, occult, and spooky. I use the term to refer to direct experiences of the unseen

Other, unmediated or influenced by religious structures, texts, doctrines, and analytical thought. Mystical encounters are often experienced as coming from beyond. They tend to be individual in nature and hard to describe or share with others (though communities of mystics are not uncommon). Mystics often run afoul of ecclesiastical authorities. Every major religious tradition has a mystical expression. In some it is valued and sought; in others it is suspect. But the experience itself seems to be universal. Many of the spiritual masters discussed in these pages have had such experiences, though coming from different traditions, they interpret their experiences differently.

Then there is asceticism. An ascetic rejects the comforts and amenities sought by others, seeking out a life of extreme simplicity, often within a monastic community or as a hermit monk. Many ascetics are also mystics. They may differ on the purpose of the spiritual quest, according to their several traditions, but all see worldly comforts as a distraction from it, and in some cases as completely illusory. Every major spiritual tradition acknowledges certain ascetics among its saints.

The importance of a moral life is another recurring theme among the world's spiritual traditions. Understandings of the moral life vary in detail, but they usually include the Golden Rule ("Do unto others as you would have others do unto you"), obedience to authority, showing hospitality to strangers and the needy, and loyalty to family, clan, or faith group. Rare is the mystic or ascetic who does not also observe a strict moral code.

Most spiritual traditions also grapple with the question of how the unseen Other is known. This question assumes different forms in different traditions. In the West, it has usually been discussed in terms of the relationship between revelation (insights seen to have come from outside) and reason (insights arising from human thinking or experience). Great energy has been expended to show that the two are compatible or even identical, but some seekers have always honored one over the other. Eastern spiritual masters tend to address the question differently, advising the seeker to clear her mind of cluttering thoughts that impede spiritual progress (some Western masters advise the same thing). Spiritual masters representing different stances on this question are discussed in the biographies comprising this book.

Given these recurring themes, some have suggested that beneath surface differences, the world's spiritual traditions are basically alike. A man seated next to me on a commercial airliner recently told me that after extensive research, he had concluded that all religions say the same thing. "Really?" I said. "What do they say?" He replied with something about how everyone is a child of God and we should all love each other. Not wishing to argue with a man who thought he knew all the answers, I mumbled something and tried to change the subject. It was clear to me that if the man had studied religion at all, he hadn't studied it much. His summary of the world's religions was a thin pabulum that avoided most of the important questions, little resembled any actual religion, and amounted to nothing more than feeling good about ourselves and being nice.

But he had raised an intriguing question. Given the themes that recur in the major spiritual traditions of the world, is there a core of beliefs and understandings common to them all? My study (unlike that of the man seated next to me on the airliner) leads me to conclude that spiritual masters the world over address similar questions—How is the unseen Other known? What or who is sacred? What is the good life? Is the world a good or a bad place? What is salvation?—but the answers they give to these questions vary widely. Some believe in one God; some believe in a multiplicity of gods; some believe in no god at all. Some teach equality of all persons; some believe in ranks or classes of persons. Some spiritual traditions are missionary faiths; others discourage the conversion of nonbelievers. Some believe in a soul that lives on after death; some say there is no soul. Some say bodily existence is good; others say it's something to escape from or an illusion. Clearly, all religions and spiritual traditions do not say the same thing.

What the world's religions and spiritual traditions have in common is their experience of an unseen Other that is mysterious, tremendous, and alluring. The only other thing they have in common is the questions they ask about the unseen Other. The answers they give to those questions, however, are so profoundly different that we shouldn't expect them simply to put their differences aside, sit down around a campfire, join hands, and sing "Kumbaya." It's not going to happen.

Is Only One Spiritual Tradition True?

The question above can be answered in three basic ways. The first is usually called exclusivism. Exclusivists say, "There is only one true faith, and it's mine. All others are wrong, so come over to where I am." This was the position of the pre-Vatican II Roman Catholic Church and is today the position of some Protestant and Islamic groups. It is unknown among Eastern spiritual traditions. Then there is inclusivism. Inclusivists say, "While there is only one true faith, there are multiple ways of entering into it, some of which may be unknown to us." This is the position of many liberal Christians in the West who see God bringing souls to Christ within the historic church but also outside it. The third way of answering the question is pluralism: "All (or most) spiritual traditions are culturally conditioned ways of encountering the same reality. Each is valid in its context." This is the classic Hindu position and is represented in the West, most notably, by the late British philosopher John Hick. (Christopher W. Morgan, of the Mid-America Baptist Theological Seminary in Cordova, Tennessee, distinguishes nine variations on these three answers, in his *Faith Comes by Hearing: A Response to Inclusivism*.)

The rest of this section will be a personal statement. In considering the question posed above, I am tempted simply to say that I don't know. That would be in keeping with the comment of my father with which I began this introduction and which my experience increasingly confirms. Moreover, in exploring spiritual traditions different from my own Christian tradition, I have often found myself saying something like, "That's a great insight! We Christians could learn something from these people." To say that truth resides exclusively within one faith tradition is, I believe, less a commentary on other faith traditions than on the narrow perspective and experience of the speaker.

But neither can I go all the way with the pluralists. Given the fundamental and irreconcilable differences among the world's spiritual traditions, they cannot all be true, or at least not all equally true. There cannot be one God and at the same time no God; bodily existence cannot be both a good thing and also an illusion. The world's faiths are not culturally conditioned roads to the same destination. Some understandings must be more accurate, more faithful, more true than others. Some questions can have only one right answer.

All this perplexes me as a Christian. I was reared by faithful Christian parents, and while I have often questioned my Christian faith, including its most basic tenets, I have never been severed from the Christian community. It is as much a part of who I am as my face and my name. I shall die a Christian—a questioning Christian, but indubitably a Christian.

Christianity is a missionary faith, and I once served as a missionary in Nigeria. The purpose of mission work is to share with others the joys of one's faith. I sought to do that in Africa and continue to seek to do it. But does that mean that I must convince others that they are wrong? I think not. I now know too much about their traditions to say that they are simply wrong. I am also learning much from others as they share with me the joys of their faith. In Zimbabwe, for example, I got to know a traditional healer (sometimes called a "witch doctor" in the West) whose approach to healing was not clinical or pharmaceutical, but relational and spiritual. Even the Western-educated physicians I spoke with there acknowledged that such traditional treatments are the most effective way to treat some illnesses. Truth is not limited to people who think as I do.

But then, what of seemingly exclusivist New Testament passages like John 14:6, where Jesus says, "I am the way, and the truth, and the life. No one comes to the Father except through me"? Or Simon Peter's statement about Jesus in Acts 4:12: "There is salvation in no one else, for there is no other name under heaven given among mortals by which we must be saved"? The Bible contains many kinds of literature, each conveying its meaning in its own way. We must not mistake one kind of writing for another. Several people have observed that verses like the two quoted above sound like what a man says to his beloved. When he tells his beloved that she is the most beautiful creature in the world, he is saying something about his feelings for her, not making a negative judgment on other women. I find this interpretation of these verses helpful.

When the day is done, I hope that I will have been as faithful a disciple of Jesus Christ as I can be. He is supremely mysterious, tremendous, and alluring to me. Each morning I pray that Christ will remake me into his own likeness and use me for his purposes. Understanding so little about those purposes, I must trust Christ to do what he will do, especially with those who have never heard his name and those who, having heard it, have rejected it. Perhaps some have not heard it because I did not speak it; perhaps some have rejected it because of what they observed in me. I entrust them, as I entrust myself and everything, to the judgment and mercy of God as disclosed in Jesus Christ.

Reading This Book

This book is not a history of the world's spiritual traditions and it omits huge chunks of material that such a history would include. The reader can, however, learn something of those traditions by reading these pages, and I hope my short biographies will capture the imagination of anyone delving into spiritual matters for the first time and prod that person to further reading and exploration.

In compiling the list of subjects for these biographies, I have sought to include masters from all the major spiritual traditions thriving anywhere in the world today, plus a few key figures from history whose legacies have died out. I also wanted to include spiritual masters from traditions leaving no written record, such as native African and native American spirituality, but the absence of a written record for those traditions posed a challenge I was not always able to surmount.

Deciding whom to write about was another challenge. The line between philosophy and spirituality, for example, is a blurry one. Several thinkers known mainly as philosophers appear in this book, and many philosophers not discussed might have been included as well (Plato, Kant, and Hegel come immediately to mind). I have written only about thinkers whose motivations were in my judgment *primarily* spiritual in nature. But it was often a judgment call and a case could be made for including many figures not discussed in these pages.

I also regret that so few women appear in these biographies (14 out of 163). That is because until very recent times, most cultures discouraged women from pursuing the spiritual quest and from writing about anything at all. The list of subjects is slightly weighted with Christians (63 out of 163) because I think it likely that the majority of my readers will come from Christian backgrounds and that Christian spiritual masters will be of particular interest to them.

The biographies are arranged chronologically to show how different traditions often developed simultaneously in different places. For a quick overview of the development of one tradition, the reader may consult the appendix, which lists separately the biographies for each of the world's major faith groups. Each biography is also written to stand alone so that a reader opening the book randomly to any page can make sense of that page without reading anything else.

Each biography, including the quotation(s) and the thought question at the end, contains no more than four hundred words. This self-imposed limit made possible the format of one subject per page, but it also required that much important material be omitted. Deciding what to omit and squeezing as much as possible into four hundred words was the most challenging part of writing this book. I sought to do three things in each biography: (1) say something about the historical context in which the subject lived, (2) bring the subject to life as a flesh-and-blood person, and (3) indicate why the subject is important.

I should say a word about the spelling of proper names. Many of those discussed in these pages spoke and wrote in languages other than English, containing consonants and vowels which English lacks and for which normal written English makes no provision. Professional linguists have developed a system of marks to indicate these consonants and vowels when transliterating a word or name from another language into English. Examples are Abū al-Ḥasan al-Ashʿarī and Hōnen. I have omitted most of these marks because I felt they would confuse most readers, but in doing so, I have also omitted indications about the proper pronunciation of such names. I encourage the reader who wants to talk about the subjects of these biographies to consult a dictionary or go online to learn to pronounce their names correctly. In most cases, I have also used modern place names to identify geographical locations.

Acknowledgments

Several people assisted me in producing this book. I am profoundly—is there an adverb stronger than profoundly?—grateful to my friend and colleague Dean Mosher of Fairhope, Alabama, whose likenesses of the subjects of these biographies adorn the pages of this book. This is the third book of mine which Dean has illustrated. When we began our first project together, he was an obscure, struggling artist and parishioner at the parish where I was rector. That was nearly twenty years ago. Dean has since risen to national prominence, most notably for his carefully researched and accurate murals of naval battles and other historic events. His work may now be seen at the Air and Space Museum at the Smithsonian Institution in Washington, D.C., the U.S. Naval Academy in Annapolis, Maryland, and elsewhere.

Whenever possible, Dean worked from photographs, paintings, and other actual likenesses of his subjects. Where these were unavailable, he researched the ethnic and cultural background of the subject, the clothing the subject may have worn, and other artists' guesses at what the subject might have looked like. Then he put pen to paper and drew a "likely likeness" of the subject. As usual, Dean's work is better than first rate and I expect that his drawing rather than my writing will most readily draw the reader into these pages.

I also thank the Wm. B. Eerdmans Publishing Company of Grand Rapids, Michigan, for returning to me the originals of Dean's drawings that first appeared in two of my earlier books published by Eerdmans, *Glorious Companions: Five Centuries of Anglican Spirituality* (2002) and *God Seekers: Twenty Centuries of Christian Spiritualities* (2008), and for their kind permission to use thirty-two of those drawings in the present volume.

Several scholars assisted me by reading and critiquing my biographies of spiritual masters in their fields of expertise. They pointed out errors of fact and emphasis which I have sought to correct, and I am grateful to them: Lucinda Mosher, faculty associate in interfaith studies and director of the Multifaith Chaplaincy Program at the Hartford Seminary in Hartford, Connecticut; Rabbi Steven Silberman, of the Ahavas Chesed Synagogue in Mobile, Alabama; Danny Fisher, coordinator of the Buddhist Chaplaincy Department at the University of the West in Rosemead, California; Wakoh Shannon Hickey, assistant professor of religious studies at Alfred University in Alfred, New York; and Amrutur V. Srinivasan, director of the Vedic Institute of Connecticut and author of *Hinduism for Dummies*.

Finally, my wife of forty-seven years, Pam, read every word of this manuscript and gently pointed out sentences that made sense only to me and others weighted down by heady thinking and expression. Rewrites at her behest have made this manuscript accessible to many readers who might have been put off by my sometimes stilted academic style. I am grateful to Pam for that, and of course for much more. But that would require another book.

Richard H. Schmidt
Fairhope, Alabama
January 2015

1
Vyasa

Born Kalpi, India (?), date unknown
Place and date of death unknown

The world's oldest living religion was a mature, sophisticated faith long before recorded history. For centuries before the Hindu scriptures were written down, priests in northern India passed them from generation to generation through memorization and chanting.

Those scriptures are called the Vedas (Sanskrit for knowledge), traditionally dated from around 3000 BCE. The Vedas are largely a collection of hymns, containing over twenty thousand stanzas. Many Hindus believe that when a previous universe was dissolved, Brahma, the Creator God, preserved the eternal Veda and transmitted it to priests in this universe when humanity was ready to receive it.

The Vedas comprise a complex text affirming life and emphasizing duty to family and the larger world. Vedic hymns address various gods who adapt themselves to times and places to meet specific human needs, but all gods are expressions of the one supreme and unknowable God, Brahman (not to be confused with Brahma). Hindus believe one may worship God under any name and in sundry ways. Affirming many paths to the divine, including other faiths, Hindus do not seek converts. Any faith teaching right conduct can lead the believer to God.

No one knows when the Vedas were written down (some speculate around 500 BCE, some say much earlier), but we know who wrote them down. His name was Krishna Dvaipayana, commonly known as Vyasa, a Sanskrit word meaning divider or splitter, since, for clarification and ease of access, he divided the original Veda into four collections with separate names (hence "the Vedas," plural).

Tradition says Vyasa was born on an island in the Yamuna River, near modern Delhi, the son of a Hindu sage and a fisherwoman. Little is known of his life, but an additional sacred epic poem, the Mahabharata, fifteen times the length of the Christian Bible, is also attributed to him. Vyasa also appears as a major character in it. The Mahabharata has helped impress on Indian society the importance of right behavior and doing faithfully what one is meant to do.

Truth cannot be suppressed and always is the ultimate victor. —Yajur Veda

Do not be led by others, awaken your own mind, amass your own experience, and choose your own path. —Atharva Veda

Let noble thoughts come from every direction. —Rig Veda

What in Hinduism has enabled it to flourish for five thousand years?

2
Abraham

Born early second millennium BCE,
at Tell el-Muqayyah, Iraq (?)
Died early second millennium BCE, possibly near
Hebrew, Israel

The mists of legend and prehistory shroud the patri-
arch revered by Jews, Christians, and Muslims as
their earliest hero of the faith. Some scholars suggest that the Abraham of the Bible
and the Quran was not a single individual, but a tribe or composite figure representing several ancient leaders whose names are lost to us. Both Jews and Arabs claim
descent from Abraham; the name means "father of a multitude."

In the Hebrew Bible, the Lord directs Abraham to "go from your country and
your kindred and your father's house to the land that I will show you." Abraham obeys
and God then gives him and his descendants the land of Canaan (modern Israel and
Palestine), promising to make of Abraham's progeny a great nation. This promise, fulfilled through Abraham's son Isaac, is the biblical basis of the modern Israeli nation's
claim to the land between the Mediterranean Sea and the Jordan River. Years later, in
a terrifying encounter, God tests Abraham by commanding him to slay the boy Isaac
on a remote mountaintop, a command Abraham was prepared to obey until an angel
stopped him at the last instant. One of the names of God in the Hebrew Bible is "the
shield of Abraham."

For Christians, Abraham is the great paragon of faith. The apostle Paul (see #23)
twice writes that "Abraham believed God, and it was reckoned to him as righteousness." Abraham was right with God, Paul says, not because of any acts of obedience,
but because he believed and trusted God. Paul contrasts this to what he perceived as
rabbinic Judaism's excessive legalism. All who trust God, not adherents of the law, are
the true descendants of Abraham and children of God, Paul says.

Arabs trace their descent from Abraham through his older son, Ishmael. Abraham
is a major figure in the Quran, which portrays him as a champion of monotheism and
the archetypal Muslim. He boldly challenges his father to abandon his idols and worship the one true God. The Quran also includes the story of the sacrifice of Abraham's
son, who is not named but whom Muslims presume to be Ishmael. Abraham's name
is closely linked with Mecca, "the city of Abraham," where he constructs the world's
first mosque, the Kaaba.

In what way was Abraham a "hero of the faith"?

3
Akhenaten

Born 1385 BCE (?), in Thebes, Egypt
Died 1336 or 1334 BCE, in el-Amarna, Egypt

Akhenaten was little more than a name until the discovery and excavation in the nineteenth century of the ruins of Amarna, his spectacular capital in the Egyptian desert. Interest in the enigmatic pharaoh and his queen, Nefertiti, grew as art from Akhenaten's reign, unlike any other in ancient Egypt, and his revolutionary religious reforms became known.

Upon becoming pharaoh around 1352 BCE, he took the name Akhenaten, which included the name of the Egyptian sun god, Aten. At court, Aten was worshiped solely and directly, while the common people also worshiped only Aten, but through Akhenaten, making him both king and priest.

Some suspect Akhenaten's motives were more political than religious. But others have seen him as the world's first monotheist. While he worshiped one god, he may have stopped short of denying the reality of other deities. Even this, however, was a radical departure from Egypt's polytheistic past, and the country's official religion became, for practical purposes, a strict monotheism. An iconoclastic campaign ensued, with temples and images of other gods destroyed and their priestly orders disbanded.

Amarna was built where the sun rose between two cliffs and Aten was always worshiped in broad sunlight rather than in dark temple interiors. Art from the era represents Aten as creator of all things and hints that no artist can begin to convey his true nature.

This sounded like genuine monotheism to nineteenth- and early twentieth-century scholars. Some, including Sigmund Freud, speculated that Akhenaten's monotheism had influenced Moses (see #4). Most scholars today, however, say a link between Akhenaten and Moses is unlikely. Jewish monotheism originated elsewhere.

Not surprisingly, devotees of traditional Egyptian religion disliked Akhenaten's reforms. Within a decade after his death, his son and successor, Tutankhamun, destroyed the temples and images commissioned by his father and the country returned to its polytheistic past. Amarna was soon a ruin and Akhenaten's name was omitted from subsequent lists of Egyptian pharaohs.

How manifold are the things you have made! They are hidden from the human face. Only god, like whom there is no other! Solely and alone, you created the world as you desired: human beings, cattle, and wild beasts, everything on earth, whether moving on feet or flying on high with wings. —from a hymn composed by Akhenaten

What similarities and differences do you see between Akhenaten's faith and later monotheistic faiths?

4

Moses

Born fourteenth century BCE (?), in Lower Egypt
Died thirteenth century BCE (?), on Mt. Nebo, Jordan

Driven into Egypt by a famine in Canaan, Abraham's (see #2) Hebrew descendants were soon reduced to slavery there, according to the Hebrew Bible. A Hebrew raised in Egypt's royal household would eventually free them. His name was Moses.

Nothing in the life of the great liberator, lawgiver, and founder of the Israelite nation can be verified from other sources, but the story of Moses, as told in the Bible and the Quran, points to a visionary leader of extraordinary energy and rugged determination.

Calling to Moses from a mysterious bush which was aflame but not consumed, God sent Moses to tell the Egyptian pharaoh to "let my people go" back to Canaan, their ancestral homeland. When Pharaoh refused, God sent ten plagues upon the Egyptians, culminating in the Passover, when the angel of death slew the eldest sons of every Egyptian household but spared the Israelites. Jews to this day commemorate this event as one of their foremost holy days. Moses then led the fleeing Israelites through the Red Sea, into the Sinai desert.

The Bible tells of God's feeding, leading, and protecting the Israelites during their forty years of desert wandering, despite their constant grumbling that they preferred slavery in Egypt to freedom in the desert. Moses chafes under the burden of caring for such a carping tribe and complains to God that he'd rather be killed than continue as their leader.

The pivotal event of the Israelites' desert sojourn was Moses's ascent of Mt. Sinai, where God initiated a covenant with the Israelites and gave Moses the Ten Commandments. "I will walk among you, and will be your God, and you shall be my people," God said.

Moses died at the age of 120, according to the Bible, on the slopes of Mt. Nebo, where he gazed across the Jordan River into the land God had promised to the descendants of Abraham and Isaac. Tradition holds that he is the author of the first five books of the Hebrew Bible, the Torah.

Much of this story is told in the Quran as well, where Moses is a great prophet, known as Musa and mentioned in the Quran more often than any other person. Muslims believe that Moses foretold the coming of the prophet Muhammad (see #45). The lives of the two prophets are parallel in many ways.

How would you describe Moses as a leader?

5
David

Born ca. 1040 BCE, in Bethlehem,
Palestinian Territory
Died ca. 970 BCE, in Jerusalem

David was a young shepherd and musician when he came to the court of Saul, ancient Israel's first king, where his music comforted the emotionally unstable Saul. David soon proved himself a gifted military leader as well, overshadowing Saul and inciting the jealous king to seek his life. Upon Saul's death, David succeeded him as king and established his capital at the Jebusite town of Jerusalem, known ever since as "the City of David."

David was passionately devoted to the God of Israel to whom he attributed his military successes, but his other passions led him into adultery with Bathsheba, whom he had seen bathing on a rooftop, and then to arrange the violent death of her husband. A tumultuous and tragic family life ensued, complete with jealousy, rebellion, and palace intrigue. David's later penitence was deep and genuine, as seen in Psalm 51, traditionally attributed to him.

The Israelite state was at its largest under David. Jews even today regard David's reign as a Golden Age and look for a future descendant of David, the *messiah* (anointed one), to inaugurate a reign of worldwide peace and well-being. Christians acclaim Jesus (see #21), a descendant of David, as the *messiah* (Christ means "anointed one" in Greek). Muslims revere David as a major prophet. He is mentioned frequently in both the New Testament and the Quran.

It was as a hymn writer, however, that David made his most enduring contribution. He is often pictured holding a lyre. David cannot have written the entire biblical book of Psalms (many psalms contain indications of later authorship), but he wrote many of them. Seventy-three of the Hebrew Bible's 150 psalms are associated with David in some way. Many are addressed directly to God, including songs of praise, penitence, petition, and thanksgiving, suggesting an intimate, multifaceted devotion to his God. The book of Psalms has been called "the hymnbook of the Jewish Temple" and is widely used in Jewish and Christian worship to this day.

> The LORD is my shepherd, I shall not want. He makes me lie down in green pastures; he leads me beside still waters; he restores my soul. He leads me in right paths for his name's sake. —Psalm 23:1–3

If you were seeking an original image to refer to God in a hymn, what would it be?

6

Isaiah

Born ca. 770 BCE, in Jerusalem (?)
Died ca. 680 BCE, in Jerusalem (?)

Following the oppressive rule of David's (see #5) son Solomon, the ten northern Israelite tribes broke away to form their own kingdom of Israel. They suffered repeated palace intrigue, violence, and coups until the Assyrian army conquered and destroyed the kingdom in 722 BCE. The southern kingdom of Judah enjoyed relative stability under the hereditary Davidic monarchy at Jerusalem until it fell to the Babylonian army in 587 BCE.

A series of colorful, outspoken personalities emerged during this time, in both Israel and Judah, calling for repentance and obedience to God. They were the Hebrew prophets. Isaiah was perhaps the foremost among them.

While in the Jerusalem temple, possibly serving there as a priest, the young Isaiah "saw the Lord sitting on a throne, high and lofty," surrounded by heavenly beings. Chastened and humbled before the majesty of God, he came to see all human allegiances as worthless beside "the holy one of Israel."

During a prophetic career encompassing six decades, Isaiah warned one ruler after another against relying on military force and foreign alliances. Real security is only found in faithfulness to God, he said, and God will not tolerate injustice, exploitation, corruption, and favoritism. Isaiah even saw the invading Assyrians as God's agent, suggesting that God works through powers that deny him as well as through those professing allegiance to him. "Do not call conspiracy all that this people calls conspiracy, and do not fear what it fears, or be in dread. But the Lord of hosts, him you shall regard as holy; let him be your fear, and let him be your dread," Isaiah warned.

Chapters 40–66 of the biblical book of Isaiah contain oracles from a later time, written by anonymous disciples of the prophet. Building on Isaiah's insights, they contain some of the most soaring expressions of monotheism ever written and several oracles beloved by Christians as foreshadowing the coming of Christ.

> Woe is me! I am lost, for I am a man of unclean lips, and I live among a people of unclean lips; yet my eyes have seen the King, the Lord of hosts!
> —Isaiah 6:5

> Thus said the Lord GOD, the Holy One of Israel, in returning and rest you shall be saved; in quietness and in trust shall be your strength. —Isaiah 30:15

To what modern governments and policies would Isaiah's judgment apply?

7
Zarathustra (Zoroaster)

Born ca. 630 BCE (?), in eastern Iran (?)
Died ca. 550 BCE (?), in Balkh, Afghanistan

The figure of Zarathustra (usually called Zoroaster in English) has had a long and varied history in the West. Many think he influenced Greek philosophy, beginning with Heraclitus and continuing later with the Platonists. Others have claimed he was a master of ancient magic and necromancy, giving him cachet among occultists. Modern scholars have speculated about a link between Zarathustra's monotheism and later Judaism and Christianity. And the nineteenth-century philosopher Friedrich Nietzsche wrote about him in his most famous work (on which the comic book hero Superman is very loosely based).

Who was the real Zarathustra? That's hard to say. We can do little more than speculate even about when and where he lived. Estimates of his dates vary by over a thousand years. What can be known is derived from the *Gathas*, the oldest text of the faith he founded, presumed to have been written by Zarathustra himself.

Zarathustra was a Persian philosopher, probably also a priest, who founded Zoroastrianism, the established faith in Persia for centuries prior to the Muslim conquest there. There are roughly 150,000 Zoroastrians today, mostly in India, where their ancestors fled when the Muslims invaded.

Zoroastrians are expected to live according to a key principle of the faith called *asha* in the Avestan language. It is often translated truth or righteousness, but no English word captures all its nuances. *Asha* refers to propositional truth, but also means order as opposed to chaos, reality as opposed to illusion, and living in accord with reality.

For Zarathustra, the world was a great battleground between cosmic good and evil. He experienced a vision of the eternal and omniscient Creator, whom he called Ahura Mazda, meaning Wise Lord. Ahura Mazda was surrounded by lesser divine beings whom he had created and whose task was to guard the world. Opposing Ahura Mazda was Angra Mainyu, also an eternal being, but evil and destructive. Each person chose one or the other.

Unlike many Easterners, Zarathustra believed history was moving toward a climactic end when Ahura Mazda would finally prevail and those who chose *asha* would be one with him.

> The two primal Spirits, who reveal themselves in vision as Twins, are the Better and the Bad, in thought and word and action. Between these two the wise chose aright; the foolish do not. —Zarathustra

Is the world a battleground between cosmic forces of good and evil?

8

Mahavira

Born 599 BCE (?), near Vaishali, India
Died 527 BCE (?), in Fazilnagar, India

Like Hinduism, Jainism is an ancient faith predating recorded history. Once the official religion of much of India, it declined during a Hindu revival in the eighth century CE and then when Muslims invaded. Jainism underwent something of a revival in the nineteenth century and today claims 4.2 million adherents, mostly in India.

Mahavira did not found Jainism, but he is its best known proponent, organizer, and reformer. Born to a noble family, Mahavira discerned at the age of thirty that worldly pleasures do not bring contentment. He renounced them, distributing his wealth to the poor and moving into the forest to begin a life of meditation and austere asceticism. He taught as he roamed eastern India, finding shelter where he could and often being taken for a spy or thief. Tradition says that after his clothing caught on thorns, Mahavira remained naked for the rest of his life.

Jainism is best known for its cardinal doctrine of nonviolence. Jains are more thoroughgoing in observing nonviolence than anyone else on earth. Not only are they vegetarians, but strict Jains avoid dairy products, viewing milking as a form of violence against cows; root vegetables since pulling them from the ground may kill tiny insects; and honey because taking it from the hive is violence against bees. Harsh speech is also seen as a form of violence and some Jains wear a cloth over their mouths to remind them to speak peaceably.

Jains forbid lying (unless truthfulness might lead to violence, in which case silence is observed), stealing, and possessiveness. Mahavira added chastity to this list. Married Jains are expected to observe these principles as rigorously as is feasible while monks (Mahavira founded an order of mendicants) observe them very strictly.

Most Jains do not believe in God. The universe is eternal and self-sufficient, they believe, requiring no God or higher power to create or sustain it. Like Hindus, Jains believe in the cycle of rebirths and see the soul as immaterial and distinct from the body.

Doctrines of other faiths are honored and dogmatism is forbidden. Jains refuse to force their views on others, even their teaching about nonviolence, because all points of view, including Jainism itself, are seen as limited.

Nonviolence and kindness to living beings is kindness to oneself. —Mahavira

Imagine a kingdom ruled by Jains. How would it fare in today's world?

9
Kongzi (Confucius)

Born 551 BCE, near Qufu, China
Died 479 BCE, near Qufu, China

Confucianism is often called a religion, but some say it shouldn't be. It says nothing about God or the transcendent and has no mystical expression. It is more a way of living than a faith, concerned more with order and behavior than with the divine. Confucianism is a philosophy for living in this world.

Kongzi (Confucius is a Western rendering of Kong Fuzi, an honorary title meaning Master Kong) is the most famous philosopher and teacher of ancient China. Kongzi's father, a poor aristocrat, died when Kongzi was three. His mother became his teacher, and the boy excelled in many disciplines. He was especially drawn to ancient Chinese poetry and history.

As an adult, Kongzi was a government administrator who soon formed his own ideas on education, government, and how to order society. Probably because he sought to halt some licentious and corrupt practices at court, Kongzi's ideas were not well received. He resigned his position and traveled to other regions of China for twelve years, seeking a place where he might implement his ideas. His reputation for integrity and vision gained him an increasingly large group of disciples, and he returned to his home at age sixty-seven. Kongzi spent the rest of his life teaching and writing. His best known literary work, the *Analects*, contains most of his famous sayings.

Although later teachers (see #15, #18) developed Confucian thought in additional directions, its basic outlines can be traced to Kongzi. He never saw himself as an innovator, however, but as the collector and transmitter of wisdom inherited from earlier generations.

Kongzi's cardinal principle has been called humaneness or benevolence. He was perhaps the first to articulate the Golden Rule, but in a negative form: What you would not like done to you, do not do to others. Kongzi had a positive view of human nature, believing that virtue could be learned and that every person was a potential sage.

For Kongzi, the virtuous life included honoring parents and ancestors, polite behavior, and doing well what is required. His goal was a harmonious society. Although Daoism (see #10) and Buddhism (see #11) also flourished in China, Kongzi's vision of a humane society became deeply rooted in the Chinese mind. Recent Communist governments have sometimes sought to root it out.

Do you see anything missing in Kongzi's understanding of a healthy social order?

10
Laozi (Lao-Tzu)

Born sixth century BCE (?), in eastern China (?)
Died fifth century BCE (?), in eastern China (?)

Dao (or *Tao*) is a Chinese word meaning "way" or "path." It is the central idea of the *Daodejing* (or *Tao Te Ching*), a book usually called in English *Book of the Way and Virtue*. Hardly a systematic treatise, the *Daodejing* contains paradox, aphorisms, rhythmic rhymes, and analogies. It has been hugely influential in shaping Chinese life and thought until recent times and is variously interpreted as a philosophical, mystical, political, and self-help book.

Scholars differ as to the date and author of the *Daodejing*. Some believe it was produced by several editors and compilers using multiple sources. Ancient tradition, however, ascribes it to a contemporary of Kongzi (see #9) named Laozi (or Lao-Tzu) who is said to have become disgusted with the corruption he saw around him and decided to flee to Tibet. A guard recognized and detained him, requiring him to write down his thoughts, thus producing the *Daodejing*.

Laozi saw the *Dao* as the transcendent origin and governing principle of the universe, but not as a personal God in the Western sense. The natural world functions in accordance with the Dao, but human beings, exercising free choice, often fail to conform to it, destroying the natural balance of the universe. The *Daodejing* points the way to restore that balance.

The key to restoring balance is "nonaction." This is not doing nothing, but quietness of mind, acceptance of reality, and diminishment of desire. Ambition, striving, and the ego are stilled. One thing is not valued more highly than another; ideological differences recede in significance.

Daoism does not compete with, but complements Confucianism (see #9) and Buddhism (see #11) in China. It is less concerned with social structures than Confucianism and less concerned with the cycle of rebirths than Buddhism. Daoism is a path for individuals to find the right balance in this life.

The Dao abides in non-action, yet nothing is left undone. —Laozi

The best leader is one people hardly know is there. When his work is done, his aim fulfilled, they say, "We did it ourselves." —Laozi

He who knows, does not speak. He who speaks, does not know. —Laozi

A journey of a thousand miles begins with a single step. —Laozi

What might account for the recent popularity of Daoism in the West?

11
The Buddha

Born early fifth century BCE (?), in Kapilavastu,
Nepal (?)
Died late fifth century BCE (?), in Kushinigar, India

The people of the Indian subcontinent have always been more interested in ideas than in history. The earliest written accounts of the man now known as the Buddha are more philosophical guides than biographies in the modern sense and come from several centuries after he lived. Scholars also differ as to the dates of his life. Nonetheless, drawing on the earliest accounts, most scholars accept the following outline of the Buddha's life.

Born to Hindu royalty, Siddhartha Gautama was sheltered from painful realities until, at age twenty-nine, he confronted old age, suffering, and death firsthand. The stunned Siddhartha then sought understanding by studying under several spiritual guides, renouncing his privileges, and embracing a life of extreme self-denial.

Enlightenment came to Siddhartha at age thirty-five as he meditated beneath a pipal tree, now known as the Bodhi tree. From that moment on he is referred to as the Buddha (Enlightened or Awakened One). The Buddha abandoned his extreme ascetic practices and adopted what is called the Middle Way, a mean between self-mortification and self-indulgence.

He also came to understand the cause and cure of suffering, the "Four Noble Truths" of Buddhism: 1) suffering (or dissatisfaction) is real, multifaceted, and pervasive; 2) it is caused by craving or desire resulting from failure to perceive the true value of things; 3) it is eliminated through enlightenment (or liberation or Buddhahood), understood as the cessation of desire; 4) there is a practical path to achieve enlightenment through right thoughts and behaviors, Buddhism's so-called "Eightfold Path."

God is not an essential part of Buddhist spirituality. The Buddha was concerned with thoughts and perceptions, not the origin or end of things. Raised a Hindu, he perceived history as cyclical and taught that the human soul lives many lives before reaching enlightenment and Nirvana, the final release from the cycle of rebirths.

The Buddha spent the rest of his life traveling through north India to teach and assist his disciples in developing a network of monasteries.

*Just as the ocean has a gradual shelf, a gradual slope, a gradual inclination,
with a sudden drop-off only after a long stretch, in the same way this doctrine and
discipline has a gradual training, a gradual performance, a gradual progression,
with a penetration to knowledge only after a long stretch.* —the Buddha

Is suffering all in the mind?

12
Ananda

Born early fifth century BCE (?), in Kapilavastu, Nepal (?)
Died late fifth century BCE (?), in northern India (?)

The Buddha's most trusted and intimate companion was his first cousin Ananda. Ananda is usually called the Buddha's "attendant," but his role was more extensive than that word suggests.

When both men were fifty-five years old, the Buddha (see #11) declared to a gathering of monks that he needed a trustworthy, reliable attendant. Most of those present quickly volunteered, but Ananda alone held back. The Buddha chose Ananda. When asked why he had not stepped forward, Ananda replied that the Buddha, knowing his disciples so well, would know whom to choose. He accepted the post on eight conditions, all designed to make clear that he would remain subservient to the Buddha.

For the next twenty-five years, Ananda accompanied the Buddha in his travels, dialogued with him privately on spiritual matters, ministered to his physical needs and comfort, and acted as go-between when someone sought a private audience with the Buddha. But most importantly, Ananda listened to what the Buddha taught—and remembered it. His memory was legendary. He was said to have been able to recite sixty thousand of the Buddha's words without missing a single syllable.

When Kashyapa (see #13) convened the First Buddhist Council, Ananda was invited to participate even though his progress on the road to Nirvana was deemed less advanced than that of other participants (it is said he reached that goal the night before the council convened). Ananda's recitations there comprise the Sutta Pitaka, a "basket" of discourses concerning methods of meditation, mindfulness, and contemplation, along with some poetry, all intended by the Buddha for his followers. It is the oldest and most complete record of the Buddha's spoken words.

Ananda began each of his recitations at the council with the words "This I have heard." He is known today as "the disciple who heard much" and as the "Guardian of the Teaching."

Ananda is also credited with persuading the Buddha to form an order of nuns, which he had at first declined to do despite repeated requests. He reminded the Buddha of women who had nurtured him as a child and asked whether only men could attain enlightenment by leaving home for the monastic life. The Buddha then relented and authorized the establishment of an order of nuns, provided certain safeguards were met.

What might account for Ananda's willingness to accept a secondary role?

13
Kashyapa

Born early fifth century BCE (?), in Mahatitta, India
Died late fifth century BCE (?), on Mount
Kukkutapada, India

In ancient times when few could read or write, disciples often memorized long passages from a teacher's discourses so as to recite them and pass them on to later generations. Such was the case with the Buddha's teachings (see #12), but at his death, Buddhist monks were scattered and none had memorized everything he had taught.

One monk is reputed to have remarked following the Buddha's death that he was relieved no longer to be obliged to follow the Buddha's rigorous disciplines. This comment alarmed Kashyapa (also called Mahakashyapa, *maha* being Sanskrit for great), the Buddha's leading disciple. He therefore proposed a gathering in the town of Rajgir of all who had memorized something the Buddha had said, a gathering known as the First Buddhist Council.

With five hundred monks in attendance and Kashyapa presiding, the Buddha's disciples recited from memory what they had heard him say, stating on what occasion the teaching had been given. Others who had heard the teaching then confirmed and added to it.

The council organized the Buddha's oral teachings into three groups: Ananda's Sutta Pitaka (see #12), a second collection of teachings on monastic discipline, and a third consisting of philosophical reflections. Because the council unified into a single community all who followed the Buddha, Kashyapa is known as the "father of the *sangha*" (Sanskrit for community).

Ch'an Buddhists, known as Zen in Japan and the West (see #58, #77), see Kashyapa as their precursor. They like to tell the story based on a (much later) tradition that one day the Buddha held up a white lotus blossom and admired it silently. Most of those present were bewildered at this, but Kashyapa smiled discreetly. Seeing Kashyapa's response, the Buddha then named him his successor because Kashyapa had discerned the truth intuitively, conveyed directly from his teacher's mind into his own, without recourse to words or scriptures. This is the method of Ch'an or Zen Buddhists.

Kashyapa is said to have been born into a wealthy family. He felt drawn to asceticism, but when his parents urged him to marry, he wedded a beautiful young woman. When his parents died, however, both Kashyapa and his wife gave their possessions away, freed their slaves, entered the monastic life, and lived separately thereafter.

Why would someone able to discern the truth intuitively want to preserve teachings remembered and taught by others?

14

Ezra

Born early fifth century BCE, in Babylon, Iraq
Died late fifth century or early fourth century BCE,
in Tedef, Syria (?)

Until the twentieth century, the most traumatic event in Jewish history occurred in the sixth century BCE when the Babylonian commander Nebuchadnezzar conquered Jerusalem and carried most of its inhabitants into exile. "By the rivers of Babylon — there we sat down and there we wept," wrote an anonymous psalmist at the time (Psalm 137). Faithfulness to their God united and preserved the exiled Jewish community until, fifty years later, the Persian emperor Cyrus conquered Babylon and allowed the Jews to return home. Many did.

Among the returning Jews was a religious scholar named Ezra. Once back in Jerusalem, Ezra pondered what had brought such tragedy upon the nation and how to prevent its happening again. He felt that infidelity to the Mosaic covenant (see #4) had weakened the nation and was appalled to discover that the Jews who had remained home had been less religiously diligent than those in Babylon, ignoring the Sabbath and intermarrying with "the people of the land." Ezra called for a renewed commitment to the Torah, or Teaching, the first five books of the Bible. These are the foundational Jewish scriptures, traditionally ascribed to Moses. As told in the Hebrew Bible, Ezra read the Torah to the people, convincing them to recommit themselves to it and dissolve their marriages to non-Jews.

Ezra was the first Jewish scribe. He not only copied the Torah but interpreted it for a new generation. Tradition credits Ezra with convening the "Great Assembly" of scholars, which continued to meet for over two hundred years, further probing the Torah and applying it to daily living. Their interpretations, handed down orally, came to be seen as authoritative as well, part of the ever-expanding study of the Torah (see #27). The Great Assembly built the framework within which later Judaism developed and which informs Jewish faith and practice today.

Controversial in his day, Ezra's policies have never lacked for detractors. Some later Jews have questioned his insistence on racial purity. Others have accused him of legalism, of "building a fence around the law," thereby tying the hands of those who followed him. But Ezra was the first to try to envision day-to-day holiness by ferreting out the meaning of the Torah and carefully answering questions like: What is God's will? What should I do? What does faithfulness look like?

Should the wisdom of the past always guide the future?

15
Mengzi (Mencius)

Born ca. 372 BCE, in Zoucheng, China
Died 289 BCE, in Zoucheng, China

The most authoritative and influential interpreter of Kongzi (see #9) is said to have been a sage named Mengzi (usually called Mencius in the West) who studied under Kongzi's grandson. After being immersed in Kongzi's thought, Mengzi served as advisor to several Chinese princes and as a teacher. He spent his last years mentoring disciples and writing a book expounding his thought, called the *Book of Mencius*.

Mengzi had a positive view of human nature. Far from being trapped in sin and in need of redemption, people are inherently good, Mengzi said, and tend by nature to be compassionate. He cited the example of a child who had fallen into a well. People naturally feel sympathy for the child, he said, even if they don't know the child or its parents. Such sympathy is inborn and genuine, not a contrived effort to gain the admiration or gratitude of the child's parents or society at large.

But people's natural goodness is not always manifest because societal influences intrude and promote bad character traits. People's innate benevolence must be awakened and cultivated through education, Mengzi said. The purpose of education is not to reform students' character, but to develop the good character to which everyone is predisposed.

Mengzi believed people sensed four things deep within them: sympathy or commiseration for the pain of others, a sense of shame, deference toward others, and the ability to know right from wrong. These four things, if properly nurtured, grew or sprouted into the four cardinal virtues of benevolence, adherence to ceremonial and social norms, behaving in ritually appropriate ways, and wisdom.

Political philosophy also engaged Mengzi. He felt common people were of higher value than their rulers (a novel view at the time) and that the people could remove a sovereign who ruled unjustly. But Mengzi was no democrat. His ideal form of government was absolute monarchy under a wise and benevolent ruler.

The way of truth is like a great road. It is not difficult to know it. The evil is only that men will not seek it. —Mengzi

Great is the man who has not lost his childlike heart. —Mengzi

The way of learning is none other than finding the lost mind. —Mengzi

Is virtue discovered from within or taught from outside?

16
Patanjali

Born fourth century BCE (?) in eastern India (?)
Died third century BCE (?) in eastern India (?)

Yoga is often practiced in the West as a means of exercise, relaxation, and clearing the mind, with no spiritual or religious intent, but yoga was originally a means of transcending the material world to achieve union with God. It still is for Hindus and many others. Yoga means "union" in Sanskrit.

The Yoga Sutras (Aphorisms or Sayings), compiled by a sage called Patanjali over two thousand years ago, convey the original yogic teaching. Virtually nothing is known of Patanjali's life, including where and when he lived. In any case, most of the Yoga Sutras antedate Patanjali. He may have written some of them and he probably edited and tweaked others, but like the Vedas (see #1), the Yoga Sutras represent a spirituality of very ancient origin.

Patanjali divides his 196 aphorisms into four books relating eight steps or stages in the spiritual quest. These steps begin with abstaining from evil and cultivating good habits. Then come sitting, posture, breathing, and other techniques to focus the mind on a fixed object. The goal, attained only after long training under an expert guide, is total detachment from the world and merging of the individual self with the divine, rather as a drop of water is absorbed into the sea. Hindus differ on the details of this process, but most believe it takes many lifetimes—reincarnations—before liberation is attained.

This contrasts with most Western spiritualities where union with the divine is also the stated goal, but is conceived as the fulfillment or perfection of the self, not its merger into the divine.

> *Undisturbed calmness of mind is attained by cultivating friendliness toward the happy, compassion for the unhappy, delight in the virtuous, and indifference toward the wicked.* —The Yoga Sutras

> *The Spirit and wisdom sit waiting patiently near those who intensely long for them.* —The Yoga Sutras

> *Sloth is the great enemy—the inspirer of cowardice, irresolution, self-pitying grief, and trivial, hairsplitting doubts. Sloth may also be a psychological cause of sickness. It is tempting to relax from our duties, take refuge in ill-health, and hide under a nice warm blanket.* —The Yoga Sutras

Do you agree that "undisturbed calmness" and the mind's losing of itself in the divine are the goals of the spiritual life?

17
Ashoka

Born 304 BCE, in Patna, India
Died 232 BCE, in Patna, India

Ashoka the Terrible or Ashoka the Great? The Mauryan Empire encompassed most of modern India, Bangladesh, Nepal, Pakistan, and Afghanistan by the year 300 BCE. At the death of Emperor Bindusara, his many sons went to war over the succession. The victor, Ashoka, is said to have personally slain several of his brothers, perhaps all of them.

Ashoka then invaded and conquered the small, peaceful, democratic kingdom of Kalinga, on India's east coast, one of the few places not already under his sway. His military campaigns killed over one hundred thousand people.

When Ashoka set out to survey his conquests, he saw miles of burned homes and rotting corpses. He heard the wailing of widows and orphans. Far from feeling jubilant at his victory, Ashoka was sickened and grieved. He vowed never again to inflict such misery on anyone.

Ashoka had been a nominal Buddhist (he had learned of Buddhism from Kalingan monks as a youth) but now he embraced the faith and became, for the next thirty-three years, one of the most generous, compassionate, fair-minded, and beloved rulers in human history—Ashoka the Great.

He published his new policies on stone pillars fifty feet high, many of which still survive. Ashoka vowed to be as a loving father to his subjects. He banned the death penalty and all forms of torture. Never again would he resort to violence, even to animals. He provided medical care not only for his subjects, but for other countries as well. He was accessible to his subjects, even when it interrupted his dinner or state business. Criminals who were elderly or had families to support, he pardoned. He dug wells and built hospitals, schools, and monasteries.

Ashoka also sent out Buddhist missionaries, including his son and daughter, who traveled to Sri Lanka to plant the Buddhist faith there. Buddhism remains today the dominant faith on that island and Sri Lanka's is the world's oldest continuing Buddhist community. Although Ashoka promoted Buddhism, including pilgrimages to Buddhist holy sites, he respected Zoroastrians, Jains, Hindus, and others.

In his *The Outline of History*, H. G. Wells comments that among all of history's "majesties" and "royal highnesses," the name of Ashoka "shines, and shines, almost alone, a star."

What have I done? If this is victory, then what is defeat? —Ashoka
(as he toured Kalinga)

Define greatness.

18
Xunzi (Hsun-Tzu)

Born ca. 300 BCE, in north-central China
Died ca. 230 BCE, in southern China (?)

Neither Kongzi nor Mengzi (see #9 and #15) was a systematic thinker. Their books contain suggestive aphorisms, anecdotes, and conversations, but Confucian thought remained elusive and tenuous until Xunzi wrote an organized, detailed, coherent, and comprehensive account of the thinking of earlier Confucian sages. But for Xunzi's work, Confucianism might not have exerted such a formative influence on Chinese life for over two thousand years.

Xunzi also was a major philosopher in his own right who differed from his predecessors in important ways. In particular, Xunzi took a far more negative view of human nature than had Mengzi. During some periods of Chinese history, this negative view of human nature has caused Xunzi to fall out of favor.

"Human nature is evil," Xunzi said. "Goodness is attained only through training." Absent such training, people would behave in selfish, destructive, antisocial ways, seeking only to gratify their instincts and the desire for bodily pleasure, position, and recognition. Chaos would ensue.

The needed training would come, Xunzi believed, from scholars versed in the wisdom of the ancient sages. By teaching the traditional norms of courtesy, ritual observances, and the harmony expressed in music, these scholars would unite the people, tame their base desires, and channel their energies into socially constructive enterprises. Since this social system was deemed immutable, Chinese culture became deeply conservative; novelty and innovation were not prized.

Like most Confucians, Xunzi was pragmatic, rational, and this-worldly. He gave little or no thought to God or the supernatural, seeing traditional religious observances as useful expressions of emotion and a means of binding people together in an orderly social structure.

The rigid cause themselves to be broken; the pliable cause themselves to be bound. —Xunzi

A person is born with desires of the eyes and ears and a liking for beautiful sights and sounds. If he gives way to them, they will lead him to immorality and lack of restriction, and any ritual principles and propriety will be abandoned. —Xunzi

When people lack teachers, their tendencies are not corrected; when they lack ritual and moral principles, their lawlessness is not controlled. —Xunzi

Do you agree that human nature is evil and that goodness results only through training?

19
Hillel

Born ca. 60 BCE, in Babylon, Iraq
Died ca. 20 CE, in Jerusalem

Judaism does not seek converts and Jews have debated to what extent converts should be welcomed. A famous story about the founders of two academies for students of the Torah (see #14) illustrates this. Both schools began in Jerusalem just before the birth of Christ. A would-be convert asked both Shammai and Hillel to teach him the entire Torah while he stood on one foot. Insulted, Shammai drove the man away with a cane. But Hillel converted the man by saying, "What you hate, do not do to your neighbor. This is the entire Torah; the rest is commentary. Go and learn it." This story and others became part of the oral tradition, adding color and detail to the written Torah.

Hillel's gentleness and simple lifestyle won him many friends, Jews and non-Jews alike. Friends wagered whether anyone could make him angry (none succeeded). Hillel was the acknowledged leader of the Pharisees, a party of devout Jews seeking holiness of life, and became the head of the Sanhedrin, the supreme Jewish governing council in Jerusalem. His descendants headed the Sanhedrin for the next four hundred years.

Hillel was once trapped on the roof of his academy on the Sabbath day, in peril and unable to climb down. His colleagues spotted him and, despite the prohibition of labor on the Sabbath, climbed to the roof and carried him to safety, then bathed and clothed him. "This man deserves that the Sabbath be profaned on his behalf," commented one of his rescuers. What they did for Hillel accorded with Hillel's own teaching that the Sabbath was made for people, not people for the Sabbath.

In time, Hillel's flexibility and his belief that Jewish law should not lay heavy burdens on anyone prevailed over Shammai's more rigid, by-the-letter approach. Hillel's view was later incorporated into the Mishnah (see #27), the first major written redaction of the oral traditions interpreting the Torah. Rabbinic Judaism to this day still follows Hillel's approach.

If I am not for myself, then who is for me? But if I am only for myself, then who am I? And if not now, when? —Hillel

Where there are no humans, you must strive to be human yourself. —Hillel

What keeps flexibility in applying a teaching from becoming an easy "anything goes" permissiveness?

20
Mary

Born ca. 20 BCE, possibly in Nazareth, Israel
Died sometime after 30 CE, possibly in Jerusalem
or Ephesus

Like most women in the Bible, Mary, the mother of Jesus, is not a major figure, but what the Bible does say of her suggests that much was left unsaid, and her place in later Christian and Muslim devotion makes her the most revered woman in history.

Mary was a complex character. The angel Gabriel visited Mary, probably a teenager at the time, to tell her that, though an unmarried virgin, she was to give birth to a boy who would be called "the Son of the Most High." She replied, "Here am I, the servant of the Lord; let it be with me according to your word," exemplifying a humility and obedience for which she has been revered ever since.

Yet the song Mary is reported to have sung after hearing this news, known as the Magnificat, suggests a political and economic revolutionary. Mary later appeared at several critical moments in Jesus's adult ministry, prompting his first miracle and weeping at the foot of the cross, where Jesus entrusted her care to one of his disciples. She is last seen in the Bible praying with the disciples in Jerusalem shortly after Jesus's ascension into heaven.

In subsequent centuries, Mary's stature in Christian devotion soared, sometimes seeming to eclipse that of Jesus himself. She is revered as the *theotokos* (God-bearer) among the Orthodox and as "Mother of God" among Roman Catholics. Hymns are sung to her; countless artists have depicted her on canvas and in stone; miracles are attributed to her intercession at shrines across the world. Mary is a perplexing figure to modern feminists, some dismissing her as unduly submissive and retiring, while others hail her as an outspoken early champion of their cause.

Mary is an important figure in Islam, the only woman mentioned by name in the Quran, where she is called Maryam. Muslims believe in the Virgin Birth of Jesus to Mary, taking that teaching more literally than some Christians do. The Quran tells the story of Jesus's birth and gives details of Mary's life not found in the Bible. Muslim women honor Mary as an example of godly living, and Muslim tradition endows her with many additional honorific names, such as Siddiqah (Woman of faith), Tahirah (She who was purified), Mustafia (Chosen woman), and Marhumah (Wrapped in God's mercy).

Can one be both humble and a revolutionary?

21
Jesus of Nazareth

Born ca. 4 BCE, in Bethlehem, Palestinian
Territory (?)
Died ca. 29 CE, in Jerusalem

No surviving record from Jesus's time mentions him. Our knowledge of the man who exerted more influence on world history than any other comes entirely from the four Gospels in the Christian New Testament and a few similar accounts, all written one or two generations later.

Jesus was born and lived his entire life in an obscure province of the Roman Empire about the size of Delaware. A carpenter by trade, he became an itinerant rabbi and healer around the age of thirty, traveling about Galilee and occasionally to Jerusalem and nearby Gentile regions.

Attracting crowds and a small cadre of disciples who traveled with him, Jesus soon aroused controversy. To some he seemed a liberator, to others an apostate. His unconventional interpretations of rabbinic law, seemingly irreverent acts, and association with disreputable characters offended both the scribes and the Pharisees (see #14, #19, #25), while his speaking of the end of the age and coming reign of God alarmed the Romans, suggesting that he saw himself as the long-awaited *messiah* (see #5) and was plotting a Jewish revolt against Roman rule. Jesus was tried and convicted as an insurrectionist, then quickly crucified.

Two days later Jesus's tomb was found empty. He then began appearing mysteriously to his disciples who, fearful and skeptical at first, soon concluded he had risen from the dead, hailed him as *messiah*, and worshiped him as Lord and Savior. The demoralized and confused disciples were transformed. Exhibiting new courage and vision, they took their good news near and far. Most were martyred for their faith.

The communities founded by the disciples eventually grew into the Christian church. It took the church three centuries to sort out who they believed Jesus had been. The eventual consensus, hammered out after much probing and debate (see #26, #29, #32) and today embraced by over two billion Christians worldwide, was that in Jesus, God had assumed human flesh.

> *Our Father in heaven, hallowed be your name. Your kingdom come. Your will be done, on earth as it is in heaven. Give us this day our daily bread. And forgive us our debts, as we also have forgiven our debtors. And do not bring us to the time of trial, but rescue us from the evil one.* —Jesus of Nazareth

Answer Jesus's question to his disciples in Mark 8:29: "Who do you say that I am?"

22
Simon Peter

Born ca. 4 BCE, near the Sea of Galilee, Israel
or Jordan
Died ca. 64 CE, in Rome, Italy

"You are Peter, and on this rock I will build my church," Jesus said. But what did he mean by giving Simon the new name Peter, meaning Rock? The remark followed immediately upon Peter's confession that he believed Jesus to be the *messiah* (see #5).

Roman Catholics believe Jesus was entrusting the leadership of the Christian church to Peter and his successors, the bishops of Rome. Others, however, see Jesus's remark as affirming not Peter personally, but the faith Jesus saw in Peter. Beyond doubt, however, Simon Peter was the preeminent leader of and spokesman for Jesus's disciples and the early Christian church. His name always comes first in New Testament lists of the disciples.

Surely no one but Jesus foresaw such a future for the rough, uneducated fisherman. Although Peter was the first to name Jesus as *messiah*, he was also noted for foolish bravado, rebuking Jesus when Jesus began to speak of his impending death, and slicing off the ear of a slave the night before Jesus was killed. He also denied knowing Jesus three times during Jesus's trial.

Following the resurrection, Peter was forgiven and empowered by an encounter with the risen Christ who three times commissioned him to "tend my sheep." He led the disciples in selecting Matthias to replace Judas Iscariot, the disciple who had betrayed Jesus. Then, at the first Christian Pentecost, Peter boldly preached that God had raised Jesus from the dead and made him both Lord and *messiah*.

Peter spent most of the rest of his life in Jerusalem, where he was twice arrested by the Jewish authorities, defying them each time. "We must obey God rather than any human authority," he said. The apostle Paul (see #23) acknowledged Peter as the apostle to the Jews as he himself was apostle to the Gentiles. Peter's memoirs are thought to be a major source of the Gospel of Mark, though the two New Testament epistles attributed to Peter are probably from another hand.

The circumstances of Peter's arrival in Rome are unknown and the New Testament does not connect him to the city. His stay there was probably brief. Ancient tradition holds that Peter was martyred in Rome by the Emperor Nero, crucified upside down because he felt unworthy to die as his Lord had died.

Why would the later church envision Peter as the admitting officer at the gates of heaven?

23
Paul of Tarsus

Born ca. 5 CE, in Tarsus, Turkey
Died ca. 67 CE, in Rome, Italy

The New Testament contains eight indisputably authentic letters from Paul of Tarsus and a detailed account of his life, written in part by a companion of Paul. These sources portray an indomitable, steel-willed Christian missionary of an introspective bent.

As a young Pharisee (see #19, #25), Paul had diligently pursued holiness and persecuted Christians. He assisted in the stoning of Stephen. Then, around age thirty, while traveling to Damascus, Paul was temporarily blinded and converted to Christianity by a vision of the risen Christ. During the next four decades, he traveled widely and planted Christianity, until then a Jewish sect, among the Gentiles.

Paul made three missionary journeys through Asia Minor, Greece, and Macedonia. He proclaimed his message, established small Christian communities, trained local leaders, and then moved on, keeping in touch through occasional visits and letters. These letters address questions and disputes in local congregations, giving them a grounded, down-to-earth quality.

Frustrated in his early quest for holiness through obedience to the law, Paul developed a theology of justification (getting right with God) through divine grace and faith in the risen Christ. The faithful Christian community, animated by the Holy Spirit, was the body of Christ, the extension of Christ's presence in the world. Within this community, social, racial, and economic barriers melted away.

Paul's theology and ethics profoundly shaped the nascent Christian church's understanding of itself and its mission. He had little interest in the details of Jesus's earthly life. Paul's Christ was the risen Lord redeeming the world from sin and death.

Shipwrecked, often driven out of town, and nearly stoned to death, Paul saw himself as a divine agent, with Christ dwelling within him to inspire and empower his work. He eventually made his way to Rome, where he was imprisoned and presumably martyred.

In Christ God was reconciling the world to himself. —Paul of Tarsus

It is no longer I who live, but it is Christ who lives in me. —Paul of Tarsus

There is no longer Jew or Greek, there is no longer slave or free, there is no longer male and female; for all of you are one in Christ Jesus. —Paul of Tarsus

And now faith, hope, and love abide, these three; and the greatest of these is love. —Paul of Tarsus

How might Christian teaching have developed differently had Paul never lived?

24

John the Apostle

Born ca. 6 CE, near the Sea of Galilee,
Israel or Jordan
Died ca. 100 CE, in Ephesus, Turkey (?)

Two sons of Zebedee, a Galilean fisherman, were among the most intimate and trusted companions of Jesus. James is said to have been the first disciple martyred for his faith, but ancient tradition says his younger brother John died a very old man, of natural causes, the only apostle to avoid martyrdom. Irenaeus (see #26) relates that John taught and preached to the church in Ephesus, where Paul of Tarsus (see #23) had earlier visited.

John is chiefly remembered for the Gospel that bears his name. The author of the Gospel of John never states his name, however, and speculation and debate have long swirled around the question of the book's origin. It likely went through several stages, with its contents based on the memories of John the son of Zebedee, and with John's students crafting and editing the subtle, polished literary work we have today. John is usually thought to have been the "beloved disciple" often referred to in the Gospel of John but never named.

Jesus, as portrayed in John's Gospel, differs markedly from the Jesus of the other three canonical Gospels. John's Jesus uses everyday language and images to deliver sophisticated philosophical discourses, but there are few parables and adages. He arrives as light in the darkness, truth confronting falsehood, self-sacrificing love defying the self-serving hatred of those around him. John's Jesus always knows who he is and where he is going. He controls everything, though others fancy themselves in control. Jesus says "I am" in a way suggesting to Jews that he sees himself as God—a blasphemous act. Underlying the entire Gospel are questions of Jesus's identity and authority: Who is this and by what authority does he do and say such outrageous things?

The answer to such questions had been given in the prologue to the Gospel of John, where the author identifies Jesus as the *logos* of God. *Logos* was a Greek term usually translated "word," but meaning far more than that English word. For John, the *logos* is God's eternal self-expression, seen in but not limited to creation and history. In Jesus "the *logos* became flesh and lived among us . . . full of grace and truth," John wrote. Later Christian theologians would further develop the *logos* theme (see #26, #29).

Some non-Christians see John's theology as demeaning to God. Why do you suppose that is?

25
Akiva

Born ca. 40 in Lod, Israel
Died ca. 135, in Caesarea, Israel

When the Jerusalem temple was destroyed in 70 CE and the Jews scattered throughout the Roman Empire, Judaism lost its center and focal point. The dispersed Jews had holy books but no established canon of scripture. With various oral traditions purporting to explain those books, order and direction were sorely needed. Akiva ben Joseph provided an early impetus to address this need.

Born to poverty, Akiva became a shepherd. At age forty, he learned to read and at the urging of his wife, Rachel, returned to his native town of Lod and spent twenty-four years away from his family, studying the Torah (see #14, #19) at the academy there. So poor was the family that Rachel sold her hair to feed their children. When Akiva returned as a renowned scholar with many disciples in train, Rachel, now aged, shabbily dressed, and nearly penniless, ran to greet him. Akiva's disciples rebuked her, but Akiva said, "Let her be. Both my learning and yours are rightly hers."

Akiva was both a scribe (see #14) and a Pharisee (see #19). Both groups were key to the development of rabbinic Judaism. The scribes studied sacred texts, and the Pharisees sought in those texts guidance to sanctify every moment of daily living. From these two impulses—study and the pursuit of holiness—Judaism as we know it today emerged.

Akiva began sifting, sorting, and organizing the oral traditions pertaining to the Torah, a process which a century or so later would lead to the defining of the Hebrew Bible (what Christians call the Old Testament). He found nuances of meaning in every word, even every letter of the Torah. His disciples continued this work after him, laying the foundation for the Mishnah, Judaism's oldest teaching text (see #27).

After supporting a rebellion against Rome, Akiva was ordered to stop teaching the Torah. When he refused, he was tortured and publicly martyred, and is reported to have said, "All my life I waited for the opportunity to show how much I love God, and now that I have the opportunity, should I waste it?"

If the dripping of this water can, by continuous action, penetrate this solid stone, how much more can the persistent word of God penetrate the pliant, fleshy human heart if presented patiently and consistently? —Akiva, observing a stone hollowed out by dripping water

Why not leave a spiritual tradition fluid and undefined?

26

Irenaeus

Born ca. 130, in Ephesus, Turkey
Died ca. 200, in Lyons, France

As a youth in Ephesus, Irenaeus had heard the preaching of Polycarp who had known the apostle John (see #24). He later traveled to Gaul, possibly commissioned by Polycarp, became bishop of Lyons, and was probably martyred there.

By the late second century, the link to the apostles had grown faint and disputed questions could no longer be resolved by appealing to those who remembered them. Moreover, various other religious and philosophical systems thrived in the Roman Empire of the time. What was Christian teaching? Who was to say?

Gnosticism was a particularly challenging rival to Christianity. Some Gnostics claimed to be Christians. All Gnostics felt that the material world, including the human body, was a tragic mistake. They sought to rise above it to commune with an entirely spiritual reality. The incarnation, the notion that God would take on human flesh, was unthinkable to them. Some claimed that Christ was God but had only seemed human, wearing human flesh as a kind of cloak but never identifying with it.

To Irenaeus, however, the incarnation was the key to everything. Irenaeus taught what he had heard as a child in Ephesus, making use of the *logos* concept, earlier articulated in the Gospel of John, in explaining his view that in Christ God had "recapitulated" or "summed up" humanity by assuming human flesh. In his obedience, Christ reversed humanity's rebellion against God and restored the human race to union with God. Irenaeus's book *Against the Heresies* provides both the first detailed explication of Christian theology and an invaluable description of alternative views prevalent at the time. He has been called the "father of Christian theology."

Irenaeus also realized that disputes about Christian teaching would continue to arise. He saw the office of bishop (Greek *episcopos*, or supervisor) as a safeguard against false teaching, especially the bishop of Rome since both Peter and Paul had visited Rome and the Roman congregation could be counted on for orthodox teaching. He also drew up a list of authoritative writings, nearly identical with what the church would later accept as the New Testament, and wrote several summaries of the faith that resemble the later creeds.

> It was necessary that the Mediator between God and human beings be kin to both, to restore friendship and concord to both, presenting humanity to God and revealing God to humanity. —Irenaeus

What modern viewpoints resemble Gnosticism?

Judah Ha-Nasi

Born ca. 135, birthplace unknown
Died ca. 219, in Beit She'arim, Israel

Jewish tradition holds that God gave both a written teaching (the Torah) and an oral teaching (the oral Torah) to Moses on Mt. Sinai. The oral Torah was to be passed down through word-of-mouth, from teacher to student, with each generation adding insights deemed to have been implicit in it from the beginning (see #14).

By the first century of the Christian era, the oral Torah had become an enormous body of material. Akiva (see #25) began organizing it and Judah Ha-Nasi took the next step: he started writing it down.

Judah lived following a brutal persecution of Jews. Knowing that persecution could arise again, he saw the danger of depending on word-of-mouth transmission to preserve the oral Torah for future generations. Working from notes on the lectures of Akiva and others, Judah organized and summarized the oral Torah, then probed its underlying ideas and surveyed various interpretations, even those long discarded and rejected. He sought to free future generations from bondage to a single viewpoint, enabling them to apply the Torah in new ways to new occasions. The result was the Mishnah, Judaism's earliest teaching text and its leading compendium of oral tradition.

The Mishnah was not quite complete when Judah died (the next generation of scholars gave it its final form), but it bears his imprint throughout. It focused and so-lidified the detailed study of sacred texts and contains prayers, blessings, and material pertaining to tithes, agriculture, the Sabbath observance, oaths, marriage, dietary law, civil law, and worship. The Mishnah gives accounts of actual legal cases and summa-rizes how learned rabbis of the past applied the Torah to them.

Judah Ha-Nasi was a political leader as well, appointing local magistrates in the Roman province of Judea. He was conversant with Roman and Greek culture and on cordial terms with the occupying Roman authorities.

Whoever chooses the delights of this world will be deprived of them in the next, and whoever renounces them will receive them. —Judah Ha-Nasi

Tell your neighbor nothing that may not fitly be listened to. —Judah Ha-Nasi

I have learned much from my masters, more from my colleagues, and more from my pupils than from them all. —Judah Ha-Nasi

How does learning from oral tradition compare with learning from a written document?

28

Nagarjuna

Born ca. 150, in southern India
Died ca. 250, in southern India

For centuries the Buddha's teachings were recited in monasteries as Buddhist spirituality spread through India and neighboring regions. Emphasizing the individual monk's quest for enlightenment, this is called Theravada (Tradition of the Elders) Buddhism and is still widely practiced in Sri Lanka and southeast Asia.

Around the beginning of the Christian era, however, a new movement emerged in India, introducing Buddhist spirituality to the common people. It is called Mahayana (the "Great Vehicle") Buddhism. Mahayana saints typically live in the world to assist others in their spiritual journeys. Compassion for others, more than individual wisdom, is the goal. Mahayana thought is based on discourses of the Buddha said to have been kept secret until the Buddhist community was ready for them. Mahayana became the dominant expression of Buddhism in China, Tibet, Korea, and Japan.

Mayahana Buddhism has also produced a diverse philosophical tradition. The best known thinker of that tradition was named Nagarjuna. Mahayana texts regard Nagarjuna as the foremost Buddhist philosopher, after the Buddha himself (though some modern scholars have suggested that his influence has been overstated).

Nothing is known of Nagarjuna's life, but several volumes of his writings survive. The most important is his *Treatise on the Middle Way*, a poetic work of 450 stanzas. Nagarjuna enlarged on the Buddha's notion of the Middle Way (see #11) to create a sophisticated philosophy based on the Middle Way between existence and nonexistence.

The Buddha had spoken of "emptiness," a concept central to all forms of Buddhist thought. He meant that people and their experiences lack permanence. Everything changes over time and hence is "empty," not real. Nagarjuna accepted this "ultimate truth" but sought to balance it with a "conventional" or provisional truth acknowledging the reality of the sense world, albeit a derivative and fleeting reality. This was his Middle Way.

Key to Nagarjuna's understanding is the notion of "derivative origin," that neither human life nor anything humans experience comes into being on its own; it is not independent or self-sufficient, but caused by something else—and hence will pass away. Like the Buddha, he saw suffering as caused by attachment to such "empty" things. Liberation or enlightenment comes from embracing and living into this emptiness.

For whom emptiness is possible, everything is possible. —Nagarjuna

If everything is empty and fleeting, does human existence have meaning?

29
Origen

Born ca. 185, in Alexandria, Egypt
Died ca. 254, in Tyre, Lebanon

Few people have heard of the man widely deemed the early Christian church's deepest thinker because he was later declared a heretic and people stopped quoting him.

Origen's father was imprisoned for his Christian faith and then martyred. The young Origen wrote to his father in prison, urging him to stand firm. He expected to be martyred himself. Origen was indeed tortured under the Emperor Decius and probably died of his wounds, but not before he had become the most influential biblical scholar in the Christian world.

Origen's mind, perhaps influenced by the Gnostics (see #26), often traveled to lofty, esoteric realms. He believed in disembodied souls and that some souls acquired material bodies because they had grown cold. They were gradually returning toward reunion with God. The divine *logos* (see #24, #26) was one soul that had not grown cold. In Jesus Christ, it lovingly assumed a human body. Humanity was thereby assumed into the *logos*, the human and divine natures becoming interwoven. Eventually, all of creation, including Satan himself, would be reunited with God, Origen believed.

Origen was a devoted and innovative Bible student. He believed the divine *logos* was present in scripture as it was present in Christ. Every bit of scripture pertained to Christ, Origen believed, and was divinely inspired. He was not a fundamentalist in the modern sense, however, because he did not believe God had dictated the Bible to its human authors and he had little use for the literal meaning of scripture. Origen developed the allegorical method of biblical interpretation which has been hugely influential in both the Eastern and the Western churches. The spiritual meaning of scripture is found beneath the surface and is not always evident to a casual reader, he said.

Controversy always swirled around Origen. Three hundred years after his death, the church condemned him as a heretic, because he believed in disembodied souls and universal salvation, among other things. But Origen had made an indelible mark on the Christian church, and future Christians would be indebted to him, even after the man himself had been banished to obscurity.

If the mystery concealed of old is made manifest to the apostles through the prophetic writings, and if the prophets, being wise men, understood what proceeded from their own mouths, then the prophets knew what was made manifest to the apostles. —Origen

Can scripture have different levels of meaning?

30
Plotinus

Born 205, near Tell El-Ruba, Egypt
Died 270, near Naples, Italy

Plotinus was the last of the great Greek philosophers and the father of neo-Platonism. He never saw himself, however, as launching an updated version of the philosophy of Plato, but rather as Plato's faithful interpreter, and for centuries thereafter readers of the great Athenian philosopher understood what they read largely as Plotinus had expounded it.

Plotinus studied under several mentors in Alexandria before seeking exposure to a wider range of ideas. He began traveling and arrived in Rome at the age of forty, spending the rest of his life in or near the city. He taught philosophy in Rome and, during the final decade of his life, let his disciple (and later biographer) Porphyry compile his lecture notes into *The Enneads*, the philosophical treatise through which his thought has come down to us.

"The One" was Plotinus's term for God, which (certainly not whom) he conceived as totally transcendent—indivisible, changeless, eternal, incomprehensible, and inexpressible. The One does not act and is even beyond self-consciousness, yet is the source of all that exists. Existing things are not created (that would imply action on the part of the One) but emanate from the One, as light emanates from the sun.

Plotinus posits a hierarchy of entities originating from the One. The first, Mind, is still outside of time, but it is here that multiplicity first appears, for Mind is conscious both of itself and of the One. From Mind proceeds what Plotinus calls the World Soul, still indivisible and immaterial, but linked at its higher level to Mind and at its lower level to the material world. The World Soul governs the realm of nature, including individual human souls which come from the World Soul and like it, relate both to Mind and to their physical bodies. Human beings err by forgetting their true nature as disembodied souls. Through contemplation, they remember and reclaim that identity. Human souls survive the death of the body. Unlike the Gnostics (see #26), Plotinus did not see the material world as a mistake or evil. As part of what emanated from the One, it was good.

Augustine (see #37) was much influenced by Plotinus, both before and after his conversion to Christianity, and Plotinus's dualistic understanding of reality has always found a following among some Christians.

Compare Plotinus's understanding of God and human nature with yours.

31

Anthony

Born ca. 251, near Beni Suef, Egypt
Died 355, on an Egyptian peak overlooking
the Red Sea

When the Emperor Constantine converted to Christianity in 313, what had been a fringe faith opposing the dominant culture instantly became part of that culture and began to resemble it. Throngs stepped forward to be baptized for political reasons. Where could those seeking to make a deeper commitment now turn? Thousands turned to the desert.

Anthony was born to a wealthy family in upper Egypt. His parents died when Anthony was about twenty, leaving him a large estate. When Anthony read "If you wish to be perfect, go, sell your possessions, and give the money to the poor, and you will have treasure in heaven; then come, follow me" (Matthew 19:21), he liquidated his estate, gave the money away, and took up residence in a solitary place outside of town. For the next eighty or so years, as he became famous and would-be disciples sought him out, Anthony kept moving deeper into the desert, finally arriving at a remote peak overlooking the Red Sea, where he spent the last fifty years of his life, alone.

Most of our information about Anthony comes from Athanasius's adoring biography, written shortly after Anthony's death. It contains colorful tales of Anthony's battling all manner of demons and devoting himself to prayer, fasting, and scripture reading. Anthony lived an extremely austere life, taking but one meal per day and declining to bathe. According to Athanasius, he exemplified inner harmony, tranquility, honesty, and simplicity.

Two additional sources of information about Anthony are a collection of tales and sayings attributed to him and other desert hermits, and seven letters probably from his hand.

Anthony was by no means the only one seeking holiness alone in the desert. Thousands did the same. The hermit monk became a model for Christian living that has ever since attracted a small but devoted number of devotees. A second model developed shortly thereafter when groups of hermits came together to seek holiness in communal living (see #32).

A time is coming when men will go mad, and when they see someone who is not mad, they will attack him, saying, "You are mad, for you are not like us."
—Anthony

Learn to love humility, for it will cover all your sins. —Anthony

When the church is too worldly, how does a Christian live faithfully?

32
Basil of Caesarea

Born 329 or 330, in Kayseri, Turkey
Died 379, in Kayseri, Turkey

Christian theology, especially in Eastern Orthodoxy, owes much to three fourth-century bishops from Cappadocia, in central Turkey—Basil of Caesarea, his brother Gregory of Nyssa (see #34), and their close friend Gregory of Nazianzus (see #33). They are known as the Cappadocian Fathers.

A gifted organizer and politician, Basil served as bishop of Caesarea, a position carrying authority over neighboring dioceses as well. He held his jurisdiction together amidst passionate theological squabbling about the Trinity, all the while advocating for what later became the orthodox understanding. He was noted for his preaching, especially on themes of social responsibility, and for his hands-on care of the poor. The Orthodox churches also revere Basil for a liturgy attributed to him.

Basil exerted a formative influence on Christian monasticism. He traveled to Egypt to study monastic life there (see #31), but thought a hermit monk living alone risked idiosyncratic extremism. Upon his return, Basil gathered into monastic communities any hermit monks he found in Cappadocia, and monasteries began to flourish there. Life in Basil's monasteries centered around prayer, manual labor, care for the poor, and obedience, a model which thrives to this day in Eastern monasticism and which greatly influenced later Western monasticism as well (see #42).

Christians had experienced God as Creator, God in the person of Jesus, and God moving in their midst. How was this to be explained? An outspoken party known as Arians (after an Alexandrian priest named Arius) maintained that since God is one, Jesus and the Spirit must be subordinate to the Creator. Basil, however, noting that Father, Son, and Holy Spirit are praised in worship as one, concluded that they must truly be one in nature. God the Father (Creator), God the Son (incarnate in Jesus), and God the Holy Spirit (active today), though distinguishable, are indivisible, Basil said.

Basil's foremost contribution was to the understanding of the Holy Spirit. He believed everyone hungers for God, a hunger satisfied only by seeking to become like God. This is the work of the Holy Spirit, giving life and then guiding persons toward holiness and union with God.

> *What does the Spirit do? His works are ineffable in majesty and innumerable in quantity. . . . Even if you can imagine anything beyond the ages, you will discover that the Spirit is even further before.* —Basil of Caesarea

Have you experienced God in different ways? Can that be explained?

33
Gregory of Nazianzus

Born 329, in Nenizi, Turkey
Died ca. 389, in Nenizi, Turkey

When an Orthodox Christian refers to "the Theologian," everyone knows he speaks of Gregory of Nazianzus. Gregory's reputation rests primarily on his five Theological Orations, delivered in Constantinople in 380 in defense of the Trinity, but he also wrote letters, sermons, and poetry. He is noted more for the elegance and clarity of his writing than for his originality.

By nature shy, trusting, and introspective, Gregory was splendidly suited for the life of a literary contemplative. But his friend Basil of Caesarea (see #32) prevailed upon him to accept a small bishopric under Basil's jurisdiction, a position Gregory intensely disliked and which he seems largely to have neglected. In 381, following the enthusiastic reception of his Theological Orations, he was made archbishop of Constantinople, but could not cope with the convoluted politics of church and empire. He resigned the position within a year, returning to his native town of Nazianzus, where he spent the rest of his life writing in seclusion. A two-thousand-line autobiographical poem, written during this time, shows his pique and his internal struggles.

The Council of Nicaea in 325 had defined the Christian understanding of the relationship of the Father and Son. Gregory and the other two Cappadocian Fathers wrote especially of the Holy Spirit. Gregory was the first to speak of the Holy Spirit's "proceeding" from the Father. In his Theological Orations, he said a godly life is the mark of a true theologian; maintained that the Son and the Spirit, though originating with the Father, are eternal; defended from scripture that Christ was fully human and fully divine; and brilliantly expounded the idea of three "persons" united in one indivisible Godhead.

Gregory also developed a view of revelation novel at the time, though commonplace later. He saw divine revelation as progressive, given in stages, as humanity is able to receive it.

> God accepts our desires as though they were a great value. He longs ardently
> for us to desire and love him. He accepts our petitions for benefits as though we
> were doing him a favor. His joy in giving is greater than ours in receiving. So let
> us not be apathetic in our asking, nor set too narrow bounds to our requests, nor
> ask for frivolous things unworthy of God's greatness. —Gregory of Nazianzus

Is understanding the nature of God possible? Is it important?

34

Gregory of Nyssa

Born ca. 335, in Kayseri, Turkey
Died ca. 395, in Nevsehir, Turkey (?)

Basil of Caesarea (see #32), seeking to promote supporters of Trinitarian theology, had named his younger brother Gregory and his friend Gregory of Nazianzus (see #33) as bishops of small dioceses under his jurisdiction. Neither flourished as a bishop, and Basil's brother's experience in Nyssa was even unhappier than that of the other Gregory in Nazianzus. He had no gift for finance, and when funds went missing, was falsely accused of misappropriating them. He was imprisoned, then escaped and wandered through central Turkey for a time. Gregory was eventually exonerated and resumed his duties as bishop of Nyssa, but ecclesiastical governance remained onerous to him.

Gregory of Nyssa lacked the political skills of his brother and the intellectual acumen of Gregory of Nazianzus, but excelled them both in the depth of his insights into the spiritual life. His thought evolved during his lifetime, culminating in his *Life of Moses*, focusing on God's self-revelation to the Hebrew lawgiver (see #4) in three key incidents: at the burning bush (Exodus 3), in the thick cloud (Exodus 20), and while passing by and showing only his back side (Exodus 33).

For Gregory, God is unknowable, but approachable. Human beings experience a desire for God which Gregory likens to hunger and erotic love. As we strive for God, we move into a holy darkness and become more and more like God. This movement toward God never ceases, even in the next life. For Gregory, human perfection was not arriving at a state of bliss, but a perpetual ascending and growing. The soul is never satisfied, for God is always more, always greater, always ahead of us. Gregory was a universalist who believed that ultimately all created beings would choose union with the divine.

All three Cappadocian theologians contributed to the Christian understanding of the Trinity. In arriving at this doctrine, the church departed from the philosophical understanding of God as existing in absolute simplicity and solitude, affirming instead that God is essentially personal, implying relationship, movement, energy, and mutuality within the being of God.

> *Hope is always drawing the soul away from the beauty it sees to what lies beyond.* —Gregory of Nyssa

> *The true vision of God is to desire to see him and never to be satisfied in that desire.* —Gregory of Nyssa

Is a satisfying knowledge of God possible?

35

Ambrose

Born ca. 335, in Trier, Germany (?)
Died 397, in Milan, Italy

Ambrose of Milan has long been seen as the model Christian bishop. Born to wealth and influence (his father was Roman governor over much of western Europe), Ambrose studied law and rhetoric and then entered public life, rising to the post of governor of the region around Milan.

The Milanese church was deeply divided by the Arian controversy (see #32) when the bishop of Milan died in 374. Both the Arians and the orthodox party wanted one of their own named to the post. The politicking became bitter. Seeking to calm the storm, Ambrose, already beloved as governor, entered the church where the election was taking place to plead for peace. Within moments, the crowd began shouting "Ambrose for bishop!" But the governor, though a believing Christian, had not been baptized and did not want the office of bishop. The crowd prevailed upon him, however, and he reluctantly agreed. Within the next eight days, Ambrose was baptized, then ordained deacon, priest, and bishop (setting a surely unbreakable record for rapid rise in the ecclesiastical hierarchy).

Once a bishop, Ambrose liquidated his vast wealth, giving it to the poor and the church, and for the next twenty-three years, oversaw the Milanese church with charity, flexibility, and fairness. He mediated the swirling theological disputes of the day with a measured hand.

Ambrose carried on a cordial correspondence with Basil of Caesarea, with whose views he strongly concurred, but never insulted his Arian opponents, who came to trust him. Unversed in theology at the time of his election, he often studied the Bible and theology far into the night, becoming particularly fond of Origen (see #29). His door was open to anyone, of whatever rank. Ambrose even rebuked the emperor when he deemed it necessary. His rebukes were accepted and the emperor repented. When some insisted on uniformity in worship, Ambrose said he always honored local custom in his travels (giving rise to the adage "When in Rome, do as the Romans do").

Ambrose is also thought to have introduced Eastern, antiphonal chant to the Western church and he wrote original hymns, some of them still sung today. So effective was he as a preacher that his sermons were instrumental in the conversion of Augustine of Hippo (see #37).

The emperor is in the church, not above the church. —Ambrose

Describe the model bishop or religious leader.

36
Ashi

Born 352, in Babylon, Iraq
Died 427, in Babylon, Iraq

Soon after the Jews left Palestine in the first century of the Christian era, the spiritual and intellectual center of Judaism shifted to Babylon, where a centuries-old Jewish community thrived (see #14). Mesopotamia remained the heart of Jewish life for the next millennium. From this community came the Babylonian Talmud, to this day the foremost compendium of Jewish thought and culture. Its primary editor was Rav Ashi. An earlier Talmud written in Jerusalem is also considered authoritative, but the Babylonian Talmud has been the more influential of the two.

Wealthy, well-connected, and the leading scholar of his day, for nearly sixty years Ashi headed an academy in Babylon for the study of the Torah and the Mishnah (see #27). He convened other scholars to probe those texts and apply their precepts to new questions and situations. Ashi collected records of discussions and viewpoints, some almost forgotten, creating an encyclopedia-length compendium of Jewish lore, including questions and answers (sometimes several answers to the same question), legends, philosophy, logic, history, science, anecdotes, and witty sayings.

Although the Babylonian Talmud is thoughtfully organized, it can read like a rambling stream-of-consciousness novel. Its conclusions are less significant than the methods used to reach those conclusions—free-wheeling discussion and debate with insights from every source given their due. No field of human knowledge or experience lay outside its purview.

Scriptural authority in Judaism can appear diffused and muddled. It may be envisioned as a series of concentric circles. At the center is the Torah (see #14), the foundational authority. A passage from the Torah is read at every Jewish worship service. In the next circle is the rest of the Hebrew Bible, known to Christians as the Old Testament. The circle surrounding the Bible contains the Mishnah, containing additional teachings given at Mt. Sinai and handed down orally for centuries. The next circle contains the Talmud, offering commentary on the Bible and Mishnah and inviting later students to add their contributions. In the outer circle are other sources of knowledge, including secular disciplines like philosophy and science. Jews see God's truth contained in the Torah as changeless, but human understanding of it as always growing and evolving as new occasions and challenges arise. Each generation of Jews is expected to reconsider what God is saying in the Torah.

Do you find the Jewish understanding of scriptural authority freeing, confusing, or both?

37
Augustine of Hippo

Born 354, in Souk Ahras, Algeria
Died 430, in Annaba, Algeria

Augustine of Hippo towers over Western Christian spirituality. It was he who posed the questions which have energized Western Christians for 1,600 years.

As a young man, Augustine enjoyed sensual pleasures, taught rhetoric, and studied philosophy, searching for the truly good. Increasingly restless in his search and inspired by the prayers of his mother and the preaching of Ambrose (see #35), he was converted to Christianity and baptized at the age of thirty-three. Augustine returned to his native north Africa, became bishop of Hippo (modern Annaba), and wrote probing, insightful books on theology, philosophy, ethics, the Bible, and his personal life. We have more literature from his hand than from any other ancient author. Augustine's contributions are enormous.

Augustine debated a British monk named Pelagius over the nature of sin and grace. He had a profound sense of human sin, insisting that it is universal and irresistible and that only an infusion of divine grace can blot it out.

He also explored the nature of the Christian church in a dispute with the Donatists, a group maintaining that only ordination at the hands of a morally worthy bishop is valid. Augustine countered that God validates the church and its sacraments and that human failings do not annul them. He wrote of four distinguishing characteristics of the Christian church—its unity, holiness, universality, and faithfulness to apostolic teaching.

In his majestic *City of God*, Augustine provided the first comprehensive Christian understanding of history, describing two radically different but intertwined "cities," each defined by what it loves, and countering those who blamed the Christian church for the decline of the Roman Empire.

Augustine also probed the Trinity, elucidating that teaching with several analogies based on human psychology. A human being, for example, exists, knows, and wills— three activities or manifestations of the soul, yet the soul is one.

Augustine's most popular work is his *Confesssions*, the first spiritual autobiography and, many would say, the best such work ever penned. Augustine's *Confessions* is intensely personal, ruthlessly honest, and psychologically penetrating. It is cast as an extended prayer of thankfulness and praise.

> *You awaken and stir us so that only in praising you can we be content. You have made us for yourself and our hearts are restless until they find their rest in you.*
> —Augustine

If you were to write a book of "confessions," what would it say?

38

John Cassian

Born ca. 360, in Dobruja, Romania or Bulgaria (?)
Died ca. 435, in Marseille, France

John Cassian studied under the hermits of the Egyptian desert (see #31) for seven years, making extensive notes on their practices and seeking simplicity of life. After later spending time in Constantinople and Rome, Cassian was invited around the year 415 to introduce Egyptian desert spirituality to Europe. This became his life's work.

Cassian preferred communal monasticism to the hermit model and set up two monasteries in southern France, one for men and one for women. He is chiefly remembered for two literary works in which he organized and adapted what he had learned in Egypt. Those books greatly influenced Benedict of Nursia (see #42) and the character of Western monasticism generally.

In his *Institutes*, Cassian tells how to structure monastic life to overcome vices such as gluttony, lust, pride, anger, and greed, or as he says, "what belongs to the outer man."

In his second book, the *Conferences*, Cassian distills the wisdom of the Egyptian hermits pertaining to "the training of the inner man and the perfection of the heart." He saw a monastery as a place for demonstrating and teaching how to partake of the love of God and described a three-step process which would be further developed by later thinkers. The first step, usually taking some years, was to subdue fleshly and material desires through ascetic disciplines. Cassian's regimen was strict but temperate, allowing for human frailty. Then came the cultivation of humility through charitable acts. The final step was mystical union with the Spirit of God, described in erotic terms and often including retreat from the world in a hermitage.

Cassian did not share the strict emphasis on divine grace of his contemporary Augustine (see #37), but found a place for human free will and prayer in overcoming sin.

> *When the vice of pride cannot seduce a man with extravagant clothes, it tries to tempt him with shabby ones. When it cannot flatter him with honor, it inflates him by causing him to endure what appears to be dishonor. When it cannot persuade him to feel proud of his eloquence, it entices him through silence into thinking he has achieved stillness. When it cannot puff him up with the thought of his luxurious table, it lures him into fasting for the sake of praise.* —John Cassian

How does the pursuit of virtue become a source of spiritual pride?

39
Buddhaghosa

Born ca. 370, in northeast India
Died ca. 450, in India (?)

The earliest Buddhist scriptures, dating from the fifth century BCE (see #12, #13), were not written down until 29 BCE. The Mahavihara Monastery in what is today Sri Lanka owned the largest collection of these sacred texts, including extensive commentaries on the Buddha's discourses. Organizing these scriptures and making them available to a wider readership was largely the work of a monk called Buddhaghosa (the name means "Voice of the Buddha" in Pali).

Buddhaghosa was an itinerant Hindu saint who traveled northern India and debated philosophical questions with other scholars. When a Buddhist monk bested him in debate, Buddhaghosa converted to Buddhism and determined to study his new faith in depth. He eventually found his way to the Mahavihara Monastery, gained access to the library, and undertook his life's work.

Buddhaghosa was not an original thinker. His gifts were for systematizing, translating, and explaining. The Mahavihara scriptures were mostly in a tongue little understood off the island of Sri Lanka. Buddhaghosa translated them into Pali, a language known nearly everywhere Theravada Buddhism (see #28) had taken root. These scriptures are now known as the Pali Canon, Buddhism's oldest anthology of sacred writings. Buddhaghosa also organized the texts and wrote commentaries of his own. So clear was his work that it quickly became—and remains—the accepted interpretation of Theravada Buddhism.

Buddhaghosa's most popular work, *Path of Purification*, is a masterpiece of Indian literature. Using sophisticated psychological categories, *Path of Purification* contains a detailed account of Buddhist meditation practices, suggesting forty different objects of meditation, each suited to a different personality type. A meditation teacher is to assess a student's personality by observing posture, eating habits, and other behaviors, then assign a topic for meditation.

The best known section of *Path of Purification* is its treatment of death. Bhuddaghosa suggests meditating on death from many vantage points: death as a murderer, as the undoing of life's accomplishments, as an inevitability that we share with animals, as an illustration of life's fragility, as entrance into reality. Buddhaghosa's meditation on death is still practiced among Theravada Buddhists to this day.

> *There is suffering, but none who suffers; doing exists although there is no doer; there is extinction, but no extinguished person; although there is a path, there is no one to travel it.* —Buddhaghosa

What would be the point of meditating on death?

40

Patrick

Born ca. 390, in Banwen, Wales (?)
Died ca. 460, in Downpatrick, Ireland (?)

Christianity probably reached Celtic Britain in the late second century. In this remote corner of the Roman Empire, the faith developed understandings often different from those on the European continent. The Celts retained many pre-Christian practices and beliefs, making no sharp distinction between paganism and Christianity and seeing conversion more as a mutual enrichment than the replacing of one faith by another. Celtic Christianity was earthy, intimate, and immediate. Every star and planet, every rock and stream, the human body and every organ of it disclosed something of the divine. The Celts had little interest in the metaphysical speculations popular elsewhere.

Patrick, born in Wales, was kidnapped as a young man and taken to Ireland, where he worked as a shepherd. Not religiously inclined at first, Patrick learned to pray during his long hours alone in the field at night. After six years, he escaped and found his way back home, but he dreamt of a man from Ireland begging him to return and evangelize his former captors. Legend says that Patrick converted the entire island, but his work was probably confined largely to the north.

In an autobiographical essay called Patrick's *Confession*, he gives a vivid picture of a humble yet extraordinarily energetic Christian missionary, but the best known work attributed to Patrick is a hymn called "St. Patrick's Breastplate." Though perhaps written sometime later, it captures the spirit of Patrick and of Celtic Christianity generally, calling upon the Trinity to act as a shield protecting the singer from dangers both physical and spiritual.

The Celtic influence on the British church subsided after the Synod of Whitby in 664, but many modern people, alienated by impersonal technology and burdened by environmental degradation, find the Celtic emphasis on the sacredness of the created order attractive and timely.

> *Christ be with me, Christ before me, Christ behind me, Christ within me, Christ beneath me, Christ above me, Christ to my right, Christ to my left, Christ in my lying, in my sitting, in my rising, Christ in the heart of all who think of me, Christ in the mouth of all who speak of me, Christ in the eye of all who see me, Christ in the ear of all who hear me.* —St. Patrick's Breastplate

Is the natural order something to be used for humanity's purposes or a manifestation of the divine and therefore sacred?

41
Bodhidharma

Born 470 (?), in southern India (?)
Died 550 (?), near Luoyang, China (?)

Accounts of the life of Bodhidharma are long on legend and short on verifiable fact. Some say he never
existed. Bodhidharma was probably born in southern
India in the fifth century, possibly to a Brahmin family.
Declining a career in politics, he became a monk and
immersed himself in Mahayana Buddhism, identifying particularly with Kashyapa
(see #13) and Nagarjuna (see #28).

At some point Bodhidharma traveled to China where, having attained some renown, he had a famous conversation with the southern Liang emperor Wu, a devout
Buddhist who had constructed temples and monasteries throughout his realm and
commissioned the translations of Buddhist scriptures into Chinese. Wu asked what
merit these actions had gained him. "None at all," said Bodhidharma. Disappointed,
Wu then asked Bodhidharma to convey to him the highest truth. "There is no truth—
just emptiness," said Bodhidharma. "Just who do you think you are?" the aggravated
Wu asked. "I don't know," said Bodhidharma, smiling. He then turned and walked out.

Bodhidharma set out again, for the Shaolin Monastery near Luoyang, in northern
China. Declining lodging within the monastery, he is said to have found a nearby
cave where he sat facing a wall and meditated for nine years, uttering not one word
during that time, despite questions posed to him by would-be disciples. Possibly concerned for Bodhidharma's health, the Shaolin monks built a room for him and finally
prevailed upon him to occupy it. He meditated silently for another four years in this
room. No one knows what meditational methods Bodhidharma used.

Colorful legends abound concerning Bodhidharma. Ch'an Buddhists (see #13,
#58, #77) look to him as their patriarch and founder. He is the model for the Ch'an
master, teaching by example and intuitive understanding rather than by the study of
scriptures and doctrines. The goal is to experience and embrace emptiness in order
to attain enlightenment and Nirvana. It is also said that Bodhidharma originated the
tradition of Chinese martial arts from which kung-fu and karate evolved, as a means
of clearing the mind.

If you use your mind to study reality, you won't understand either your mind
or reality. If you study reality without using your mind, you'll understand both.
—Bodhidharma

Freeing oneself from words is liberation. —Bodhidharma

**If "there is no truth, just emptiness," do study, work, and life itself have
significance?**

42

Benedict of Nursia

Born 480, in Nursia, Italy
Died 543, on Monte Cassino, Italy

For roughly 600 years, until about 1300, spirituality in the West meant just one thing: living according to a slender little book known as the Benedictine Rule. It was a handbook for structuring the life of a "school for the Lord's service," as Benedict of Nursia called a monastery.

Nothing is certain about Benedict's early life, but it was later said that after studying in Rome, he grew disgusted by the scandalous behavior he witnessed there and retreated to the Italian countryside to become a hermit. But he soon began to found monasteries, including what became and remains the mother house of the worldwide Benedictine movement, on Monte Cassino in central Italy.

Benedict's Rule draws on Basil (see #32) and John Cassian (see #38) and is noted for its brevity, flexibility, and moderation. Each of Benedict's monasteries, consisting of twelve monks, was autonomous. Each house chose its own abbot; there was no superior or centralized authority. Benedict urged that allowance be made for the weakest brother so as to avoid embarrassing him. "Nothing harsh, nothing burdensome," he said.

Benedictine monks take a vow of "stability, conversion of life, and obedience," as outlined in the Rule. Stability includes living harmoniously with others in the community, allowing for the idiosyncrasies of each. Conversion of life means allowing oneself to be shaped by the community and not asserting one's own opinions. Obedience is submission to one another and to the abbot who, once elected by his fellows, is to be obeyed without question.

All this is designed to lead to humility, a key theme in the Rule. Private property is not allowed in the monastery; all things are owned in common. Hospitality, especially to pilgrims and the poor, is always extended.

Monastic life was a balance of work, rest, study, and prayer. The community gathered seven times a day for worship, consisting of scripture readings, hymns, and prayers, all based on the church seasons.

The Benedictine movement quickly spread. Today there are roughly a hundred Benedictine monasteries and retreat houses in the United States alone, and hundreds more worldwide.

The brothers demonstrate pure love to one another, loving fear to God, sincere and humble love to their abbot. Let them prefer nothing whatever to Christ, and may he bring us all together to everlasting life. —Benedict of Nursia

What would you emphasize in a "rule" for communal living?

43
Gregory I

Born ca. 540, in Rome, Italy
Died 604, in Rome, Italy

Pope Gregory I—Gregory the Great—is revered not for his theological contributions (he was not an original or deep thinker), but for his administrative gifts, his personal character, and for laying the foundation on which the medieval papacy would later be erected and which undergirds the Roman Catholic Church to this day.

Born to a wealthy patrician family, Gregory at first pursued a government and diplomatic career, serving for several years as papal liaison to the imperial government in Constantinople. But Gregory was soon drawn to the monastic life. He converted his villa in Rome into a monastery and founded six new monasteries on the family's extensive estate in Sicily. When the papacy became vacant in 590, the clergy and people unanimously chose Gregory. He was the first monk to hold the office.

For the next fourteen years, despite frequently poor health, Gregory worked tirelessly. He reformed the administration of the papal estates and finances by insisting on efficiency and honesty; held bishops and other officials accountable for their work; sent teams of missionaries far afield (he is especially remembered for sending the monk Augustine to found the see of Canterbury in England); and cared for the poor who resided near him, requiring other church officials to do the same.

Although the extent of Gregory's contributions to the church's worship life are uncertain, it was during his time that seasonal variations were introduced into the liturgy of the Western church, and the form of chant developed at this time bears Gregory's name.

Gregory envisioned church and empire as separate but mutually supportive realms. He rejected any imperial attempt to interfere in church affairs and assumed that all provinces of the Western church were subject to papal authority. His book on the office of bishop, emphasizing the bishop's role as shepherd of souls and outlining the qualities expected of those called to that office, is still cited today.

When we attend to the needs of those in want, we give them what is theirs,
not ours. More than performing works of mercy, we are paying a debt of justice.
—Gregory I

Anger is an expensive luxury which only those of a certain income can afford.
—Gregory I

Given the choice, would you choose a spiritual master or a gifted administrator as church leader? Why?

44
Khadijah bint Khuwaylid

Born 566, in Mecca, Saudi Arabia
Died 619, in Mecca, Saudi Arabia

Detractors of the Prophet Muhammad (see #45) often point to his multiple marriages to suggest that he was a womanizer, but that judgment ignores three facts: First, polygamy was not questioned in Muhammad's day. Second, all but one of Muhammad's marriages came late in life and were forged for largely political reasons, to unify the warring tribes of the Arabian peninsula. Third, prior to his other marriages, Muhammad was faithfully married for twenty-five years to one woman until her death when he was fifty, a year he referred to thereafter as his Year of Sorrow.

That wife's name was Khadijah. The daughter of a wealthy merchant of the Quraysh tribe, she inherited her father's business interests at his death, running them very successfully, and was known for feeding and clothing the poor and sharing her wealth with needy relatives.

Fifteen years Muhammad's senior according to most sources, Khadijah hired him to travel to Syria and oversee a business transaction there. Impressed by Muhammad's conscientiousness and honesty, the twice-widowed Khadijah proposed marriage. By all accounts, the marriage was a very happy one. It produced two sons who died in infancy and four daughters, only one of whom survived her parents. That daughter, Fatima, married Muhammad's cousin Ali (see #47), a union producing all the Prophet's descendants, including several key Muslim leaders of later times.

Khadijah also served as Muhammad's chief spiritual advisor. After the Prophet's first revelation, received while alone in a cave, he returned home to Khadijah, then fell ill. When Khadijah suggested bed rest, he replied that there was no time for resting, that he had been commanded to call the people of Arabia to turn to God but was unsure whether anyone would listen to him. Khadijah thought for a moment and then said that she would be the first to listen to his message. His wife was Muhammad's first convert and stood by him even in the face of forceful opposition. She is known today as the "mother of Islam."

The Prophet's later wives were sometimes jealous even of his memory of Khadijah. One objected when he continued to support Khadijah's relatives financially. Muhammad replied, "She believed in me when no one else did. She accepted Islam when others scorned me and helped and comforted me when no one else would lend a helping hand."

What was Khadijah's greatest gift to her husband?

45
Muhammad

Born ca. 570, in Mecca, Saudi Arabia
Died 632, in Medina, Saudi Arabia

Muslims see their book, the Quran, as the definitive revelation of God and Muhammad as the agent through whom it was given. Muhammad received the Quran (meaning recitation) in a series of visions beginning in his fortieth year and continuing until his death.

Muslims believe the Quran contains the literal words of God. It discloses a God of goodness and mercy and is uncompromisingly monotheistic. The Quran can be read on several levels and is the source of Muslim theology, anthropology, law, ethics, and the Muslim understanding of history. Reciting passages from it is a major part of Islamic education and worship, and Islamic art is resplendent with graceful, ornate renderings of its verses.

Though not divine or to be worshiped, Muhammad himself is also the object of veneration. Knowledge of the Prophet comes not only from the Quran itself, but also from the many anecdotes and stories handed down by those who knew him. In matters of faith and practice, these accounts rank just below the Quran in authority. Muslims revere Muhammad as exhibiting the highest degree of every virtue, especially humility and submission to God. At the mention of his name, Muslims typically say, "Peace be upon him."

Following his first revelation (see #44), Muhammad remained quiet for a time, finally sharing his experience with his close family. They became his first converts, but many citizens of Mecca, where the family lived, were polytheists who profited from the city's numerous pagan shrines. Muhammad's strict monotheism was not well received and a violent conflict ensued. Muhammad sent some of his followers across the Red Sea to Ethiopia, where a Christian king protected them.

In the year 621, Muhammad was transported first to Jerusalem and then to heaven itself, a gripping and formative experience known as the Prophet's Night Journey. A year later, the entire Muslim community migrated to the town of Yathrib, north of Mecca, renaming it Medina an-Nabi (City of the Prophet). The name was soon shorted to al-Medina (the City).

Spread by both conversion and conquest, Islam grew into a vibrant monotheistic community that, by the time of Muhammad's death, extended throughout Arabia and would soon stretch from the Atlantic in the west to the Pacific in the east.

Compare the place of the person (Jesus, Muhammad) to the place of the book (the Bible, the Quran) in Christianity and Islam.

46
Abu Bakr

Born ca. 573, in Mecca, Saudi Arabia
Died 634, in Medina, Saudi Arabia

The Prophet Muhammad (see #45) exercised both spiritual and political authority over the Arabian peninsula, but he left no instructions as to a successor. At his death, the Prophet's followers convened and chose Abu Bakr, his closest friend and confidant, as the first caliph (successor).

Abu Bakr's ties to Muhammad ran deep. Some say he was the Prophet's first convert outside his family and he was with Muhammad during his three days in a cave while fleeing from Mecca to Medina, a pivotal moment in the Prophet's life. His daughter was Muhammad's most beloved wife after Khadijah (see #44), and Muhammad often referred others to Abu Bakr for guidance.

Many Arabian tribes, however, regarded Muhammad's death as terminating their participation in the Muslim community. New would-be prophets arose and old tribal and regional tensions resurfaced. Some tribes withheld the *zakat*, an obligatory payment by all Muslims for the support of the poor. In just twenty-seven months as caliph, until his own death, Abu Bakr succeeded in subduing the peninsula's warring factions. He also orchestrated campaigns against the two great empires of the day, the Persian and the Byzantine, securing the borders of the Islamic community from their incursion and preparing it for its imminent expansion into three continents. He forbade Muslim soldiers from committing crimes against captive peoples and guaranteed the safety of Byzantine Christian monasteries.

The Quran is the ultimate authority for Muslims. Scholars had memorized its passages for recitation, but as they died or were killed in battle, Abu Bakr formed a group to collect, verify, and transcribe every word of the Quran. He is today revered for his faithfulness, wisdom, and strength of character. Umar, successor of Abu Bakr as caliph, said, "If the faith of Abu Bakr were weighed against that of everyone on earth, Abu Bakr's would outweigh all the others."

Such is the view of all Sunni Muslims. Sunnis (from the Arabic word for example or customary practice) comprise Islam's largest denomination, roughly 85 percent of all Muslims. However, Shia Muslims (see #47, #61, #141), Islam's second largest group, see Abu Bakr as an opportunist who usurped the caliphate from its rightful heir, the Prophet's son-in-law Ali (see #47).

There is greatness in the fear of God, contentment in faith in God, and honor in humility. —Abu Bakr

How would you provide continuity of authority in a spiritual community?

47
Ali ibn Abi Talib

Born ca. 599, in Mecca, Saudi Arabia
Died 661, in Kufa, Iraq

Choosing the first three caliphs, successors to Muhammad, was dicey. None was a unanimous choice and two died violently. Not until the fourth caliph did the man some had always regarded as the obvious choice assume the post. This was Muhammad's nearest blood relative, his cousin and son-in-law Ali.

While Muhammad lived, Ali showed himself courageous in battle and a diligent worker. Once, upon learning that the Prophet's enemies intended to slay him during his sleep, Ali enabled Muhammad's escape by spending the night in his bed.

Although convinced of the legitimacy of his claim to the caliphate following Muhammad's death, Ali declined to press his case, perhaps because he was barely thirty at the time, but also because of his aversion to infighting among the Muslim faithful. He retired from public life, devoting himself to his family, farming, and digging wells for public use.

When, finally, Ali became the fourth caliph, he proved himself a wise and compassionate ruler. He treated conquered peoples with compassion, distributed public revenues evenly among the populace, decentralized the government, and (unlike his immediate predecessor Uthman) declined to fill top positions with his relatives.

Ali's letters are devotional classics. In one, he urges the governor of Egypt to deal fairly and mercifully with everyone because "all are either your brothers in religion or your equals in creation" and "you are above them; he who appointed you is above you; and God is above him who appointed you."

For Muslims, Ali's words and deeds have authority in matters of belief and practice second only to the Quran and the Prophet's own example.

Ali was assassinated by supporters of his assassinated predecessor Uthman. Uthman's family, the Umayyads, then seized the caliphate and held it for ninety years. The minority Shia Muslims maintained Ali's line for centuries and continue to regard him as Muhammad's true successor. Among Shias to this day (as in Iran, see #141), religious and secular authority are often combined in one person.

Do not be too hard, lest you be broken; do not be too soft, lest you be squeezed.
—Ali

Regarding this life, act as if you will live forever; regarding the next life, act as if you will die tomorrow. —Ali

How did Ali exhibit the teachings of Muhammad?

48

Appar

Born 600, in Thiruvamoor, India
Died 681, in Thiruvamoor, India

Marulneekkiyar, later known as Appar (Tamil for father), was still a boy when his father died. Following a now illegal Indian custom, his mother incinerated
herself on her husband's funeral pyre. Soon thereafter,
his older sister, at age twelve, was betrothed to a military
commander who was killed in battle. She too prepared to be incinerated. But Marulneekkiyar, pleading that his sister was now the only mother he had, prevailed upon
her to remain alive and raise him.

As a young adult, Appar was a Jain (see #8), mastering their scriptures and disciplines. But when he fell out with the Jains, his sister urged that he embrace the Hindu
god Shiva.

Appar began writing hymns to Shiva, of which 3,130 survive, many still sung today. He was called "King of divine speech" and "Lord of language." Appar's hymns
are personal, with mystical overtones, incorporating facts and incidents in Appar's life
while exploring the inner, psychological, and emotional dimensions of faith. Common people readily identify with Appar's agrarian images and accessible language.

Before his death at the age of eighty-one, Appar visited 125 Shaivite (devoted to
Shiva) temples in southern India and consecrated them with song. His music, and
that of several other Shaivite poets, countered the Jain influence and helped reestab-
lish Shaivite Hinduism as the prevailing faith of south India.

Most Hindus recognize many gods. One will be the focus of worship in one place
and another in another place. They see no contradiction in this since all gods are
manifestations of Brahman, the one supreme god (see #1).

Hindus also view time as cyclical, not linear. Like the seasons, everything comes
around again. Some cycles take millions of years. History neither begins nor ends.
Shiva, one of three chief Hindu gods, dissolves or liberates the universe when it has
run its course and another universe begins. Together with Brahma the Creator and
Vishnu the Sustainer or Protector, they continually make, maintain, and dismantle
creation. A human self may be born and die many times during one of these cycles.
The goal of the spiritual quest is liberation from this cycle of rebirths through union
with God.

Lord, I am caught in the wheel of births and deaths. I am tired of this.
Show me a way to get out of it. —Appar

Have you ever felt "caught in a vicious cycle"?

49
Xuanzang

Born 602, near Luoyang, China
Died 664, in Tongchuan, China

Few pilgrimages have encompassed so many miles and years as that of the Chinese Buddhist monk Xuanzang. Beginning in Ch'ang An (modern Xi'an) in eastern China in the year 629, he headed west along the Silk Road, reaching modern Uzbekistan, then turned southeast and crossed the Kyber Pass into Pakistan and Kashmir, finally arriving in India, which he crisscrossed for several years, before returning to Ch'ang An nearly twenty years later. Xuanzang traveled in excess of ten thousand miles, experiencing opposition, typhoons, imprisonment, and near starvation, all in lands where he was a complete stranger. He was often a fugitive and had to travel under cover of darkness.

Xuanzang was not seeking fame or fortune, but books, specifically the classic texts of Mahayana Buddhism (see #28). He had embraced the monastic life at age twenty and then traveled China searching for the best Buddhist literature. He was dismayed at the fragmentary and confusing nature of what he found and determined to go to India to study the originals of books he had read and to seek additional texts. The emperor, however, had forbidden travel outside the country, so Xuanzang became a fugitive.

Finally in India, Xuanzang was welcomed at Buddhist shrines and monasteries, including the famous Nalanda Monastery in northern India, a renowned learning center where he studied for several years. He collected Buddhist manuscripts wherever he went and learned the languages in which they were written.

When Xuanzang finally arrived back in Ch'ang An, he brought with him wagonloads of books and was hailed as a hero by the same emperor who had sought to forbid him from leaving the country years earlier. He spent the rest of his life in a monastery translating into Chinese the texts he had collected. His work helped root Mahayana Buddhism in China and prepare for its later spread to Korea and Japan.

Xuanzang is remembered for the twelve-volume account of his journey, *Records of the Western Regions of the Great T'ang Dynasty*, dictated to a disciple the year after his return. It describes in detail the geography, culture, politics, economy, and religion of the lands Xuanzang visited. *Records* is today an invaluable resource for archaeologists and historians seeking to reconstruct the history of ancient Asia.

Imagine a world with few books, most of them not helpful. Would you spend twenty years searching for better books?

50
Abu Hanifa

Born 699 (700?) in Kufa, Iraq
Died 767, in Baghdad, Iraq

By the early 700s, the Umayyad conquests (see #47) stretched from Spain to Central Asia. An Arab Muslim aristocracy ruled this vast domain, but the conquered peoples were not Arabs, nor did many convert to Islam. The Umayyads sought a legal system based on the Quran and Muhammad's words and deeds, but much of this material from an earlier, simpler time was unsuited to the Umayyads' imperial needs.

Abu Hanifa was the first to address this problem, founding the first of what would become four main schools of Sunni jurisprudence (see #52, #53, #55). He was also the only non-Arab among early Islam's prominent jurists (he was probably of Persian descent).

Flexibility in the law was Abu Hanifa's goal. What matters is the orientation of the heart, he said, not the letter of the law. Abu Hanifa allowed local customs to be integrated into Islamic law and permitted adaptation as times changed. He urged jurists to exercise independent reasoning in their rulings, even when the Quran contained nothing to support them. Using analogy and hypothetical cases to seek the reason behind a law, Abu Hanifa's approach was seen as moderate and gentle. Some would have expelled from the community persons guilty of usury, consuming alcohol, and other offenses. To them Abu Hanifa said, "Those who face Mecca at prayer are true believers, and no act of theirs can remove them from the faith."

Abu Hanifa wrote nothing himself, but his many disciples jotted down his comments and in later decades elaborated upon them.

The flexible Hanifite approach attracted a large following. It is probably the most widely followed legal school in the Muslim world today, predominating in Turkey and much of central and southeast Asia. More conservative scholars, however (see #52), favored laws based on a stricter interpretation of Quranic passages and Muhammad's example, accusing the Hanifites of valuing their own opinions over divine law.

It is reported that Abu Hanifa declined appointment as chief judge on the grounds that he was unworthy. When caliph Al-Mansur said he was lying, Abu Hanifa replied that if he were lying, he would be doubly unworthy, for "why would you appoint a liar as judge?" Incensed at this seemingly flippant reply, Al-Mansur sent Abu Hanifa to prison. He died while incarcerated.

Could Abu Hanifa's flexibility in moral teaching open the door to abandoning moral standards entirely?

51
Rabia

Born ca. 715, in Basra, Iraq
Died 801, in Jerusalem

While all things Muslim arise from the Quran, Islam is hardly an arid, lifeless adherence to a written text. Alongside Quranic study and devotion, mysticism has flourished in Islam almost from the beginning. The best known expression of Muslim mysticism is called Sufism. One of the earliest Sufis was Rabia.

An ascetic who, until near the end of her life, rarely left her hometown of Basra, Rabia was born into desperate poverty and later sold into slavery. She sought, even as a slave, to give her life to God. It is said that her master, overhearing her praying late one night, freed her so that she might devote herself entirely to God and even offered to exchange roles with her and become her servant.

Rabia loved God alone; earthly things did not attract her. She declined several marriage proposals and owned nothing but a broken water pitcher, a mat on which to sleep, and a brick for a pillow. Rabia wrote passionate poems suggesting that no thought be given either to any benefit that serving God might bring or to possible punishment for refusing to serve him. Rather, God should be loved for himself—for his mercy, goodness, and beauty.

Rabia longed passionately for union with the God she loved and came to understand that the distinctions between Creator and creation, between Lord and servant, ultimately melt away until the faithful find their place within God himself where they can never again be separated from God.

> O God, whatever you have apportioned to me of worldly things, give to your enemies, and what you have apportioned to me in the hereafter, give to your friends, for you alone are sufficient for me. —Rabia

> O God, if I worship you for fear of hell, burn me in hell, and if I worship you for hope of paradise, exclude me from paradise. But if I worship you for your own sake, grudge me not your everlasting Beauty. —Rabia

> Prayer should bring us to an altar where no walls or names exist. Is there not a region of love where . . . ecstasy is poured into itself and lost, where the wing is fully alive but has no mind or body? In my soul there is a temple, a shrine, a mosque, a church that dissolve in God. —Rabia

What is the purest motivation for worship?

52

Malik ibn Anas

Born 716, in Medina, Saudi Arabia
Died 795, in Medina, Saudi Arabia

Many Westerners scorn Islamic law, called *sharia* (path), because a few Muslim zealots misuse it to justify acts of terror and repression. But *sharia* law is intended as a blueprint for a just society and a holy personal life. It resembles Jewish law (see #36) in both content and the role it plays in the lives of Muslims. Like Judaism and Christianity, Islam seeks to sanctify all of life. It makes no distinction between sacred and profane—everything is subject to the divine will and guidance.

Sharia is applied in various ways. Less than 10 percent of the Quran pertains to legal matters, and much of that concerns issues in seventh-century Arabia. If Muslims were rightly to order their lives and societies, additional guidance was needed. Various schools of jurisprudence arose in the first two Muslim centuries. Four have lasted and predominate today. They are considered canonical by Sunni Muslims. All four recognize the others as valid paths to a holy life. The first was the Hanifite school (see #50); the second was the Malikite.

Much like the Christian apologist Irenaeus (see #26) centuries earlier, Malik ibn Anas sought to establish right belief and root out heresy by emphasizing consensus within the community, especially among those who had known the founder of the faith. Many such companions of Muhammad still lived in Medina during Malik's youth there. He consulted with them (one source says over three hundred of them), sifted through their reminiscences to eliminate inauthentic tales, and composed the first compendium of Islamic custom and law, which he called *The Approved*.

Malik's approach was more conservative than that of his older contemporary Abu Hanifa. He insisted on fidelity to the Quran and the authentic traditions pertaining to Muhammad, emphasizing consensus and a reduced role for logic. His disciples traded barbs with the Hanifites, yet Malikites could also be flexible in interpretation when circumstances required it. The Malikite school is strong today throughout much of Muslim Africa.

> *Arguing about religion fosters self-display, darkens and hardens the heart, and leads to aimless wandering.* —Malik

> *Knowledge does not come to you; you come to knowledge.* —Malik

Do you see knowledge as something fixed with which all must come to terms, or as evolving with the times?

53
Muhammad al-Shafii

Born 767, in Ashkelon, Gaza strip
Died 820, in Cairo, Egypt

As the Islamic world expanded and conversions to the faith became more common, each locality began to develop its own understanding of *sharia* law (see #52) and fragmentation threatened the Muslim community. The need for common norms to determine what was required grew critical. Muhammad al-Shafii, born to poverty though distantly related to Muhammad's family, developed a method of determining *sharia* law. He also founded one of the four canonical Sunni legal schools (see #50, #52, #55), which bears his name.

Al-Shafii spent several years in Mecca studying under Malik and eventually settled in Cairo, a growing Islamic center founded a decade after Muhammad's death. Tradition says that he had memorized the entire Quran by the age of seven and Malik's *The Approved* by ten. He was the first Muslim jurist to write a book, eventually producing over a hundred works noted for their exquisite style and lucid expression.

Al-Shafii's best known book, *Al-Risala*, outlines four "roots" of Islamic law, a scheme that became widely accepted among Sunni jurists. The first root is the Quran, believed by Muslims to have come directly from God. While obedience to the Quran is primary, it does not address every legal question.

Second are traditions concerning the life and teachings of Muhammad. The Prophet's life is seen as the authoritative commentary on and supplement to the Quran. Al-Shafii insisted that such traditions be authenticated by an unbroken string of testimonies reaching back to Muhammad himself.

Third is analogy, a method first developed by Abu Hanifa (see #50) nearly a century earlier. Al-Shafii often deferred to the work of Abu Hanifa, saying that everyone was Abu Hanifa's child when it came to determining the content of *sharia* law.

Finally, there is the consensus of the Muslim community (not merely those in Medina, as Malik had taught). Later generations understood this to mean consensus among qualified scholars. Al-Shafii said that a ruling embraced by the entire community was valid even if it lacked support from the other three "roots" because God would not allow his entire people to fall into error.

I would like people to learn what I have to give without attributing it to me.
That way, my reward will come from God himself, not from people's praise.
—Muhammad al-Shafii

What personal qualities does a consensus-builder require?

54
Kukai

Born 774, in Zentsuji, Japan
Died 835, at Mt. Koya, Japan

Indigenous Japanese religion, today called Shintoism, was comprised of hundreds of local cults deifying Japanese culture. Mahayana Buddhism (see #28) arrived in Japan from Korea during the sixth century. The broader Buddhist vision quickly took root and within decades several Buddhist schools of thought emerged in Japan, drawing upon but moving beyond older imported schools. Among the most important and lasting was the Shingon school, founded by a scholar, poet, monk, calligrapher, and civil engineer named Kukai.

Born to an aristocratic Japanese Confucian family, Kukai was drawn to Buddhism as a young adult and began chanting Buddhist mantras. A mantra is a word or syllable which, when chanted over time, clears the mind of cluttering thoughts and concerns and moves one toward enlightenment or liberation from suffering. Mantra-based Buddhism is called "esoteric" because it accesses insights unavailable to rational thought. At the age of thirty, Kukai went to Ch'ang An, China, where in two years he mastered the disciplines of esoteric Buddhism taught there.

After his return to Japan in 806, Kukai taught widely, wrote extensively, designed several civic building projects which still survive, created works of art, and founded the Shingon (Word of Truth) school of Buddhism. He is one of Japan's foremost systematic philosophers.

An expression of Mahayana Buddhism, the Shingon school sees enlightenment as attainable in this life, not at the end of a long series of rebirths. The Shingon route to enlightenment is through bodily disciplines and rituals, not the study of sacred texts and doctrines. The human body is the medium through which the unity of all things is experienced. Ultimate reality transcends this transient world (the doctrine of emptiness is as central in Shingon as in other Buddhist thought) but the movements and forms of this world express ultimate reality and offer an experience of it.

The Buddha was for Kukai not primarily a historical figure, but a cosmic reality and immanent presence within every person, accessible through ritual meditation.

Kukai's most important literary work, *The Ten Stages of Consciousness*, discusses in ten volumes other religious traditions, including other Buddhist schools, as sequential steps to spiritual maturity, culminating in the Shingon school.

Do not seek to follow in the footsteps of the men of old; seek what they sought.
—Kukai

Is the human body a means of access to spiritual truth?

55
Ahmad ibn Hanbal

Born 780, in Baghdad, Iraq
Died 855, in Baghdad, Iraq

The word "fundamentalist" originated with a group of conservative Protestant Christian scholars in the early twentieth century who sought a return to the "fundamentals" of their faith in the face of a growing modernist movement. It is today applied, often pejoratively, to such movements in other faiths as well, including the Hanbalites, the last of the four Sunni Muslim schools of jurisprudence to develop (see #50, #52, #53).

Ahmad ibn Hanbal spent his younger years traveling through Mesopotamia and Arabia amassing a huge collection of authentic traditions about the Prophet Muhammad. Many regard it as his major legacy. But Ibn Hanbal valued such traditions only as commentary on the Quran, which he insisted contained the uncreated, eternal words of God. To say otherwise, he felt, would invite people to alter the Quran. The Quran was, moreover, to be taken at face value, absolutely literally. The plain words of the text, clarified when necessary by traditions about Muhammad, were Ibn Hanbal's authority, his only authority. He shunned reason and consensus, often cited as authorities by the other three Islamic legal schools.

Many early Muslims, like Ibn Hanbal, had believed the Quran was eternal and uncreated, but a group called the Mutazilites arose in the eighth century and maintained that to say that anything other than the one, indivisible God is eternal is to compromise God's unity and freedom. The Quran must therefore have been created in time, they said, adding that Quranic references to God's speech, hands, throne, and the like are metaphorical, not literally true. The Mutazilites were extreme rationalists who maintained that all moral and theological truth was accessible to human reason. Reason was deemed the judge of all things.

Unfortunately for Ibn Hanbal, the ruling Abassids aggressively promoted Mutazilism. Ibn Hanbal refused to yield. He was lashed to a post and flogged, reportedly three hundred times, until he lost consciousness. Then he was imprisoned. During his incarceration Ibn Hanbal's popularity soared and after two years he was released. When he died, hundreds of thousands thronged to his funeral, and his popularity has hardly waned since. Many today revere him as a heroic defender of Islamic orthodoxy.

If you want God to be persistent in granting you what you love, be persistent in doing what God loves. —Ibn Hanbal

What is worth being tortured for?

56
Shankara

Born 788 (?), in Kaladi, India
Died 820 (?), in Kerala, Kanchipuram,
or Kedarnatha, India

Although he died at age thirty-two, Shankara was a key
figure in the eighth-century Hindu revival in India
and its survival during the Muslim invasion a century
later. He traveled throughout India debating (probably) Muslims, Buddhists, Jains, and
Shaivite Hindus (see #48). Monasticism was not widespread in India at the time, but
Shankara founded four monasteries, reviving the monastic movement among Hindus.

The prevailing Hinduism of the day was dualistic, sharply contrasting the spiritual
and the material, the eternal and the passing. Shankara, however, found in the Vedas
(see #1) an affirmation that all things are one.

Shankara interpreted the Vedic motto "Thou art that" to mean that what one thing
is, everything is. Souls do not exist independently or separately—nothing does. He
likened perceived reality to ocean waves which are not separate entities, but part of
the one sea. Everything not only derives from, but *is* the one supreme, unknowable
God. Shankara's philosophy is called "Advaita." The term literally means "not two."
In Advaita, liberation comes from awareness of the unity of all things.

Shankara dismissed yogic meditation, mystical experiences, and devotional acts.
They might be helpful, but could not lead to knowledge and liberation from the cycle
of rebirths. That came only through the study of the Vedas. Advaita remains a major
expression of Hinduism to this day.

The similarity of Shankara's views to those of Nagarjuna (see #28) illustrates the
cross-fertilization which for centuries took place between Hinduism and Buddhism in
India. Shankara was sometimes called a "Buddhist in disguise," although he rejected
what he saw as Buddhist dualism.

The body is merely the vehicle of the immortal spirit. —Shankara

*Souls are in bondage because they mistake their body for themselves. They
become enmeshed in it like a caterpillar in its cocoon. And so they get swept
here and there, rising and sinking in the ocean of death and rebirth. In reality,
only the body dies. The inner being is forever.* —Shankara

*The air inside an empty jar is the same as the air outside the jar. . . . Smash
the jar, and the air inside it merges seamlessly with the air outside. Smash the
illusion that you exist apart from God, and you merge into that divine reality.*
—Shankara

What do you believe about the soul?

57
Yaqub ibn Ishaq al-Kindi

Born ca. 805, in Kufa, Iraq
Died ca. 870, in Baghdad, Iraq

When the Abbasid caliph al-Mansur founded the city of Baghdad and transferred his capital there in 762, he set the stage for a five-hundred-year period often called the Golden Age of Islam, a time of stunning scientific and intellectual creativity. Islamic and other scholars in Baghdad studied and enlarged upon ideas and insights from many nations. The pace-setting Islamic thinker was Yaqub ibn Ishaq al-Kindi, often called the "father of Islamic philosophy." He wrote on a range of topics, including logic, ethics, psychology, theology, medicine, astronomy, zoology, and meteorology.

Al-Kindi saw truth as multisourced. Seek it everywhere, he said, including among non-Muslim thinkers. Al-Kindi was particularly impressed with Aristotle and other ancient Greeks and oversaw a team of scholars who translated their philosophical and scientific works into Arabic, thus bringing them for the first time to the attention of Islamic, Jewish, and (somewhat later) Christian scholars.

Revelation (or prophecy) and philosophy lead to the same truth, said Al-Kindi, though the differences between them are important. Philosophers, for example, study for years, arrive at their insights on their own, and often express themselves in demanding treatises, whereas prophets receive the truth instantaneously and directly from God and write more clearly and simply. But the philosopher can bring to the truth many whom the prophet cannot reach.

The central theme of Al-Kindi's most important work, *On First Philosophy*, is the absolute unity of God. Everything else, though it may appear to be one thing, consists of parts, Al-Kindi said. The human body, for example, is comprised of various limbs and organs. God, and only God, is one, without parts. This understanding is one reason Muslims object to the Christian doctrine of the Trinity, which seems to introduce the notion of divine multiplicity.

Although later Muslim philosophers have not always acknowledged their debt to him, it was Al-Kindi who paved the way for all their work.

We must not be ashamed to admire the truth or to acquire it, from wherever it comes. Even if it should come from far-flung nations and foreign peoples, there is for the student of truth nothing more important than the truth, nor is the truth demeaned or diminished by the one who states or conveys it. —Al-Kindi

If truth comes to us from many sources, is one source more authoritative than others?

58
Pu-tai

Born ninth century, in Fenghua, China
Died 916, in Checkiang Province, China

The Ch'an saint (see #13, #41, #77) most recognizable in the West is the potbellied, dancing figurine available from New Age curio shops. This figurine represents a legendary figure (some say he never existed) named Pu-tai. Ch'an Buddhism (called Zen in Japan and the West) certainly produced no more unconventional figure.

Little is known of Pu-tai's life. His name is actually a nickname meaning "hemp bag," for the bag of sweets he carried on the end of a staff to give to children as he wandered about. When his sweets ran out, he begged for more and then gave them to the next children he met.

Typical of Ch'an Buddhists, Pu-tai did not define things or study doctrines. He played and laughed. Pu-tai's was an intuitive, iconoclastic, antirationalistic, undogmatic spirituality. Reveling in the comic, the earthy, and the nonsensical, Pu-tai relished ambiguity and absurdity, refusing to absolutize any teaching, experience, or ecclesiastical system. He is the patron of children, bartenders, fortunetellers, and politicians.

Pu-tai illustrates Ch'an's approach to scripture. The classic Ch'an texts are not seen as the last word on anything. Truth is always fluid and unfolding. As Ch'an remembers the Buddha (see #11), he preached no sermons and issued no pronouncements, saying little and often answering a disciple's question with a mere smile or the wave of a hand (see #13).

Ch'an and Zen art broke at this time from traditional Buddhist art which depicts the Buddha bedecked in gold and jewels, surrounded by heavenly beings. Pu-tai is a bald figure, pictured dancing with his clothing barely clinging to his rotund belly, surrounded by romping, squealing children, as if flouting authority and hoping to be laughed at—or with.

It is often said that Ch'an and Zen Buddhism make no sense. Pu-tai and other Ch'an and Zen masters would agree. Ch'an is known for its senseless riddles called koans. Ch'an Buddhists believe that trying to make sense of things is not how ultimate reality is approached, not how enlightenment is attained. Rather, embrace life's mysteries and perplexities. Enjoy every moment, invite others to enjoy it with you, and don't get bogged down trying to distinguish right belief from heresy or drawing up creeds, catechisms, and doctrinal statements. The Ch'an or Zen Buddhist seeks to celebrate life, not understand it.

Is truth something to be known and understood, or something to be lived and enjoyed?

59
Mansur al-Hallaj

Born ca. 858, in Tur, Iran
Died 922, in Baghdad, Iraq

Mansur al-Hallaj rejected all the Sunni legal schools (see #50, #52, #53, #55), even criticizing the legal framework of mainline Sunni Islam as a "hidden idolatry" and endorsing a symbolic pilgrimage made at home rather than the customary (and expensive and often dangerous) journey to Mecca. True faithfulness, Al-Hallaj said, is a matter of the heart, not outward observances.

He is perhaps best known for his spectacular death. When Al-Hallaj began to attract followers, Baghdad's Muslim establishment decided to do away with him. Before a large crowd, they stabbed him repeatedly, then severed his legs, arms, and tongue, then beheaded him and cut him into pieces, burned the pieces, and scattered his ashes in the Tigris River. All the while, so long as he was able, Al-Hallaj kept smiling and praying that God forgive his persecutors.

As a youngster, Al-Hallaj began to experience ecstatic trances leading to loving union with the divine. Unlike many other Sufis, however (see #51), he did not keep to himself, but traveled throughout the Middle East and central Asia, attracting followers everywhere, and wrote and circulated poetry speaking rapturously of God's love. Al-Hallaj's poems are replete with vivid, concrete images of his union with God. Such imagery became a feature of much later Sufi poetry.

Al-Hallaj often said (including while being dismembered), "I am the Truth," a confession suggesting to his followers that God had emptied Al-Hallaj's heart of everything but God but which his critics saw as heresy.

Facing a grisly end, he said he hoped to die "in the supreme confession of the cross" and spoke of his death as redemptive for his followers, leading his critics to deride him as a "crypto-Christian."

Most Sunni Muslims today regard Al-Hallaj as a deviant, but he remains an exemplar to some Sufis, especially for his calm serenity at the time of his death.

There is nothing wrapped in my turban but God. —Al-Hallaj

I wonder at you [God] and me. You annihilated me out of myself into you. You made me near to yourself, so that I thought that I was you, and you were me. —Al-Hallaj

My spirit mixes with your Spirit, in nearness and separation, so that I am you, just as you are I. —Al-Hallaj

How are love of God and love of self related?

60
Abu al-Hasan al-Ashari

Born 874, in Basra, Iraq
Died 936, in Baghdad, Iraq

By the ninth century, Islamic thought had grown very sophisticated, and thorny questions were hotly debated. Abu al-Hasan al-Ashari, born to an aristocratic Muslim family, had the leisure to pursue such questions from his youth. At first he defended Mutazilite rationalism (see #55) against conservative traditionalists, but by age forty, he had concluded that the rationalists' God was a mere abstraction that could never energize the faithful. He sought a synthesis of rationalist and traditionalist thought by using rationalist methods and terminology to promote an essentially traditionalist theology.

What of the Quran's anthropomorphic language when speaking of God? Traditionalists accepted it literally, insisting that God has actual hands, eyes, and the like, and sits on an actual throne. Rationalists saw such language as figurative. Al-Ashari affirmed that anthropomorphic language points to real qualities of God, but that since God is one, eternal, and self-contained, divine attributes cannot be separated out from the divine essence, which is, in any case, beyond human understanding.

In a related and ongoing debate, Muslim traditionalists asserted that the Quran, including its letters, words, and sounds, was part of God's essence, and therefore eternal, whereas the rationalists said references to God's speaking are figurative. To say otherwise, they insisted, would introduce the notion of multiple divine actions and compromise the indivisible unity of God. Al-Ashari and his disciples struck a middle position that God had created the words and sounds of the Quran in time but that their meaning was contained in the eternal, uncreated divine essence.

Human free will was perhaps the thorniest problem addressed by Al-Ashari. He devised a subtle (some would say too subtle) middle course between the traditionalist view that God determines everything and the rationalists' affirmation of human free will. All power comes from God and God causes everything that happens, he said (agreeing with the traditionalists), but God exercises his power by giving human beings the ability to choose good or evil. People are therefore responsible for their choices, although the power both to decide and to act comes solely from God and God knows throughout eternity what everyone will decide.

Most Sunni Muslims accepted Al-Ashari's conservative synthesis of the traditionalist and rationalist positions. It remains the dominant theology among Sunnis today.

How do debates between Muslim literalists and rationalists compare to similar debates among Christians?

61
Abu Nasr al-Farabi

Born ca. 875, probably in Central Asia
Died ca. 950, in Damascus, Syria

As the Golden Age of Islam approached its height (see #57), Abu Nasr al-Farabi's star shone brightly in Baghdad's vigorous philosophical circles. Little is known of his early life, but as an adult Al-Farabi's contemporaries called him "The Second Teacher," exceeded only by Aristotle. Al-Farabi drew on Plato, Aristotle, and others, but also plowed new ground in his wide-ranging studies on philosophy, theology, psychology, ethics, government, logic, grammar, music, physics, and cosmology. He exerted an enormous influence on Maimonides (see #76).

Human reason reigned supreme for Al-Farabi. He saw reason not merely as helpful in understanding revealed truth but as superior to it. Revelation, he said, used images and symbols to express the truth for those unable to understand its more refined expressions. The uneducated required the authority of revelation, with its attendant rewards and punishments, to accept what the philosopher discerned through rational reflection. Al-Farabi saw Islam as the most rational religion, unburdened with illogical teachings such as the Trinity.

But Al-Farabi was no ivory tower thinker. He sought a philosophy with practical uses, calling those who declined to apply their wisdom to practical matters "futile philosophers." Much of his writing discusses how government should be conducted. Al-Farabi's best known work, *The Virtuous City*, draws on Plato's *Republic*. In place of Plato's philosopher-king, Al-Farabi envisions the prophet-imam as head of state, ruling according to reason—wisely, fairly, and in keeping with divine law. This, he said, would lead to true happiness. He was probably thinking of the city of Medina when the Prophet Muhammad combined the roles of spiritual leader and political ruler there. The triumph of Islam, Al-Farabi hoped, would produce such enlightened rulers to preside over the ideal society, "the virtuous city."

Philosophy, including that of the ancient Greeks, has always been important to Shia Muslims, less so to the dominant Sunnis. To this day, Shia communities frequently vest the secular and sacred authority in a single person, often a cleric deemed to possess great wisdom. This is seen in Shia Iran today (see #141).

We can achieve happiness only when we have beauty and we have beauty thanks to philosophy. The truth is that only because of philosophy can we achieve happiness. —Al-Farabi

A man becomes a person thanks to the intellect. —Al-Farabi

What is the most effective means to "the virtuous city"?

62
Saadia Gaon

Born 892, in Dilaz, Egypt
Died 942, in Baghdad, Iraq

Tenth-century Baghdad was the most cosmopolitan city in the world, a dazzling center of art, culture, science, architecture, and intellectual inquiry. Ideas flowed freely as the ruling Muslims mingled with people of other traditions. The city's thriving Jewish community was integral to this scene.

In Baghdad, both Muslim and Jewish thinkers encountered the newly rediscovered Aristotelian philosophy which sought truth through human reason, not divine revelation. Were religion and philosophy incompatible, or could philosophy suggest new ways to understand the sacred tradition? Advocating the latter position, Saadia Gaon began to integrate Jewish and Greek thought, the first to understand rabbinic Judaism in philosophical terms.

Born to humble Jewish parents, Saadia quickly distinguished himself as a scholar, producing the first Hebrew dictionary and grammar at the age of twenty. He later translated the Hebrew Bible into Arabic, introducing it to the wider Arabic-speaking world. His translation is still used today. Saadia was eventually named *gaon* (dean or principal) of Baghdad's prestigious school for the study of the Torah, the first foreigner to hold the position.

A group called the Karaites, who might be deemed early Jewish fundamentalists (see #55), scorned the new philosophy. They denied not only the validity of human reason, but the Mishnah as well (see #27), accepting no authority beyond the written Torah. Saadia countered that to deny reason was to deny God, the creator of reason.

When people lack the time or ability to reason things out, Saadia said, revelation serves as a guide, but the truth of the Torah and the truth of reason were one for him; everything in rabbinic Judaism was also, at least potentially, accessible to reason. This understanding enabled Saadia to affirm that the rabbinic tradition was completely reliable and that the devout Jew need look no further, though the philosophically inclined might wish to do so. Saadia made a space for the budding Jewish philosophical movement to blossom under the tent of rabbinic Judaism.

> *My heart aches to see so many Jews engulfed in oceans of doubt, floundering in the raging waters of error. There is no diver to pull them out of the depths, no swimmer to lend them a hand. Since the Almighty has taught me how to help them, I feel it my duty to extend my hand to them.* —Saadia Gaon

Is denying reason to deny God?

63
Symeon the New Theologian

Born 949, in northern Turkey
Died 1022, in Istanbul, Turkey

At the beginning of the second millennium of the Christian era, the Byzantine Empire and church were both prospering. Order, tradition, and stability were prized. A young monk named Symeon did not fit well in this picture. Although his theology was orthodox, Symeon's spirituality was shaped not by the church hierarchy but by his personal mystical encounters. He found the organized church lifeless and criticized its leaders for their lack of a personal experience of Christ.

For twenty-five years, Symeon was abbot of a small, struggling monastery in Constantinople. Symeon demanded a rigorous discipline from those under his supervision, and he began attracting new professions. His *Catechetical Discourses* are mainly talks on monastic life and discipline, given to his monks. They are redolent with Symeon's charismatic personality and accounts of his mystical encounters with Christ.

Not surprisingly, Symeon fell afoul of the church authorities and in 1009 was banished across the Bosphorus to Asia Minor, where he founded another monastery and lived the rest of his days. There he wrote his other major work, *Hymns of Divine Love*, a collection of fifty-eight poems, some running several hundred lines in length. The hymns address many of the same themes found in the *Catechetical Discourses*, but are less didactic and analytical, revealing Symeon's inner life more intimately, with passages of tearful penitence and soaring, even erotic adoration.

Symeon experienced Christ as light and the light imagery in his poetry is vivid and varied. This experience, he said, is not just for monks or the spiritually advanced, but for everyone. Begin with genuine penitence, which leads to detachment from worldly cares. This is the work of the Holy Spirit, culminating in a "second baptism," Symeon said, in a foreshadowing of modern Pentecostalism (see #117, #126, #128). The ultimate goal is deification, a key concept in Orthodox spirituality generally, as the soul grows more attuned to and united with God.

> [Christ] himself is found in me, radiating in the interior of my miserable heart, illuminating me on every side with his immortal splendor. He is completely intertwined with me, totally embracing me. He gives himself to me, the unworthy one, and his love and beauty fill me. I am utterly satisfied and overwhelmed by the divine delight and sweetness. I share in the light and participate in the glory. —Symeon the New Theologian

Under what circumstances should ecclesiastical authorities suppress individual expression?

64
Abhinava Gupta

Born ca. 950, in Kashmir, India
Died ca. 1020, in Kashmir, India

Abhinava Gupta was one of Hinduism's greatest thinkers. He wrote over thirty-five books on philosophy, theology, music, drama, logic, and aesthetics. His commentaries elucidate ancient Hindu texts in the light of reason and mystical experience. Abhinava was also a major force in the acceptance of Shaivism (see #48) in Kashmir.

Abhinava was born to a family of Hindu scholars and mystics dating back several centuries. He is said to have withdrawn into himself after the death of his mother when he was two years old. His father, raising his three children alone with help from an extended family, introduced Abhinava to ascetic disciplines at an early age. He soon embraced the ascetic life and the world of books and study. He lived at home all his life, but traveled often, mostly within Kashmir. He did not marry.

Kashmiri Shaivism differs from that of Appar (see #48) and shares with Shankara (see #56) a monistic understanding of reality. Both Shankara and Abhinava sought liberation through merger with Brahman (see #1), understood as universal consciousness, but whereas Shankara believed the material world was an illusion and Brahman inactive, Abhinava and other Kashmiri Shaivists affirmed the reality of material things and saw Brahman as active in the world. For Adhinava, merger with Brahman, represented by the god Shiva, affirmed each individual's true identity and was an act of divine grace.

Abhinava's most important work was *Light on the Tantra*. Tantra is the name of a Hindu spiritual discipline teaching that all human experience is the manifestation of divine consciousness or energy and seeking through ritual and mystic experience to merge with that consciousness. Abhinava's book, a 5,859-verse poem, deals with both philosophical and ritual questions. It contains a coherent synthesis of the various expressions of Kashmiri Shaivism practiced in Abhinava's day. One chapter offers guidance on ritualized sexual activity. He also wrote a shorter prose summary of the work called *The Essence of Tantra*.

> *Nothing perceived is independent of perception and perception differs not*
> *from the perceiver. Therefore the universe is nothing but the perceiver.*
> —Abhinava Gupta

> *Other achievements are in vain if one has missed the supreme reality, the Self.*
> *But once one has attained this reality there is nothing left that one could desire.*
> —Abhinava Gupta

What for you is "the supreme reality" and how is it attained?

65

Abu Ali al-Husayn ibn Sina (Avicenna)

Born 980, in Afshaneh, Uzbekistan
Died 1037, in Hamadan, Iran

Many regard Ibn Sina as the greatest thinker of Islam's Golden Age (see #57).

Also known by his Latinized name Avicenna, he mastered virtually every field studied in his day. Westerners would call him a Renaissance man. He wrote dozens of ground-breaking treatises on medicine, philosophy, mathematics, physics, musical theory, astronomy, alchemy, geology, psychology, theology, law, and logic. Ibn Sina's fourteen-volume *The Canon of Medicine* was a standard medical text throughout the Muslim and Christian worlds until the eighteenth century. He was also a gifted poet. His greatest contribution was his ground-breaking work seeking to reconcile rationalist philosophy and theology in Islamic terms.

By his twenties Ibn Sina had become a renowned physician. He traveled throughout central Asia, practicing medicine, teaching, and writing until finally settling in the Iranian town of Haradan.

Scholars debate whether Ibn Sina was a mystic, but he was certainly sympathetic to Sufi devotion and (unlike Al-Farabi, whose work he knew, see #61) held revelation and prophecy in great esteem. Ibn Sina called prophets "inspired philosophers" to whom God gave insights which, though consistent with philosophy, were unavailable to it.

Building on the work of Aristotle and Al-Farabi, Ibn Sina distinguished between essential being and possible being. Essential being simply and eternally is, depending on nothing outside itself, whereas possible beings may or may not exist, depending on whether an outside cause has resulted in their existence. They have a beginning and an end. This line of thought led Ibn Sina, again adapting Aristotle, to a proof for the existence of God. An endless chain of possible beings is nonsense, he said. At some point a necessary being must have caused the first in that chain of possible beings. This "first cause" argument for the existence of God would later be adapted by Thomas Aquinas (see #85).

Is the human soul eternal? Ibn Sina imagined a man suspended in the air while experiencing nothing through the senses. Such a man, he said, would still have self-consciousness—hence the soul or intellect must exist independently of the body and is an immortal substance. A human person is a soul aware of itself, Ibn Sina said; the physical body is, strictly speaking, unnecessary.

I prefer a short life with width to a narrow one with length. —Ibn Sina

Must one choose between reason and revelation, or are the two compatible?

66
Anselm

Born 1033, in Aosta, Italy
Died 1109, in Canterbury, England

Anselm left his native Italy for France at the age of twenty-three to study under the renowned scholar Lanfranc. He later succeeded Lanfranc as abbot of the monastery at Bec and in 1093 succeeded him again as archbishop of Canterbury, a post Anselm disliked because its political demands interfered with his scholarship and devotional life.

At a time when others supported their views largely through citations from scripture and the early church fathers, Anselm sought to solve thorny theological dilemmas solely through rational demonstration. In his *Cur Deus Homo* (*Why God Became Man*), for example, Anselm appealed to the medieval understanding of honor and propriety to show that the only way human sin could be overcome was for God to assume human form and give his life to pay the required penalty for it. This "satisfaction theory" of the atonement has been hugely influential in the Western church, though some have seen it as overly legalistic and based on a faulty concept of honor.

Anselm also devised a new proof for the existence of God. Called the "ontological proof," it defines God as "that than which nothing greater can be conceived." Since to exist is greater than not to exist, Anselm said, a being than which nothing greater can be conceived must, by definition, exist. Some find this argument almost mystically compelling, while others see it as a verbal sleight of hand.

Above all, Anselm was a man of prayer. Most praying in his day was done in unison by groups of Benedictine monks. Anselm wrote intensely personal prayers, ranging from lofty paeans of praise and thanksgiving to profound expressions of grief and penitence. Anselm's *Prayers and Meditations* were widely circulated and often imitated, though rarely equaled. They have become a Christian devotional classic.

> *Perfect what you have begun, and give me what you have made me long for,*
> *not because I deserve it, but because of your kindness that came first to me.*
> *Most merciful Lord, transform my tepid heart into one that loves you ardently.*
> —Anselm

> *Whatever you cause me to desire for my enemies, give it to them and give the*
> *same to me, and if what I ask for them is ever outside the rule of love, whether*
> *through weakness, ignorance, or malice, give it neither to them, good Lord,*
> *nor to me.* —Anselm

Compose a prayer expressing your relationship to God.

67
Milarepa

Born 1040 (?), in Kya Ngatsa, Tibet (China)
Died 1123 (?), in Driche Cave, Tibet (China)

When Buddhism reached Tibet from India in the seventh century, it encountered an established native religion called Bon, based on shamanistic invocations and sacrifices to spirits deemed to inhabit Tibet's austere plateau. Tibetan Buddhism incorporated elements of Bon religion, producing the distinctive Buddhist expression for which the region is known.

In the following centuries, Buddhist monasteries were established throughout the country, some housing thousands of monks. The most beloved figure from early Tibetan Buddhism is a legendary poet and yogi known as Milarepa. Many of his poems were set to music and are still sung today.

Tibetans often tell the story of Milarepa's life. An unscrupulous aunt and uncle had cheated Milarepa's family out of their assets. Seeking revenge, Milarepa mastered sorcery and caused a building to collapse during a wedding celebration, killing thirty-five friends of the aunt and uncle. Then he conjured up a violent hailstorm that devastated that year's barley crop.

Milarepa later repented of the destruction he had caused and sought a spiritual guide, eventually coming under the tutelage of Marpa the Translator, a renowned scholar. Recognizing Milarepa's need for penance, Marpa set him at demanding, repetitive physical labor, instructing him three times to build a stone tower on a nearby hilltop, then dismantle it and rebuild it. Although his back ached from carrying and lifting heavy stones, Milarepa obeyed and remained composed. Finally, at the instigation of his wife, Marpa relented and began to instruct Milarepa.

Under Marpa's guidance and after twelve years meditating in a cave, Milarepa attained complete enlightenment and detachment from worldly things. He began traveling across the Tibetan plateau, teaching and acquiring disciples. He subsisted on nettle tea, which is said to have turned his skin a waxy green. During this time Milarepa inhabited several caves on Mount Everest and in nearby Nepal. He was poisoned by a jealous rival and died at the age of eighty-four.

There's no point of view or theory in reality itself. —Milarepa

I have no desire for wealth or possessions, and so I have nothing. I do not experience the initial suffering of having to accumulate possessions, the intermediate suffering of having to guard and keep up possessions, nor the final suffering of losing the possessions. —Milarepa

What would Milarepa say in a letter to twenty-first-century America?

68
Rashi

Born 1040 in Troyes, France
Died 1105 in Troyes, France

While western Europe's Christians were still emerging from what some have called the Dark Ages, Muslim and Jewish scholars were reaching exalted heights. The foremost Jewish scholar of the day was the French Rabbi Shlomo Yitzhaki, usually known by the acronym Rashi, who wrote what is still the definitive commentary on the Hebrew Bible and the Babylonian Talmud (see #36). Rashi's commentary was the first dated Hebrew printed book (in 1475) and most editions of the Talmud ever since have printed Rashi's comments alongside the text itself. Even today traditional Jews deem Rashi indispensible to biblical and Talmudic study.

Rashi studied in Worms for several years but returned at age twenty-five to his native Troyes, where he taught scripture and later founded his own rabbinic school, attracting hundreds of disciples. Remembered as a humble man unwilling to take payment for his academic services, Rashi is said to have supported his family as had his father, by growing grapes and selling wine.

In the six centuries since the compilation of the Talmud, successive rabbis had copied the text by hand, and then the copies were copied. Errors and discrepancies eventually crept in; an accurate text was sorely needed. Rashi led the successful effort to establish that text and then added his commentary, noted for its clarity and succinctness. He covered the entire Talmud and all the Hebrew Bible except for Chronicles, explaining difficult interpretations in down-to-earth ways that made the meaning accessible not only to fellow scholars, but to beginning students as well. Rashi elucidated obscure words and complex passages, often using analogies drawn from the crafts and amusements of the day and in the language of the time, an early form of French. His work is a key source of information on the history of that tongue.

After his death, Rashi's descendants carried on his work. It is a testimony to his stature that they wrote little commentary of their own, producing instead mere "addendums" to Rashi's definitive work.

I come only to present what the text says directly and such interpretative narrative that sets the wording of the text on its proper bearings. —Rashi

Receive with simplicity everything that happens to you. —Rashi

The world exists for the sake of kindness. —Rashi

Is a definitive commentary on scripture possible?

69
Abu Hamid al-Ghazali

Born ca. 1056, in Tus, Iran
Died 1111, in Tus, Iran

After the Quran and the traditions pertaining to the Prophet Muhammad, the works of Abu Hamid al-Ghazali are the most widely quoted of all Muslim writings. Al-Ghazali has been called "the proof of Islam" and the "man who saved Islam." For most Sunni Muslims, he settled the long simmering dispute between philosophers and mystics and defined Muslim orthodoxy for subsequent generations.

Al-Ghazali was chief professor at the prestigious Nizamiyah college in Baghdad when he wrote *The Intentions of the Philosophers*, a clear and balanced summary of Muslim philosophy which, in its Hebrew and Latin translations, influenced later Jewish and Christian thinking in the West.

A year later, in 1095, Al-Ghazali underwent a wrenching crisis of faith. Temporarily paralyzed and unable to speak, he was convinced that after all his studies, he knew much about God but did not know God. Al-Ghazali then set out on a ten-year search for the truth that led him throughout the Middle East and eventually to Sufism (see #51, #59).

When he returned, Al-Ghazali wrote *The Incoherence of the Philosophers*, affirming human reason for the sciences but not for matters pertaining to God. To know God, Al-Ghazali said, one must turn to prayer and worship.

Two years later, Al-Ghazali produced *The Revival of Religious Sciences*, usually regarded as his masterpiece. A 1,500-page tome, it continues where *The Incoherence of the Philosophers* had left off, adding a blistering attack on the superficiality of Muslim legal scholars. Al-Ghazali gave a devotional interpretation to *sharia* law, stating that its purpose was not merely to regulate outward behavior, on which Muslim jurists had dwelt obsessively, but to cultivate an inner awareness of the presence of God. This book probed and integrated Islamic jurisprudence, theology, and worship and brought Sufism from the fringe into the mainstream of Islamic life.

The Revival of Religious Sciences became a standard text among Sunni Muslims. It remains so today. Some, especially those of a conservative bent, have gone so far as to claim that after Al-Ghazali, the door closed on the development of Muslim teachings, that no further interpretations of truth can be received, and that subsequent jurisprudence should be limited to applying the faith to specific cases.

Today's taboos are tomorrow's norms. —Al-Ghazali

Do you feel Al-Ghazali would have agreed that his work is the final word on divine truth?

70
Ramanuja

Born 1077 (?), in Sriperumbudur, India
Died 1157 (?), in Srirangam, India

Hinduism is remarkably flexible in its teaching about God. Hindus may be monotheists, polytheists, or a variant or combination of those basic stances. Ramanuja, one of the faith's greatest philosophical minds, was the first Hindu to espouse an active, personal God similar in some ways to the gods of Western faiths.

Philosophically, Ramanuja built on the work of Shankara (see #56) in his interpretation of the Vedas (see #1), but departed from Shankara's strict monism. While affirming with Shankara that all things are fundamentally one, Ramanuja said that didn't mean individual souls and sense objects are illusory.

For both Shankara and Ramanuja, liberation from the cycle of rebirths was attained through union with the supreme God, but souls remain distinct and are not subsumed in God, according to Ramanuja. As the soul is the enlivening agent within the body, united with it yet distinguishable from it, God is the enlivening agent of the material world, Ramanuja said. God is one, but is modified by matter and soul. This philosophy is known as Visistadvaita, "qualified monism," the second major Veda-based expression of Hinduism, after Shankara's Advaita.

Ramanuja also differed from Shankara in playing down the role of the intellect in liberation from the cycle of rebirths. He was devoted to Vishnu, the sustaining and protecting god in the Hindu pantheon (see #48), and acts of devotion to Vishnu were far more important to Ramanuja than intellectual pursuits. He also felt an infusion of divine grace was needed to attain liberation, though his disciples later differed on the role of human effort in appropriating that grace.

Hindu social structure was built around the caste system, and Ramanuja rejected this as well. The caste system had begun in prehistoric times as a means of enabling all people to fill the role where their skills could best be utilized for the community. In time, however, it had become a rigid hereditary hierarchy. Ramanuja flatly rejected this, using persons of lower castes to assist him in writing his nine books. When Ramanuja's wife took offense at his dismissing of the caste system, he sent her back to her parents and became an ascetic. He is therefore remembered as a social reformer as well as a philosopher and advocate of the devotional life.

Can a faith be "true" if it affirms monotheists, polytheists, and atheists?

71
Bernard of Clairvaux

Born 1090, in Fontaine-lès-Dijon, France
Died 1153, in Ville-sous-la-Ferté, France

Benedict of Nursia (see #42) would hardly have recognized most of the monasteries called by his name six hundred years later. Europe's Benedictine monasteries had gradually acquired large estates. Many monks lived luxuriously and spent more time managing finances than praying. Liturgical additions had transformed the simple prayer life Benedict outlined into a complicated and sometimes lifeless routine.

Bernard was twenty-one years old when he became a Benedictine monk. Disgusted by what he saw around him, he chose the small, poor, remote Cistercian monastery of Cîteaux. It is a testimony to his powerful personality that he convinced thirty family members, including his father and all his brothers, to join him there. The Cistercians sought a return to the simple observance of the Benedictine Rule.

Three years later, Bernard founded his own monastery of Clairvaux (Clear Vision). At his death, nine hundred monks resided at Clairvaux, practicing Bernard's simple, humble devotion. Through Bernard's influence, the Cistercian order soon spread throughout Europe.

Bernard was anything but grim, however. He manifested a seemingly boundless joy in the love of God, and his writings, which have become devotional classics, radiate with an almost erotic fervor. In his sermons on the Song of Songs, he (like others before him) sees that biblical book as an allegory of the love of God and the human soul. God woos the human soul through Jesus Christ, Bernard says, and our love for God is but our response to that divine wooing. People progress through four stages in their love for God, according to Bernard, beginning with self-love, then love of God because of what God has done for us, followed by love of God for God himself, and finally love of ourselves as God loves us and for God's sake.

Unlike most Benedictine monks, Bernard was also a man of the world, sought out by popes and kings to mediate disputes and for his savvy political advice. He was often away from Clairvaux, proving himself a persuasive polemicist and debater, eventually becoming the most powerful man in Europe.

Immeasurable and eternal God, unimaginable love, boundless majesty, infinite wisdom—God loves us! Can we then love God grudgingly, doling out our love for him bit by bit? O Lord! My strength and support, my liberator, my most adorable all, most loving—I need and long for nothing but you! —Bernard of Clairvaux

Can one love God grudgingly?

72

Abu al-Walid ibn Rushd (Averroës)

Born 1126, in Cordoba, Spain
Died 1198, in Marrakech, Morocco

When Abu al-Walid ibn Rushd reached maturity, dusk was already descending on the Golden Age of Islam (see #57). For nearly five hundred years, Islamic scholars had expanded the boundaries of thought in many fields. But a conservative reaction, led by Al-Ghazali (see #69), had emerged and the times did not favor freewheeling theological and philosophical thinking.

Ibn Rushd was a prominent Islamic legal scholar. Like most Sunni Muslims, he espoused *sharia* law as the route to true happiness because it leads to knowledge of God, but he is chiefly remembered as the last of the great Islamic philosophers.

Ibn Rushd wrote a sharp, point-by-point rebuttal to Al-Ghazali's *The Incoherence of the Philosophers*, calling his own work *The Incoherence of the Incoherence*. Whereas Al-Ghazali had dismissed reason as a means of knowing God, Ibn Rushd embraced it and labeled Al-Ghazali's arguments "sophistical" and "feeble." There is one truth, he said, and the trained philosopher can discern it through reason, while for others, the same truth is conveyed through the vivid imagery of the Quran. It is from philosophers, not theologians, that one learns the "unvarnished" truth. Philosophy, he said, is the "companion" and "foster-sister" of *sharia* law.

Like Ibn Sina before him (see #65), Ibn Rushd wrote on an extraordinary range of topics. His most influential writings were his commentaries on Aristotle. They were of three kinds: short paraphrases of the philosopher for those with little schooling, moderately challenging works with some analytical comments on the text, and advanced commentaries with critical analysis on every point Aristotle had made.

With Muslim interest in philosophy on the decline, few of his fellow Muslims paid attention to Ibn Rushd. But the Christian West was emerging from several centuries when creative thought had centered largely on monastic spirituality. Christian (and Jewish) scholars found Ibn Rushd fresh and challenging and it was largely through him that the West rediscovered ancient Greek philosophy. He is known in the West by the Latinized version of his name, Averroës. So influential was he that Western scholars called him "the Commentator" (on the works of Aristotle, "the Philosopher") and those who would soon appropriate Aristotle's ideas to interpret Christian teaching were known not as Aristotelians, but as Averroists.

Two truths cannot contradict one another. —Ibn Rushd

Would Christians today be willing to learn from a Muslim?

73
Mahadevi

Born 1130, in Udutadi, India
Died 1160, in Srisailam, India

Mahadevi had been a devout Hindu girl from early childhood. When her parents arranged her marriage to the local king, the wedding took place but since the king was a Jain (see #8) and an atheist, Mahadevi soon left the royal household to become a mendicant and began writing poetry, singing songs of praise, and wandering through south India to find other seekers after the divine.

So began a life that would feature numerous challenges to accepted ways. Even many of Mahadevi's sympathizers sometimes grew alarmed at her unconventional behaviors. She dismissed the caste system that suppressed women, farmers, and artisans, and wore no clothing as an expression of humility, a common practice among male Hindu saints but previously unknown among females. She became an outspoken advocate for women and was given the nickname Akka (elder sister), by which she is often referred to today.

Mahadevi is mainly remembered, however, for her literary contributions. Veera Shaivism is a monotheistic expression of Hinduism established during Mahadevi's lifetime, emphasizing loving devotion to God and rejecting the authority of the Vedas (see #1). Mahadevi was its most notable devotional writer. Veera Shaivism is widely practiced today throughout the Indian subcontinent.

Mahadevi's often haunting poems speak of awe, wonder, longing for union with God, taming of the ego, unselfish love, and her inner struggles against the external forces that sought to constrain her. Her longing is said to have been fulfilled when she finally attained union with God at her death.

> I am without pride of caste. Without pride of resolute will am I. I have cast away the arrogance of riches. Of the pride of learning also I have none. No manner of pride dare draw near to me, for you have blest me with your grace. —Mahadevi

> The arrow that is shot should penetrate so deeply that even the feathers do not show. Hug the body of the Lord so tightly that the bones are crushed and crumble. Weld yourself to the divine until the very welding disappears. —Mahadevi

> Like treasure hidden in the ground, like flavor in the fruit, like gold in the rock and oil in the seed, the Absolute is hidden in the heart. —Mahadevi

If both saints and lunatics decline to wear clothing, how do you tell the difference?

74

Honen

Born 1133, in Okayama Prefecture, Japan
Died 1212, in Kyoto, Japan

As Buddhism spread through east Asia, various sects and schools of thought developed. All sought enlightenment resulting in release from the cycle of rebirths and entrance into Nirvana, but they differed on the way to reach this goal. Many advocated purity of life, study, and/or meditation in a monastic setting.

But in fifth-century China, a new Buddhist expression began to emerge, teaching that enlightenment resulted not from human activity, but from divine grace. Called Pure Land Buddhism, it reached its greatest influence in China in the eighth century and arrived in Japan in the ninth century. It is widely practiced in Japan today.

The two foremost Pure Land teachers in Japan were Honen and Shinran (see #79). Honen pursued enlightenment in a monastery until he was around forty years of age but grew increasingly frustrated when his efforts failed to achieve it. Like many others at the time, he was also troubled by the decline in Buddhist devotion in the broader Japanese culture, seeing it as a possible sign of the end of the age. He sought a means of reviving Buddhist practice among the general populace.

Honen had a sudden insight while reading the Chinese scholar Shan-tao. He came to understand that enlightenment was a gift from a radiant, cosmic Buddha figure called Amidabha and was available to anyone who sincerely asked for it and called upon Amidabha's name. Those who invoked the divine name would be reborn at the time of death into the "Pure Land," a transcendent realm of resplendent beauty.

Breaking with his past, Honen left the monastery, lived simply as a hermit, and eventually wrote devotional works. He advocated chanting or speaking the divine name many times each day to focus attention, deepen devotion, and open one's heart to the gift of enlightenment. Honen's disciples repeated the name in group ritual observances, in private prayers, and under their breath while performing daily chores. This simple and accessible faith attracted a huge following, largely from among the working classes and dispossessed.

Honen had his critics. They accused him of being a libertine and ignoring the importance of ethics and morality. He was exiled for a time from Kyoto, his home. Honen answered by stressing the importance of holy living, though not as a means of attaining enlightenment.

Do you feel that enlightenment or wisdom is given or achieved?

75
Basava

Born 1134, in Bagewadi, India
Died 1196, in Kudalasangama, India

Basava was an idealistic visionary whose administrative skills enabled him to implement his vision. Born to an upper caste family, he was an accountant to his king in southwest India. The king, impressed with Basava's honesty and diligence, named him prime minister. In that capacity, Basava founded an academy for spiritual seekers and philosophers with equal numbers of men and women and including students from every caste. He entertained members of the untouchable caste in his home and endorsed the marriage of a Brahmin woman to an untouchable man. Basava also created a parliament including men and woman and representatives from all castes and stations of life.

All this violated centuries-old Indian taboos and aroused fierce opposition. Basava was forced to flee. He spent his remaining years studying, refining his views, and teaching about the dignity of all persons and all forms of work.

A Hindu monotheist, Basava saw God in every person. One night Basava awoke to find a burglar trying to remove the jewelry from his sleeping wife. Seeing a glimpse of God in the burglar, he removed the jewelry himself and gave it to the burglar. When thieves stole cows from Basava's fields but left the calves behind, the calves began crying for milk from their mothers. Basava located the thieves and gave them the calves as well.

Basava believed that ability and the willingness to work, not birth, should determine one's station in life. All work, he said, was holy and no work was degrading or demeaning. Known for his humility, Basava often said that a cow gives milk only to one who sits at its feet, not to one who sits on its back. He expressed these views in poems and sayings which have inspired Hindu reformers ever since.

Why should you grow angry at those who are angry at you? What do you gain? What do those others lose? Physical anger diminishes your nobility and mental anger diminishes your wisdom. The fire doesn't burn anyone else's house until it first burns the house in which it was lit. —Basava

Whatever happens to me, happens. Whatever comes to me, whether pain or pleasure, I accept as my lot. I ask no favor, Lord, even of you, nor shall I stray from your path. —Basava

How would Basava be received today?

76
Moses Maimonides

Born 1135 in Cordoba, Spain
Died 1204 in Cairo, Egypt

Was Moses Maimonides a devout rabbi seeking to bring rationalist philosophers to accept the Torah as divinely revealed truth? Or was he a philosopher seeking to convince rabbinic Jews to embrace human reason? Even today, scholars disagree on Maimonides, but all concur that he was the most influential Jewish philosopher ever to live.

When radical Muslims began persecuting the Jews in Cordoba, Maimonides's family fled to Morocco and eventually to Egypt, the young Moses studying under rabbis at every stop along the way. Following the tragic death of his brother, leaving Maimonides with the care of his extended family, he took up medicine, gaining renown in that field and eventually becoming court physician to the sultan Saladin.

Maimonides is chiefly remembered, however, as a rabbinic scholar and philosopher. His two most important books reveal the two sides of his mind. The *Mishnah Torah* is a concise, clear summary of the Mishnah (see #27). Maimonides grouped Talmudic rulings (see #36) under topical headings, omitting the lengthy debates and alternative viewpoints to eliminate the need for those seeking guidance to plough through the entire Talmud. Some criticized Maimonides as an arrogant threat to traditional Judaism, but many traditionalist Jews to this day regard the *Mishnah Torah* an authoritative summary of Jewish law.

In Maimonides's other major work, *Guide for the Perplexed*, he develops his philosophical ideas, beginning from the conviction that truth cannot contradict truth (see #62). Science, philosophy, and religion are therefore not opposed, but complementary. Maimonides integrated Aristotelian ethics with scripture, discussing the attributes of God, proofs of the existence of God, and other scientific and philosophical questions. Architectonic in structure, restrained in its rhetoric, and consistently logical, the *Guide* is an early example of the scholastic approach. It would profoundly influence later thinkers, including Thomas Aquinas (see #85).

> *It is better to acquit a thousand guilty persons than to put a single innocent one to death.* —Maimonides

> *Anticipate charity by preventing poverty.* —Maimonides

> *Give a man a fish and you feed him for a day; teach a man to fish and you feed him for a lifetime.* —Maimonides

> *Teach your tongue to say "I do not know," and you shall progress.* —Maimonides

If truth cannot contradict truth, where do disagreements about truth come from?

77
Myoan Eisai

Born 1141, in Okayama, Japan
Died 1215, in Kyoto, Japan

By the twelfth century, Mahayana Buddhism had become solidly established in Japan and some Buddhist monasteries enjoyed imperial patronage and could exert political and military leverage. Myoan Eisai saw a need for reform.

Eisai had been a monk for fourteen years in the capital of Kyoto when, in 1168, he sailed to China to study at the great Buddhist center on Mt. Tiantai. There he learned of Ch'an Buddhism (see #13, #58). After just six months, Eisai returned to Japan with sixty books of Buddhist sacred writings and introduced the Ch'an school to his native land, where it became known as Zen.

Eisai was politically astute. Back in Japan, he traveled and taught, cultivating good relations with the government authorities and never directly challenging the Japanese Buddhist establishment or rejecting their practices. In 1187 he was able to return to China, this time remaining there for four years, during which he studied under the Ch'an master Huai-chang.

Upon returning home the second time, Eisai introduced green tea to Japan, grown in Kyoto from seeds he had brought from China, as a means of helping monks meditate. This is the basis for the Japanese tea ceremony today.

On his second tour in China, Eisai had also noted the importance of monastic discipline, which had lapsed in Japan, and upon returning home, he made it central to the Zen movement. Opposition quickly ensued. To avoid confrontation, Eisai withdrew to the relatively remote southern island of Kyushu, where he wrote his most influential work, *The Propagation of Zen and the Protection of the Nation*, stressing the importance of discipline. This drew the attention of Japan's shogun and samurai warriors, who embraced Eisai. In time, some came to see Zen as linked to Japanese nationalism.

Zen Buddhism relies on what in the West are perceived as paradoxical, even senseless riddles, called koans (see #58). The best known koan: "You know the sound of two hands clapping. What is the sound of one hand clapping?" Koans are meant to point to the uselessness of analytical thought that seeks to break things down and dissect them. Guided by a skilled teacher, pushed to meditate on koan after koan, and finally relying on intuitive insight alone, the Zen student attains enlightenment, recognizing the essential unity of all things.

What kinds of insights lie beyond analytical thought?

78
Muhyiddin ibn Arabi

Born 1165, in Murcia, Spain
Died 1240, in Damascus, Syria

Thirteenth-century Spain was home to a vibrant spiritual and intellectual culture where Jews, Christians, and Muslims freely exchanged insights and learned from each other. Muhyiddin ibn Arabi, a Spanish Muslim mystic, visionary, and teacher, produced a literary output that was huge, intellectually demanding, and wide ranging, on topics like the names of God, the relationship between divine transcendence and divine immanence, modes of knowing, and the unity of the created order.

Ibn Arabi traveled widely. His writings include an exposition of Jewish, Christian, and Islamic teaching and an encyclopedia of insights from many sources. He engaged Christian theology openheartedly, rather than dismissively or polemically. God is manifest everywhere and in everything, Ibn Arabi said. The believer can therefore be at home anywhere—in a synagogue or church as well as in a mosque. He saw the fundamental insight, the unity of God manifest in his creation, as common to various faith traditions, not merely to Islam.

Ibn Arabi never called himself a Sufi (see #51, #59), but he used philosophical terms to describe mystical experiences and understandings. The divine essence is indivisible and completely beyond human knowing, he said, but God manifests himself by inscribing one of the divine attributes or "names" in every human being and created thing. Therefore anyone, not just the enlightened or the educated, may discover the manifestation of God within him by cultivating his imagination. The only God anyone can know is the God already present within him, and this divine manifestation is unique to each individual. To know God, therefore, one must know oneself.

Ibn Arabi also wrote poems, sometimes bordering on the erotic, to describe the love of God and his experience of encountering God on his journey within.

My heart can assume any form: a meadow for gazelles, a cloister for [Christian] monks, a temple for idols, the Kaaba for Muslim pilgrims, the tablets of the law for Jews, the scrolls of the Quran. My creed is love, and wherever its caravan may turn, there is my religion, my faith. —Ibn Arabi

The Beloved becomes a mirror reflecting the secret face of the mystic lover, while the lover, purified of his dense ego, becomes in turn a mirror of the attributes and actions of the Beloved. —Ibn Arabi

If Ibn Arabi is right, are all faiths equally true?

79
Shinran

Born 1173, near Kyoto, Japan
Died 1263, in Kyoto, Japan

Shinran carried the teachings of Honen (see #74) to what many see as their logical conclusion.

Orphaned at nine, Shinran was entrusted to an uncle who enrolled him at a Buddhist temple, where he resided and studied for the next twenty years. Like Honen, he was frustrated at his inability to attain enlightenment through monastic disciplines. Instructed in a dream to seek out Honen, he became Honen's disciple in 1201 and soon attained enlightenment.

When two other Pure Land disciples fell afoul of the law because of reputed sexual crimes, the military banned prayer through the name of Amidabha and both Honen and Shinran were forced to leave Kyoto. They would not see each other again, and Shinran's understanding of Pure Land Buddhism began to diverge from his master's and develop into a movement of its own. He founded a second Pure Land sect, which his disciples later called the True Pure Land.

Shinran turned his back on monasticism as the preferred route to enlightenment, taking a wife with whom he had six children and thereby setting up a hereditary succession of leaders which later disciples firmly adhered to. He disregarded the distinction between ordained and lay believers and began referring to himself as "the bald-headed fool." Shinran was noted for his humility, gratitude, and humor.

Divine grace was key for Shinran, as for Honen before him. Shinran felt that human selfishness and delusion made enlightenment impossible in this life, but a spiritual awakening through the gift of faith in Amidabha would lead to deeper insights and gain the believer entrance into Nirvana in the next life. Assertion of "self power" would tie a believer to this empty existence, Shinran said, while calling upon Amidabha's "other power" would lead to release from the cycle of rebirths.

Unlike Honen, Shinran saw no need for repeated invocations of the divine name. Call upon Abidabha once in your life, he said, and Abidabha in his loving graciousness will come to you. He suggested, though, that the name be invoked often, as an expression of joy and gratitude, not as a means to attain enlightenment.

Although I too am within Amidabha's grasp, passions obstruct my eyes and I cannot see him. Nevertheless, great compassion is untiring and illumines me always. —Shinran

Is divine love a given, or must one do something to access it?

80
Francis of Assisi

Born 1181/2, in Assisi, Italy
Died 1226, in Porzioncula, Italy

Francis of Assisi is known to many as the small statue standing among the flowers in a suburban garden and the saint who converted a hare, tamed a wolf, and preached to the birds. It is true that Francis saw God in every creature, but he also possessed a granite-like stubbornness that irked many, even of his admirers.

Son of a well-to-do merchant, Francis as a young adult was a dapper man about town who dreamt of glory on the battlefield. But a year spent as a prisoner of war in a wretched dungeon effected a profound change in Francis. He learned to endure suffering with serenity, befriended even the most disagreeable of his fellow-prisoners, and upon his release embraced "Lady Poverty." Francis learned to love the poor, even lepers with runny sores whom he hugged and kissed until "what had been bitter became sweet."

Francis is often seen as the Christian whose life and character most resemble those of Jesus himself. The key to Christlike living for Francis was love of everyone and everything, including thieves, infidels, murderers, and authority figures who took offense at his challenges to established mores.

Love is expressed by voluntary poverty, Francis believed. He shunned personal property, owning not even the smallest memento. To own something, he said, is to grasp for a security that comes only from following Christ and would lead to disputes, lawsuits, and arms to protect one's possessions. Insisting on total poverty for his followers, he instructed them to support themselves solely through begging. The only time Francis is recorded as having grown angry is when his standard of absolute poverty was questioned.

The poverty that mattered most to Francis, however, was poverty of spirit. He saw humility as the sister of poverty. Francis turned his back not only on material things, but on inner possessions as well, such as honor, knowledge, talents, and virtue. He advised his followers not to think back on their sacrifice after renouncing their possessions, lest it become a source of spiritual pride.

Francis's reputation quickly spread and led to the founding of three orders, the Friars Minor (Little Brothers) for men, the Poor Clares for women, and the Third Order for those choosing to follow a Franciscan life while living fully in the world. All three orders thrive throughout the world today.

How would Francis of Assisi be received if he lived today?

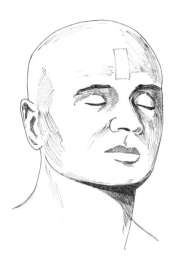

81

Madhva

Born ca. 1199 (?), near Udupi, India
Died ca. 1278 (?), in Karnataka, India

Born to a noble family, Madhva was a scholar and an athlete as a boy, but left school in his teens to travel about south India studying the Hindu scriptures. At twenty-five, he took monastic vows and devoted himself to the study of Shankara's monistic philosophy (see #56).

Like Ramanuja (see #70), Madhva eventually departed from Shankara, but he went even further, founding the third major branch of Veda-based Hindu spirituality (see #56, #70), known as Dvaita, or dualism.

In Western terms, Madhva would be called a philosophical realist. He affirmed the reality of individual souls and sense objects. Common sense tells us that what our senses experience is real, he said, and the Vedas themselves could teach us nothing if real eyes were not reading real documents. One's reading of the scriptures must be consistent with everyday experience, he said.

Madhva was a monotheist who saw the many gods worshiped by Hindus as expressions of the one supreme God and dismissed many popular devotional practices as superstitions. He saw three kinds of reality, each eternal and distinct from the others—God, human souls, and inanimate matter.

Souls are infinite in number and are like particles emanating from God and dependent upon God, Madhva said. They are not identical to God—Madhva was no monist (see #56)—but distinct, individual entities that remain distinct throughout eternity. Even when, by God's grace and spiritual discipline, souls return to God after being liberated from the cycle of births and rebirths, they are not subsumed into God, but retain their individuality.

Souls do not necessarily return to God, however. Some will never be interested in more than material things. Madhva affirmed something like what Westerners would call heaven, hell, and purgatory, the last state being an eternal transmigration of souls from one lifetime to another. Moreover, some of the stories told of Madhva's life are remarkably similar to those told of Jesus, and like many Christians, he saw souls having attained union with God as intercessors for the living. Some scholars have speculated that Indian Christians may have influenced Madhva, but most doubt the connection.

Later in life Madhva traveled about the entire Indian subcontinent and acquired a wide following. Dvaita remains today one of Hinduism's most vibrant expressions.

Can one be a Hindu and a Christian at the same time?

82

Dogen

Born 1200, in Kyoto, Japan
Died 1253, in Kyoto, Japan

Westerners are taught to conceptualize, analyze, and dissect, but this is precisely what Buddhists do not do. Many Westerners therefore associate Buddhism with practices they deem inexplicable or even ridiculous, such as the continual repetition of a sacred syllable or mantra (see #54), pondering senseless riddles (see #77), and sitting for hours while thinking of nothing. This last Buddhist practice was developed and promoted by Dogen.

Already marked as a bright student, Dogen rejected the influence and wealth of a position at the imperial court and became a disciple of Eisai (see #77), entering his monastery at age seventeen. Like Eisai, he traveled to China, studying under the Ch'an masters there for five years. Returning to Japan at age twenty-seven, Dogen began teaching meditation in the Kyoto area. In 1243, he relocated to a remote area north of Kyoto where he and his followers built a temple called Daibutsu-ji, later renamed Eihi-ji. It is today a major center of Soto Zen, the school that emerged from Dogen's witness and teaching.

As related in his masterpiece *Shobogenzo* (*Treasury of the Eye of the True Teaching*), Dogen approached enlightenment by "just sitting." He had noted the traditional Buddhist teaching that people are endowed at birth with an awareness of truth. If they already knew the truth, why, Dogen asked, did the Buddhist masters throughout history need to seek it through spiritual practices?

Dogen concluded that they didn't. Such practices were unnecessary. All one needed—and this was true for the humblest layman or woman as well as the most advanced monastic—was to "just sit" with legs crossed and back straight, in what is called the lotus position, and clear the mind of all thought. This is not how one seeks enlightenment. Rather, it is living into the enlightenment that has been there all along. It is the manifestation of one's true nature. Dogen advised finding a quiet room, eating and drinking moderately, and then "just sitting" to clear the mind—no analyzing, evaluating, or planning.

This is no easy task. Repeated practice and discipline are required. It was perhaps the demanding discipline of Dogen's practice that attracted the Japanese warrior class, or samurai, who incorporated it into their training, resulting in the unlikely embrace by a powerful military aristocracy of a religious movement centered on "just sitting."

What if "just sitting" were taught in Western schools?

83
Jalal al-Din Rumi

Born 1207, in Balkh, Afghanistan
Died 1273, in Konya, Turkey

Jalal al-Din Rumi was perhaps the greatest mystical poet of all time, in any language. His masterpiece, the *Mathnawi* (*Couplets*), contains roughly twenty-seven thousand lines of poetry. It is a rambling work, speaking through various voices with different points of view, and covering a range of topics. It includes stories and dialogues, drawing upon both contemporary and traditional Muslim sources. The *Mathnawi* is today beloved by Sufis and other Muslim mystics, adherents of other religions, and the nonreligious. Rumi wrote other poems and prose works as well.

Rumi was born in Central Asia just as the Mongols swept in, destroying the major Muslim centers there. When he was a small boy, his father, a Muslim scholar, fled with his family and wandered for over a decade, finally settling in Konya, in modern Turkey, where Rumi eventually succeeded his father as professor at the local Muslim academy.

At the age of thirty-seven, Rumi's life took an abrupt turn when he became an ascetic and embraced Sufism (see #51, #59). Much of his work expresses a deep loneliness and the absence of God, perhaps harking back to the destruction of his boyhood home. That experience of loss and longing for God, he said, was vital to the spiritual life. Rumi sought God through dancing, singing, poetry, and music, which led him to moments of ecstasy in the presence of God, also described in his writing. With his son, Rumi founded the order known in the West as "Whirling Dervishes," who attain union with the divine through stately, spinning dance. The order remains prominent in Turkey today.

Like many mystics, Rumi was peaceful and accepting of others. He focused on the inner, personal experience of God and embraced Jews and Christians who had similar experiences.

When I am with you, we stay up all night. When you're not here, I can't go to sleep. I praise you for those two insomnias, and the difference between them!
—Rumi

If you are irritated by every rub, how will your mirror be polished? —Rumi

Dance, when you're broken open. Dance, if you've torn the bandage off. Dance in the middle of the fighting. Dance in your blood. Dance when you're perfectly free. —Rumi

Can the loss of God be a good thing?

84
Louis IX

Born 1214, in Poissy, France
Died 1270, in Tunis, Tunisia

France's King Louis IX was beloved during his lifetime and has ever since been revered as the model medieval sovereign. His virtuous life, benevolence, and passion for justice embodied everything the medieval church understood Christian living to require.

Louis reigned for forty-four years during a time when France was Europe's dominant power. He fed beggars from his table and sometimes made his meal of their leftovers, washed the feet of lepers, founded hospitals and homeless shelters, and forbade usury. He made time for any subject, however lowly, who came to him seeking justice.

When a Flemish count executed three young men for hunting rabbits on his property, Louis arrested the count and tried him in the civil courts, not (as was the custom at the time) by a jury of other noblemen. The count was convicted and sentenced to death, but Louis then pardoned him, imposing instead a stiff fine used for charitable work and to endow masses to be read on behalf of the three deceased young hunters.

Louis was noted for his piety, spending long hours in prayer and penance, often fasting, and attending two masses daily. This devotion was not disclosed to the public until after the king's death. His courtiers and associates said they never once heard him swear. Louis built the splendid Sainte-Chapelle in Paris as his personal chapel and founded the theological college which later became the Sorbonne. Even when held captive during the Seventh Crusade, he read the Daily Office twice each day in his cell.

History has not looked favorably on everything Louis did, such as his leading of crusades, his burning of twelve thousand copies of the Talmud and other Jewish books, and his promoting the Inquisition in France. But Louis was a child of his times and even these initiatives were undertaken because Louis believed that in doing so he served the cause of Christ. He died from dysentery in Africa while leading the Eighth Crusade.

Louis's character can be seen in the letter he wrote from his deathbed to his son Philip, who would succeed him as king. He urged his son to love God first, bear adversity patiently, confess his sins frequently, associate only with godly men, administer justice fairly, defend the poor, give thanks constantly, and go to war only as a last resort.

Would you want Louis as your king?

85
Thomas Aquinas

Born 1225, in Roccasecca, Italy
Died 1274, in Priverno, Italy

Thomas Aquinas was a Dominican friar whose intellectual gifts made him a renowned author, preacher, and professor, first in Paris, and later in Naples and Rome. During his lifetime, some faulted Thomas for appropriating insights from Muslim and Jewish thinkers, but his reputation steadily grew until, in 1879, Pope Leo XIII declared Thomas to be what he has been ever since, the definitive theologian of the Roman Catholic Church.

Thomas drew upon Augustine (see #37), John Cassian (see #38), and other Christian thinkers, but his great achievement was to reconcile Christian teaching with Aristotelian philosophy. Muslim and Jewish scholars (see #72, #76) had rediscovered Aristotle and Thomas learned of the ancient Greek philosopher from them. He adapted Aristotle's thought, making it a suitable vehicle for expressing Christian teaching. This philosophical approach is called scholasticism.

Thomas's two major works are the *Summa Contra Gentiles*, explaining Christian faith to nonbelievers, and the *Summa Theologica*, a lucid and comprehensive exposition of Christian theology and philosophy in Aristotelian terms. He also wrote Eucharistic hymns that are still sung today and commentaries on Aristotle and the Bible.

Thomas believed both in rationally discerned truth and in supernaturally revealed truth. The two were complementary. Human reason could determine that God exists, Thomas said, and that God is one, good, omnipotent, and all-knowing. Reason is God-given, so the knowledge it yields is a form of revelation, called "natural" revelation. Other aspects of divine truth, however, such as the Trinity, the Incarnation, and the Atonement, are disclosed only by supernatural revelation through prophets, the Bible, and church teaching. Supernatural revelation also corrects and refines natural revelation when human beings misinterpret it.

Drawing on Aristotle, Thomas developed five proofs for the existence of God. To oversimplify Thomas's carefully nuanced thought, his proofs are based on the logical progression of cause and effect: Things move or happen because something moves them or causes them to happen. Logic requires at some point a Prime Mover and First Cause that was not itself moved or caused—what is usually called God.

Thomas was deeply prayerful. On December 6, 1273, he had an experience while praying of which he never spoke or wrote but which caused him to say, "Everything I have written now seems to me like straw." He did not write another word for the remaining three months of his life.

In what areas can non-Christian thought elucidate Christian teaching?

86
Moses de León

Born ca. 1250 in Guadalajara, Spain
Died 1305 in Arevalo, Spain

Around 1280 in Moorish Spain, a Jewish man discovered an esoteric book by a second-century Palestinian rabbi, hidden for over a thousand years—a lost part of the oral Torah (see #14, #27). Or so said Moses de León, who claimed to have found the book. Modern linguistic studies, however, suggest that Moses de León himself was almost certainly the book's author (or possibly its compiler).

The book is called the Zohar (radiance or splendor in Hebrew). Nearly 1,500 pages in length, it is a collection of tales, commentaries, and sermons on various topics and in various literary styles. Though much of it, like classical rabbinic writing, is a commentary on the Torah, it emphasizes mystical, individual, immediate, unmediated communion with God.

The Zohar has attained near-canonical status in Orthodox Jewish circles, and not merely because of its presumed antiquity. It can stimulate readers' emotions and imaginations and deepen their prayer life. The God of the Zohar is on intimate terms with humankind, with influence flowing in both directions. Through virtuous living, one may increase the flow of divine grace; God sometimes delays doing something until it has been prayed for. The Zohar sought to counter the rationalism then fashionable among European Jews, Christians, and Muslims. Critics have faulted the Zohar for favoring mystical speculations over the use of reason.

The Zohar became the foundational text of the Kabbalah, a Jewish renewal movement originating in Spain and southern France at the time. The term "kaballah" (tradition in Hebrew) originally referred to the Torah, received by Moses (see #4) and expounded by later rabbis, but came to refer primarily to the Zohar, deemed a supplementary tradition long hidden but now disclosed. In recent times Kabbalah has become a blanket term applied to a range of Jewish mystical sects and movements seeking to penetrate beyond rabbinic Judaism, which emphasizes the law of God in the Torah, to the deeper secrets of God discerned in spiritual signs and symbols also found in the Torah.

> The tales related in the Torah are merely her outer garments. . . . Just as wine must be kept in a jar, so the Torah must be contained in an outer garment. That garment consists of tales and stories, but we must penetrate more deeply.
> —the Zohar

Are tales and stories merely the "outer garments" of the truth they convey?

87
Ahmad ibn Taymiyyah

Born 1263, in Harran, Turkey
Died 1328, in Damascus, Syria

The thirteenth-century Mongol invasion destabilized the Muslim world. Once united and flourishing, Islam now appeared fragmented and vulnerable.

Ahmad ibn Taymiyyah hoped to set things right with a "back to basics" appeal. His family had fled to Damascus from their upper Mesopotamian home when invaders burned the region. Ibn Taymiyyah studied Hanbalite jurisprudence (see #55) in Damascus and then Islamic philosophy, Sufism, and Christian thought. He never wavered, however, from the conservative Sunni Islam in which he had been schooled.

Modern militant Islamists often cite a famous legal ruling by Ibn Taymiyyah stating that any Muslim living under a non-Muslim government that infringes on his religious freedom should resist that government or emigrate. But Ibn Taymiyyah's concern was not primarily political. The true emigrant, he said, is not one who departs from his land, but one who departs from his sin. He was not a rigid thinker, but sought pragmatic, useful solutions to problems.

Ibn Taymiyyah believed that God had from eternity ordered the best possible world. That conviction led him not to rational inquiry or rapturous adoration but to moral rigor. He saw God as just and wise, requiring obedience above all else. Like many Islamic legal scholars, Ibn Taymiyyah took literally the verses in the Quran suggesting that the disobedient were consigned to eternal punishment.

Ibn Taymiyyah was a sharp, provocative author who often fell afoul of the governing authorities, in particular for opposing the invocation of ancient saints and prophets, a practice that gave employment to many Muslims at the time. He was twice imprisoned and died in prison. But Ibn Taymiyyah was beloved by the common people who thronged to his funeral and made pilgrimages to his Damascus grave for centuries thereafter.

The real prisoner is the one whose heart is imprisoned from God and the captive is the one whose desires have enslaved him. —Ibn Taymiyyah

What can my enemies do to me? I have in my breast both my heaven and my garden. If I travel they are with me, never leaving me. Imprisonment for me is a chance to be alone with my Lord. To be killed is martyrdom and to be exiled from my land is a spiritual journey. —Ibn Taymiyyah

How would you respond to a government that denigrated your faith?

88
Gregory Palamas

Born 1296, in Istanbul, Turkey
Died 1359, in Thessaloniki, Greece

"Lord Jesus Christ, Son of God, have mercy on me, a sinner."

That was the prayer of a nineteenth-century Russian pilgrim who walked from Siberia to Jerusalem. Known as the "Jesus Prayer," it expresses a centuries-old spirituality in the Eastern Orthodox churches called "hesychasm" (after the Greek word for stillness). Constant recitation of the prayer, with relaxed breathing, focuses the mind on the name of Jesus and brings a direct experience of Christ in the heart.

Hesychasm was once controversial. A fourteenth-century monk named Barlaam insisted that God was completely unknowable. The hesychasts, led by Gregory Palamas, claimed a direct experience of God through the senses, particularly through the sacraments and relaxed breathing.

Palamas had studied secular disciplines before choosing a monastic vocation at the age of twenty. He spent several years in one of the large, rambling monasteries on Mt. Athos, looming over a remote peninsula in the Aegean Sea. To this day, Mt. Athos is home to thousands of Orthodox monks devoted to holiness. The dispute with Barlaam, however, drew Palamas to Constantinople and eventually to Thessaloniki, where he became a beloved bishop.

Hesychasts agree that God is unknowable in his essence, but Palamas distinguished between the essence of God and the energies of God. Through God's energies, such as his goodness, wisdom, providence, and majesty, God discloses himself to human beings. These energies are not created beings distinguishable from God, but manifestations of God himself, though not of the unknowable divine essence. When they flow through the believer, the believer is "deified"—drawn into God and transformed—a key concept in Orthodox spirituality based on the conviction that when the Son of God stooped to unite himself to humanity, he also raised humanity to God.

Little in Palamas's thought is original. He is remembered for developing a theological framework affirming the paradox that God is transcendent and inaccessible, yet also immanent and close at hand.

> God presents himself to everything by his manifestations, his creative and providential energies. We must seek a God in whom we can participate in some way, so that each of us, by the way proper to us and by the analogy of participation, may receive being, life, and deification. —Gregory Palamas

Write a prayer or poem expressing the paradox that God is both transcendent and immanent.

89
Sergius of Radonezh

Born 1314, in Varnitsy, Russia
Died 1392, Sergiyev Posad, Russia

The first east Slavic state, Kievan Rus, was founded in the ninth century, and the city of Kiev flourished as a center of trading and of Slavic Orthodox Christianity for four hundred years. But much of Kiev was destroyed in 1240 when it fell to the Mongol invasion. To the north, however, the undistinguished little settlement of Moscow had escaped the Mongol hordes. Its leaders negotiated with the invaders and soon Moscow's political and religious influence surpassed that of Kiev.

Slavic Orthodoxy is conservative and monastic. Its foremost personality was a monk named Sergius. At the age of twenty, Sergius and his brother Stefan retreated forty miles into the forest where they built two small huts, became hermits, and undertook a life of austere simplicity. They also built a modest chapel dedicated to the Holy Trinity.

Stefan soon returned to Moscow, but as with Anthony in the Egyptian desert a millennium earlier (see #31), others soon heard of Sergius's holiness and joined him, building huts of their own. The forests surrounding Moscow became home to hundreds of hermit monks.

A group of these monks approached Sergius about founding a monastery and becoming its superior. Never ambitious and prizing humility (he would later refuse appointment as Metropolitan of Moscow), Sergius at first declined but later reluctantly agreed. A monastery was built around the chapel constructed by Sergius and his brother, eventually known as Trinity Lavra of St. Sergius (later monks added their founder's name). Sergius's followers also founded forty other monasteries near Moscow.

Sergius aided in the unification of Russia under Moscow's rule, giving his blessing to the Muscovite army that defeated the Tartars in 1380. The victory established Moscow as the center of Russian life, and Trinity Lavra of St. Sergius became the most important monastery in Russia and the spiritual heart of the Russian Orthodox Church.

Sergius's institutions would not live off endowments, gifts, or managed estates. He insisted that each monk work to contribute to the monastery's life, and Sergius himself was noted for his industry. Along with his discipline of prayer and fasting, Sergius baked bread, made candles and shoes, chopped wood, and cooked for the monks under his care.

God's grace cannot not be given without trials. After tribulation comes joy.
—Sergius of Radonezh

In your experience, is grace only given accompanied by trials? Does joy come only after tribulation?

90
Abd al-Rahman ibn Khaldun

Born 1332, in Tunis, Tunisia
Died 1406, in Cairo, Egypt

By the fourteenth century, the Muslim world's Golden Age (see #57) had passed. Culturally, politically, and spiritually, Islam had entered a period of retrenchment. When he was born, Abd al-Rahman ibn Khaldun's family had fled from Spain to Tunis as Christian forces were reconquering the Iberian peninsula. Living in northern Africa, he witnessed the rise and fall of several minor dynasties, resulting in a roller-coaster career in which he served as teacher and judge, was then imprisoned, and then restored to favor. Ibn Khaldun also experienced grievous personal losses. His parents died in the plague in 1349, and his wife and children perished in a shipwreck in 1384.

Ibn Khaldun longed to understand the apparent whims of historical events. His monumental history of the world traced the rise and fall of empires from earliest times. The best known section of the work is its introduction, often published separately and known in English as *Prolegomenon* or *An Introduction to History*. It has been called the world's first philosophy of history and the first book of sociology. Partisanship for a particular creed or ideology, Ibn Khaldun said, obscures judgment, but impartial investigation leads to the truth.

Although he knew and respected both the Quran and Muslim philosophy, Ibn Khaldun sought to uncover recurring patterns in history that neither the Quran nor philosophy alluded to. Key to his understanding is his concept of social cohesion, which might also be called group solidarity, tribal loyalty, or nationalism. Nomadic peoples, he felt, easily develop such bonds and become brave, hardy, and frugal. These qualities enable them to conquer and subjugate neighboring peoples. But after their triumphs, the nomads build cities or inhabit the cities of their subjects. Their social cohesion weakens as they acquire a taste for higher culture, hire mercenaries to do their fighting, rule through bureaucracies, and are corrupted by luxury. This opens the way for the cycle to repeat itself when a new, stronger, and more cohesive nomadic people appears on the scene.

Thus Ibn Khaldun saw history as cyclical and governed by universal laws similar to the laws of nature, not by the decrees of an inscrutable deity. He also developed a sophisticated theory of economics and believed human beings had evolved from monkeys. These ideas, revolutionary in his day, have led some to call him the world's first modern thinker.

Is history cyclical or linear?

Julian of Norwich

Born 1342, in Norwich, England (?)
Died ca. 1420, in Norwich, England (?)

Julian of Norwich told a memorable story. A servant loved his master and wanted to please him. The master sent his servant on a distant mission. The servant hurried off but fell into a ravine and was badly injured. He grieved over his injuries not because of the pain, but because they rendered him unable to carry out his master's mission. Upon learning of his servant's misfortunes, the master comforted him, rewarded him, and promoted him to a higher position.

This story captures the understanding of sin and divine love found in *Showings* (also known as *Revelations of Divine Love*) by Julian of Norwich, who spent the last four or so decades of her life in a ten-by-ten-foot cell built into the wall of St. Julian's Church in Norwich, England. Many sought her counsel there, where she meditated on a series of sixteen visions she had received on May 13, 1373. The visions included some gory details, but their thrust was that God loves humanity profoundly and unfailingly. *Showings* is based on those visions.

Julian's times hardly suggested a loving God. England was mired in a long, grinding war with France. Church leaders were corrupt and worldly. The bubonic plague had wiped out perhaps half the British population between 1348 and 1362. Yet Julian's faith was confident and serene, based on a joyful, radiant Christ who had suffered for his people and would gladly suffer more if need be. She saw sin not as disobedience, but as the result of naiveté, ignorance, blindness, foolishness, and weakness. Humankind was not to blame for sin, but its victim. The master in Julian's story represents God, embracing, healing, and loving sin's human victims.

Julian envisioned Christ as Mother, making her a favorite of modern Christian feminists. As a human mother hurts for her injured or maligned children, so does Jesus hurt for us, Julian said. She is also known for her statement that "every kind of thing will be well," which was not an expression of naïve optimism, but a statement of confidence that God will prevail against every evil.

We may laugh to comfort ourselves and rejoice in God, because the devil is rendered impotent. —Julian of Norwich

Our courteous Lord shows himself to the soul, gladly and with the happiest smile. —Julian of Norwich

What keeps Julian from being a naïve optimist?

92

Tsongkhapa

Born 1357, in Xining, China
Died 1419, in the Ganden Monastery, near Lhasa,
Tibet (China)

Tibetan Buddhism underwent a resurgence beginning around the year 1000 with the building of
monasteries and temples, the creation of the Tibetan
calendar, and the emergence of Tibetan Buddhist sects. This resurgence culminated
four hundred years later with Tsongkhapa, the last of Buddhism's formative thinkers.

Tsongkhapa is remembered for four accomplishments: restoring a large statue in
Lhasa of Maitreya, a Buddha figure expected to appear in the future; strengthening
monastic discipline; beginning the Great Prayer Festival in Lhasa during the Tibetan
New Year, when the faithful pray for universal well-being; and establishing the Ganden Monastery near Lhasa which housed thousands of monks until destroyed during
the Tibetan rebellion against Chinese rule in 1959. Out of the Ganden Monastery
came the Gelug sect, to this day the predominant Buddhist sect throughout Tibet.

Building on the work of Nagarjuna (see #28), Tsongkhapa sought a middle position between wisdom and behavior, insight and compassion. He also sought to unify
the traditions deriving from available Buddhist scriptures and those deemed to have
been revealed only later to a select group of devotees.

Tsongkhapa left eighteen volumes of writings, emphasizing the unreality of all
sense objects, including the person experiencing them. Like Nagarjuna, he said that
since sense objects derive their existence from beyond themselves, they are fleeting,
empty, or unreal. What is experienced as real does not differ from what is experienced
in a dream; the perceived difference is a mere human convention. Similarly, statements deemed true and those deemed false are all alike false. Tsongkhapa acknowledged, however, that for purposes of day-to-day living, people act as if sense objects
are real and statements true, but there is no reality corresponding to this perception.

Tsongkhapa developed a step-by-step approach to enlightenment, teaching his
disciples through yoga to attain the experience of emptiness and bliss by visualizing
themselves as an enlightened buddha.

> *Meditate again and again until you have turned your mind away from the
> activities of this life, which are like adorning yourself while being led to the
> execution ground.* —Tsongkhapa

> *To be attached to one's own happiness is a barrier to the true and perfect path.
> To cherish others is the source of every admirable quality.* —Tsongkhapa

**The Declaration of Independence says the pursuit of happiness is an inalienable
right. Tsongkhapa says it's a barrier to truth. What do you think?**

93
Kabir

Born 1440, in Lahartara, India
Died 1518, in Maghar, India

Wit, banter, sarcasm, earthy images—these were the linguistic tools of an illiterate, lower-caste fifteenth-century Indian mystic named Kabir. A weaver by trade, Kabir composed couplets and poems in his head, put them to music, and sang them as he walked about. His disciples wrote them down.

Kabir was abandoned as an infant and raised by a Muslim family, but whether he received a religious upbringing is unknown. He never embraced Islam or any other religious tradition. Though using Hindu vocabulary in his poetry, he dismissed ritual, philosophy, dogma, the Vedas, the Quran, and every form of caste and hierarchy. Kabir rejected no religion as such but scathingly denounced hypocrisy masquerading as religious devotion.

Kabir's poetry quickly found a following at a time when the Hindu priesthood had become professionalized and the Muslim insistence on an exclusive truth did not mesh with India's traditional religious inclusiveness.

True spirituality for Kabir was the total love of a formless supreme God who was found by searching within. Shrines, chanting, rituals, diets, ascetic practice, prayer techniques and postures—these do not lead to God. Kabir experienced a simple, natural oneness with God and sought to lead others to discover the same within themselves. Look, he said, for "the breath within the breath."

Kabir revered all life and was a strict vegetarian. Hindus especially, but also Sikhs and others have been influenced by him. Roughly ten million people today, mostly in India, are part of the "Path of Kabir," a religious community recognizing Kabir as its founder.

If I say God is within me, it sounds like blasphemy. If I say God is not within me, I lie. In God the inner and outer worlds are one. He rests his feet on both.
—Kabir

I went to search for the beautiful color of my beloved and saw that color everywhere. Then I found that I myself have been colored with the same beautiful color. —Kabir

Make the whole earth into paper, all forests into pens, and the seven oceans into ink. You still cannot describe the greatness of God. —Kabir

Everyone knows that the drop merges into the ocean, but few know that the ocean merges into the drop. —Kabir

How does the belief that God is within differ from self-adoration?

94

Nanak Dev

Born 1469, in Nankana Sahib, Pakistan
Died 1539, in Kartarpur, Pakistan

Nanak Dev was reared a Hindu and mastered the Vedas. The new faith which he founded incorporated many Hindu teachings, including the cycle of rebirths and the acceptance of other faiths as legitimate paths to God, but departed radically from Hindu metaphysics, rituals, and social structures. It is called Sikhism (after a word meaning student or disciple).

Married and the father of two sons, Nanak was working as an accountant when, at around thirty years of age, he disappeared while bathing in a river. He was feared drowned. When he reappeared three days later, he had experienced a mystical conversion. Soon thereafter Nanak departed on the first of four missionary journeys, accompanied by a low-caste Muslim companion. These travels consumed twenty-five years and took Nanak throughout the Indian subcontinent and to Sri Lanka, Tibet, and Arabia. While traveling, Nanak wrote hymns that are still sung today. When he finally returned, he reunited with his family and founded the city of Kartarpur, where he spent the remainder of his days as a peasant farmer, devoting his evenings to teaching the many disciples who came to sit at his feet.

Nanak rejected priestcraft, monasticism, and asceticism. He saw living simply and honorably in the world as the path to holiness and release from the cycle of rebirths. The three pillars of modern Sikhism originated with Nanak: (1) meditation on the name of God by recitation and chanting, (2) earning one's living through honest work, and (3) sharing of resources with others. He instituted a communal meal where all dined together. Nanak also rejected religious hypocrisy and social inequality, including the Indian caste system and the dominance of men over women.

Nanak was a monotheist who understood God as incomprehensible, formless, and genderless, yet interpenetrating nature and manifest in all people, of whatever faith.

Sikhs today number roughly twenty-four million worldwide, three-fourths of them in the Punjab province of northwest India, where they constitute a majority.

Even kings and emperors with heaps of wealth and vast dominion cannot compare with an ant filled with the love of God. —Nanak Dev

Sing the songs of joy to the Lord, serve the Name of the Lord, and become the servant of his servants. —Nanak Dev

What would "living simply and honorably in the world" look like for you? What would have to change in your life?

95
Martin Luther

Born 1483, in Eisleben, Germany
Died 1546, in Eisleben, Germany

The young Martin Luther, son of a Saxony peasant, struggled to get right with God through rigorous acts of devotion as an Augustinian monk. Yet he felt increasingly estranged from God. Then he read "The one who is righteous will live by faith" in Romans 1:17 (NRSV) and concluded that getting right with God was not something people do, but something God does.

The medieval Christian church, however, offered justification for sin in exchange for works of devotion and monetary offerings to the church. Luther's new understanding moved him to nail ninety-five theses to the door of the church in Wittenberg on October 31, 1517, calling for a reconsideration of this system. He did not intend to launch a major religious or political movement, but the Protestant Reformation is usually said to have begun that day.

If Luther's Bible reading had convinced him that one gets right with God through faith rather than through good works, what is faith? And if the pope speaks contrary to the Bible, must one bow to him? Faith for Luther was not merely acceptance of the truth of Christian teachings, but trust in the promises of God even through times of confusion and doubt. "When I realized this, I felt myself born again," Luther said. "The gates of paradise had been flung open and I had entered." He felt himself justified while yet a sinner and came to see devotional acts and good deeds not as a means of earning divine favor, but as the work of Christ in the believer's heart to bring the believer's behavior into line with his new status.

Luther was in many respects a conservative thinker, but he soon broke with Rome and launched a new church. "Here I stand. I can do no other. God help me. Amen," he famously said. Most of northwestern Europe would follow him.

Luther had a gift for vivid writing and within four years of nailing his theses to the church door had written a series of major theological works. He also translated the Bible into German, which had a huge impact on the development of that language.

God's promises give what God's commandments require; they fulfill what the law decrees. Everything is God's and God's alone, both the commandments and the obeying of the commandments. God alone commands; God alone obeys. —Martin Luther

Where or who was Luther's ultimate authority in spiritual matters?

96

Huldrych Zwingli

Born 1484, in Wildhaus, Switzerland
Died 1531, in Kappel am Albis, Switzerland

Born to a farming family, Huldrych Zwingli was ordained a priest in 1506. As a pastor in Zurich, he
began advocating for church reform in 1517, accusing
monks of indolence, rejecting the veneration of saints,
questioning the church's power to excommunicate, and
denying the biblical basis for the tithe.

As with many other Protestant reformers, Zwingli based his thinking on the Bible as the only authority for Christian belief and practice. He often quoted the early
church fathers, but only in support of biblical ideas. Zwingli was not, however, a
biblical literalist and his study of Erasmus and other humanist thinkers informed his
interpretation of scriptural texts.

Zwingli's most distinctive contribution was in the area of sacramental theology.
He rejected the term "sacrament" because it suggested to many people a quasi-mag-
ical ceremony with the power to bestow divine grace on the worshiper. Zwingli saw
sacraments as purely symbolic acts.

Baptism for Zwingli was a sign of God's covenant with the baptized person, much
as circumcision had been a sign of God's earlier covenant with the Jews. It did not seal
the covenant, bestow grace, or wash away sins, as the Catholic Church taught. Zwingli did not, however, reject infant baptism, as other "radical reformers" did (see #99).

Perhaps no topic so divided sixteenth-century Christians as the Eucharist, the sacrament of Christ's body and blood. The Catholic understanding, drawing on Aristotelian philosophy and called transubstantiation, sees the bread and wine as transformed
into the "substance" of Christ's flesh and blood, though their outward form remains
unchanged. Many Protestant reformers, including Luther, also affirmed a "real presence" of Christ in the Eucharist (though not the theory of transubstantiation), but for
Zwingli, the Eucharist was a memorial meal, nothing more. The word *is* in the words
of institution ("This is my body; this is my blood") actually meant *signifies*, Zwingli
said. The Holy Spirit changed believers' hearts, not the eucharistic elements. This
view has found a wide following among Protestants ever since.

Zwingli died of wounds suffered during a battle against Catholic Swiss cantons in
which he was serving as chaplain.

*I beseech Christ for this one thing only, that he will enable me to endure
all things courageously, and that he break me as a potter's vessel or make
me strong, as it pleases him.* —Huldrych Zwingli

What do you understand sacramental acts to be?

97
Thomas Cranmer

Born 1489, in Aslockton, England
Died 1556, in Oxford, England

When Henry VIII named an obscure Cambridge don as archbishop of Canterbury in 1532, he was seeking to annul his marriage to Catherine of Aragon. Thomas Cranmer promptly issued the annulment. Cranmer also cooperated with Henry's abolishing papal authority over the English church and reconstituting it as an independent church.

Henry's death in 1547 provided Cranmer the opportunity, under Henry's son Edward VI, to reform the worship of the Church of England. Sifting and choosing among materials from Catholic, Protestant, Orthodox, and other sources, he produced the first Book of Common Prayer.

Cranmer translated everything into English, made worship simpler and easier to follow, emphasized Bible reading, involved laypeople in worship, and modified the medieval understanding of the Eucharist. Although revised several times since, Cranmer's work remains the standard for liturgical prose in the English-speaking world.

Cranmer's devotion to his monarch was more than personal. He believed God intended the king to guide both church and state. But when Mary Tudor, a Roman Catholic, ascended to the throne at Edward's death in 1553, she determined to reverse all that Cranmer had done. Mary imprisoned and tortured Cranmer and the profoundly conflicted archbishop signed several recantations. But when he was tied to the stake to be burned as a heretic on March 21, 1556, he astonished the gathered crowd by recanting his recantations and holding his right hand into the rising flames, saying, "This hand hath offended!" Cranmer became England's most renowned Protestant martyr.

Almighty God, which dost make the minds of all faithful men to be of one will; grant unto thy people, that they may love the thing which thou commandest, and desire that which thou dost promise; that among the sundry and manifold changes of the world, our hearts may surely there be fixed, where true joys are to be found; through Christ our Lord. —Thomas Cranmer

Almighty God, whose kingdom is everlasting, . . . so rule the heart of thy chosen servant Edward the sixth, our king and governor, that he (knowing whose minister he is) may above all things seek thy honor and glory: and that we his subjects (duly considering whose authority he hath), may faithfully serve, honor, and humbly obey him, in thee, and for thee. —Thomas Cranmer

Is a head of state accountable to the people or to God?

98
Ignatius of Loyola

Born 1491, in Azpeitia, Spain
Died 1556, in Rome, Italy

The Roman Catholic Church did not sit idly by while much of Europe abandoned its embrace, but undertook reforms and underwent a spiritual renewal of its own.

The leading figure in the Catholic Reformation was Ignatius of Loyola. His early life resembled that of Francis of Assisi (see #80). Both dreamt of chivalrous military exploits but soon met severe adversity. In Ignatius's case, a cannonball shattered one of his legs and he spent months in recovery with little to do but read the lives of the saints. He was transformed and soon determined to become one.

After a period of depression, Ignatius began receiving mystical revelations which gave him a positive, joyful outlook. He experimented with various devotional practices and jotted down notes on his experiences. These notes eventually became the *Spiritual Exercises*, a classic manual for spiritual directors guiding persons on retreat. The retreat is intended to last for four weeks, with each week devoted to a theme and building on earlier weeks, but it can be spaced out over a longer time for those who cannot devote an entire month to it.

The purpose of the *Exercises* is to lead the retreatant to live "for the greater glory of God," a phrase that appears often in the *Exercises*. They suggest particular biblical texts for meditation. In his imagination, the retreatant places himself in the biblical scene and becomes part of the story. Ignatius did not share Luther's suspicion of works righteousness (see #95), but commended an activist form of devotion, including acts of service and charity.

Ignatius attracted followers. A small group at the beginning, they quickly grew into the Society of Jesus, usually called the Jesuits. Today, the Jesuits operate hundreds of colleges, universities, and retreat centers throughout the world, and spiritual seekers—Catholics, Protestants, and others—often seek out a Jesuit director to work through the *Spiritual Exercises* "for the greater glory of God."

> *Take, Lord, and receive all my liberty, my memory, my understanding, my will—all that I have and possess. You, Lord, have given all to me. I now give it back to you, O Lord. All is yours. Do with it as you will. Give me only your love and your grace, for that is enough for me. —Ignatius of Loyola*

Imagine yourself in a favorite biblical scene. Then converse with the characters.

99
Menno Simons

Born 1496, in Witmarsum, the Netherlands
Died 1561, in Wüstenfelde, Germany

The Protestant Reformation might not have occurred without the printing press. Before the sixteenth century, few people had read the Bible and the Catholic Church taught that to do so would open the door to dangerous misinterpretations. When people began reading and interpreting the Bible for themselves, a perhaps predictable splintering of the Western church occurred. Leaders of the three largest branches of the Reformation—the Lutheran (see #95), the Reformed (see #100), and the Anglican (see #97)—retained much of the teaching and practice of the medieval church, but so-called "radical reformers" (see #96) rejected much more.

Several such groups are designated by the umbrella term "Anabaptists" (rebaptizers) because, finding no explicit reference to infant baptism in the New Testament, they reject it. Anabaptists see the church as a fellowship of disciplined believers who have made a mature commitment and manifest signs of holiness, something infants obviously cannot do. They practice "believer baptism." One of the most notable Anabaptists was Menno Simons.

Menno was ordained a priest around 1515 without having read the Bible. When he started to do so, he said, "I did not get very far in it before I saw that we had been deceived." He labored over having to decide between the authority of the scriptures and the authority of the church. Finally, in 1536, he broke with the Catholic Church, was rebaptized, and became the leader of a group of Anabaptists in the Low Countries which came to be called Mennonites. Menno was forced to flee with his family from place to place to avoid arrest and execution. Several followers were executed for providing him shelter. Many Mennonites fled to Ukraine, the Americas, and elsewhere. There are 1.7 million Mennonites in the world today.

In addition to practicing believer baptism, Mennonites accept the Bible as the sole rule of faith, see the Eucharist as a symbolic meal, and affirm the liberty of the individual conscience and strict separation of church and state. They are best known for their pacifism and skill in conflict resolution.

The true evangelical faith cannot lie dormant, but spreads itself out in all kinds of righteousness and fruits of love. . . . The persecution, suffering, and anguish that come to it for the sake of the Lord's truth have become a glorious joy and comfort to it. —Menno Simons

Should spiritual fellowships embrace everyone or only the seriously committed?

100
John Calvin

Born 1509, in Noyon, France
Died 1564, in Geneva, Switzerland

One central conviction undergirded everything John Calvin did, that God—glorious, honored, exalted—reigns over all. The absolute sovereignty of God was like a wall enclosing Calvin's Christian faith. When pursuing a line of thought, he would sooner or later bump up against the sovereignty of God and correct his thinking accordingly.

Calvin was born to a working class family near Paris, but his obvious intellectual gifts soon won him the patronage of the local bishop, enabling him to study both theology and law. Sometime around 1530, however, Calvin experienced a conversion to "evangelical" Christianity, as Protestant thought was called.

For several years, Calvin moved from place to place. He wrote the first edition of his *Institutes of the Christian Religion* in 1536, intended as instruction to faithful Christians on matters theological and moral. Twenty-five more editions would follow during Calvin's lifetime, adding new topics and expanding on those addressed in earlier editions. Calvin's *Institutes* became a Protestant theological classic. The standard edition runs to 1,500 pages and is daunting—not because its thought is imprecise, but because it is uncompromisingly clear: everything revolves around the sovereignty of God.

Calvin spent his final twenty-five years as a pastor in Geneva. He was the city's leading citizen, working (and occasionally tangling) with the civil authorities to create a model evangelical community. Someone once said that during Calvin's time, Geneva was "a Protestant convent." The Presbyterian and Reformed churches of today trace their origins to Calvin.

Calvin was hardly a dour figure. He formed close and lasting friendships and was known for his warm, outgoing nature. His published works contain many passages of joy and thanksgiving for the grace of God. Even ideas that some modern Christians find difficult, like humanity's "total depravity" (that no part of human nature has escaped sin's stain), divine providence (that everything that happens accords with the divine will), and "double predestination" (that God has determined from all eternity which souls will be saved and which will not) were to him indications of the goodness and mercy of God.

The first part of a good work is the will to do it, the second a strong effort to do it. God is the author of both. —John Calvin

Calvin believed in the sovereignty of God and in human free will. Is that a paradox or a contradiction?

101
Teresa of Ávila

Born 1525, in Gotarrendura, Spain
Died 1582, in Alba de Tormes, Spain

Teresa of Ávila had a colorful, earthy personality. Her writings abound with homespun images and humor and read like transcripts of a conversation. After *Don Quixote*, Teresa's *Life* is the most read book in Spanish literature. She was one of the two founders of Spanish Carmelite spirituality (see #103).

Teresa entered the Carmelite order, founded in the twelfth century on a discipline of personal, contemplative prayer. When she saw that the nuns spent more time gossiping than praying, Teresa sought to reform the order. She was constantly at odds with the powerful Spanish Inquisitors because her grandfather had been Jewish, she based her teachings on visions over which the Inquisitors had no control, and she was a woman.

Teresa develops several extended analogies in discussing prayer. In her somewhat autobiographical *Life*, she writes of the stages of prayer leading to spiritual union with God in terms of a barren land being transformed into a garden. First it is watered laboriously from buckets carried from a well, then by a windlass, then by a stream, and finally by rain, at which point earth and water are one and human effort ceases.

In her *The Interior Castle*, Teresa writes of a Spanish castle with many "mansions" flowing into one another. Here she pictures seven stages in the spiritual life, each drawing the seeker deeper into the castle. The light shining from the center grows brighter and brighter until finally a spiritual marriage occurs in the seventh mansion. It is like holding the ends of two lit candles together so that the flames become one.

A third image is that of a silkworm building a house of silk in which it will die, only to reemerge as a beautiful butterfly.

Teresa believed spiritual union with God wasn't just for monastics, but for everyone. She wrote to explain how to get there.

I see mental prayer as simply a friendly interchange and frequent solitary conversation with him who, we know, loves us. —Teresa of Ávila

I so long to see God that I forget everything, and this abandonment and loneliness seem better to me than all the company in the world.
—Teresa of Ávila

Think of an image or metaphor for the life of prayer and write a paragraph developing it.

102
Akbar

Born 1542, in Umerkot, Pakistan
Died 1605, Fatehpur Sikri, India

For over two hundred years beginning in 1526, a Muslim tribe from central Asia known as the Mughals ruled most of India. The Golden Age of the Mughal Empire began with the accession of Akbar the Great in 1556. Although said to be illiterate, Akbar was a gifted general, administrator, artist, theologian, and a patron of literature, religion, architecture, and the arts. His religious policy was revolutionary for its day, particularly for a Muslim ruler.

Probably a Hanifite Sunni Muslim (see #50), Akbar abolished the special tax on non-Muslims and appointed members of many faiths to government posts. He caused the Hindu scriptures to be translated and took part in a variety of religious festivals. This earned Akbar the trust of the non-Muslim population, but conservative Muslims deemed him a heretic.

Spirituality intrigued Akbar. In 1575, he built an academy called the House of Worship and invited theologians and mystics of various Muslim schools to an open investigation and discussion of their faith. When bickering and shouting broke out, Akbar opened the discussions to members of all faiths and to atheists. He sought to find common ground among the world's faiths and even condoned questioning the validity of the Quran, further angering conservative Muslims and arousing rumors that he was about to forsake the faith, rumors eagerly entertained by Portuguese Jesuit missionaries at Akbar's court.

Including devotees of other faiths in discussions at the House of Worship only exacerbated the level of acrimony, however, leading Akbar to close the House of Worship in 1582. Still undaunted, he launched a new movement called the Religion of God with no scriptures or clergy. It was largely an ethical system, promoting purity of life and openness to God and teaching that no creed contained all truth. Most people, however, remained committed to their previous faith tradition and the Religion of God gained few adherents. It died out soon after Akbar's death.

> *It cannot be wise to assert the truth of one faith over another. In a world so full of trouble and contradictions, the wise person makes justice his guide and learns from everyone. Perhaps this will open once more the door whose key has been lost.* —Akbar

How would you respond to an invitation to abandon your faith for a new faith combining elements of many faiths?

103
John of the Cross

Born 1542, in Fontiveros, Spain
Died 1591, in Úbeda, Spain

Thin and just four feet, eleven inches tall, John of the Cross was a giant of mystical theology. Raised by his destitute, widowed mother, John was known for his gentle patience and keen mind. He excelled in philosophy and theology at the renowned university in Salamanca, but longed for the contemplative life.

In 1567, John met Teresa of Ávila (see #101) and immediately joined her in seeking to reform the Carmelite order. Although Teresa was twenty-seven years John's senior, the two became fast friends, colleagues, and confidants. John often served as Teresa'a confessor and spiritual director. The pair founded a total of thirty-two new Spanish convents and monasteries restoring the original, strict Carmelite rule.

The Carmelite reform movement aroused intense opposition. A group of monks and others broke into John's quarters in 1577, dragged him away, and imprisoned him in a dark, unventilated, six-by-ten foot cell in Toledo. He was frequently flogged. After twenty months, he escaped and took refuge in a nearby monastery.

John was one of Spain's finest lyric poets. During his incarceration, he wrote and memorized (he had no pen or paper) most of his *Spiritual Canticle*. In this poem, a bride (representing the human soul) searches for her lost bridegroom (representing Christ). Another poem, *The Dark Night*, tells of the journey of the soul to union with God. The dark night of the soul is not a time of painful experiences, but of nothing, of emptiness, created by God because of his love for the soul. Only when God has emptied the soul of all earthly thoughts and attachments can God bring joy by filling the soul with himself.

John also wrote prose treatises expounding the spiritual dimensions of his poetry. In his *Ascent of Mount Carmel*, he describes in detail the stages of spiritual growth leading to union with God and the various pitfalls encountered along the way.

> *Souls cannot reach perfection unless they strive to be content with having nothing, so that their natural and spiritual desire is satisfied with emptiness. This is necessary in order to reach the highest tranquility and peace of spirit.*
> —John of the Cross

> *The soul that is attached to anything, however much good may be in it, will not arrive at the liberty of divine union.* —John of the Cross

Is being content with having nothing the mark of spiritual perfection?

104
George Fox

Born 1624, in Fenny Drayton, England
Died 1691, in London, England

Most of Europe's Protestant reformers appealed to scripture as their authority, rejecting anything they deemed contrary to it. But then came an uneducated English shoemaker and grazier who subjected scripture itself to the authority of his own insights and experiences. It is little wonder that George Fox aroused opposition.

While Fox was never one to compromise his principles, he was hardly a combative figure. His morals were above reproach, and the inner voice which guided him led him to respect all people equally—lay and ordained, women and men, the unlettered and the scholarly—and to eschew violence and argumentation. This voice, he was convinced, was that of the Holy Spirit.

Fox claimed that a preacher need not be ordained or have a theological degree and that churches (or "steeple-houses," as he called them) were mere human constructions in which God did not dwell. God dwelt, Fox said, in every human heart. This was "the true light, which enlightens everyone" (John 1:9). The inspired word could come to anyone.

Fox traveled throughout Great Britain and later the American colonies preaching this simple message, and a powerful preacher he was, attracting crowds of a thousand or more on street corners and by the roadside. So moving were his sermons that Fox's listeners often shook with emotion, giving rise to the derisive nickname "Quakers." They called themselves the Society of Friends.

A law outlawing non-Anglican religious gatherings of more than five people resulted in the frequent imprisonment of Fox and his followers, but he held his ground to the end.

Fox left an account of his experiences in his *Journal*, dictated to others at the end of his life. It shows a man of granite-like persistence, never repenting of sin or admitting error, accepting persecution with patient serenity, and confident of the ultimate triumph of right over wrong.

> *Do not think that anything will outlast the Truth. For the Truth standeth sure; and is over that which is out of the Truth. For the good will overcome the evil; the light, darkness; the life, death; virtue, vice; and righteousness, unrighteousness. The false prophet cannot overcome the true; but the true prophet, Christ, will overcome all the false. So be faithful, and live in that which doth not think the time long.* —George Fox

How does one know when to compromise and when to stand firm?

105
John Bunyan

Born 1628, in Elstow, England
Died 1688, in London, England

For over two hundred years, the most popular devotional book among English-speaking Protestants was an allegorical tale of a Christian soul on a pilgrimage to the Celestial City. The author of *The Pilgrim's Progress*, published in 1678, was a self-educated Baptist preacher named John Bunyan.

Because preaching by those not ordained in the established Church of England was illegal, Bunyan spent thirteen years behind bars for preaching without a license. He said that being separated from his wife and children was "like the pulling of the flesh from my bones." But Bunyan met fellow Christians while incarcerated and in his long hours alone developed a remarkable gift for writing. His best-known works are *The Pilgrim's Progress* and *Grace Abounding to the Chief of Sinners*, an account of Bunyan's inner struggle to determine the fate of his soul.

The protagonist of *The Pilgrim's Progress* is aptly named Christian. On his journey from the City of Destruction to the Celestial City, Christian slogs through the Slough of Despond, climbs Hill Difficulty, is detained in Doubting Castle, braves the Valley of the Shadow of Death, is dazzled by the charms of Vanity Fair, and fights off drowsiness in the Enchanted Ground. He is tempted by Mr. Worldly Wiseman, Flatterer, Ignorance, Timorous, Little-Faith, Faint-Heart, and Giant Despair. Bunyan himself had no doubt visited these locales and confronted these tempters in his own soul. Christian is also encouraged and strengthened along the way by fellow believers and wise counselors like Evangelist, Faithful, Hopeful, and Great-Heart.

But Bunyan's chief concern was the salvation of individual souls, not the least of them his own. Christian's journey is therefore essentially a solitary one. Like Bunyan himself, Christian must carry on without the strength and comfort others drew from accustomed ceremonies and conventional pieties.

Mr. Worldly-Wiseman is not an ancient relic of the past. He is everywhere today, disguising his heresy and error by proclaiming the gospel of contentment and peace achieved by self-satisfaction and works. If he mentions Christ, it is not as the Savior who took our place, but as a good example of an exemplary life. Do we need a good example to rescue us, or do we need a Savior? —John Bunyan

In prayer it is better to have a heart without words than words without a heart. —John Bunyan

Name the locales through which your spiritual journey has taken you.

106
Johann Sebastian Bach

Born 1685, in Eisenach, Germany
Died 1750, in Leipzig, Germany

The Bachs were a musical dynasty, producing over fifty outstanding composers and performers in the seventeenth and eighteenth centuries. The greatest was Johann Sebastian, renowned in his day for his organ playing but today revered as the foremost composer of music for Christian worship ever to live.

Bach twice worked as a court musician, playing the organ and composing orchestral suites, secular cantatas, and works for solo instruments. But his first love was sacred music, and he was willing to work for less pay in order to pursue that love. Bach served at several Lutheran churches, spending his last twenty-seven years as organist, teacher, and composer at the St. Thomas Church and School in Leipzig.

Bach wrote over three hundred sacred cantatas keyed to the seasons of the church year. They include vocal solos, orchestral passages, and choruses which often incorporate familiar German hymn tunes, but with new harmonies. His Christmas Oratorio is a set of six cantatas. Bach also composed two grand musical settings of the biblical Passion story, and although a devout Lutheran, he produced a setting of the Catholic Mass, the Mass in B Minor. Written during the final months of his life and using some melodies Bach had earlier used in other works, it is regarded by many as Bach's greatest choral masterpiece.

Music was not Bach's only passion. He was also a man of profound faith who saw his work as an act of devotion. He carefully studied Luther's translation of the Bible and taught Luther's Small Catechism to his Leipzig students. Despite personal tragedies (Bach's first wife died, then he remarried, and of his twenty children, he buried eleven), his music conveys gratitude and joy.

Bach had an engaging humility, choosing to spend most of his life serving in unremarkable church positions when he could have attained fame and fortune elsewhere. When one observer praised his skill at the organ, he said, "There's nothing remarkable about it. You just have to hit the right notes at the right moment, and the instrument does the rest."

The aim and purpose of all music should be the glory of God and the refreshment of the soul. —Johann Sebastian Bach

I play the notes as they are written, but it is God who makes the music.
—Johann Sebastian Bach

Should all music glorify God?

107
The Baal Shem Tov

Born ca. 1700 in Okopy, Ukraine
Died 1760 in Medzhybizh, Ukraine

By the early eighteenth century, life had grown grim for eastern Europe's Jews. Study of the Torah seemed to offer little to the struggling farmer or cobbler, and besides, how could a man straining to feed his family find time to study anything? If learning was the only pathway to God, many would not walk it.

In this unlikely setting appeared a captivating and unabashedly joyful personality named Israel ben Eliezer. He is usually called the Baal Shem Tov (Master of the Good Name) or simply the Besht (from the Hebrew initials BST). There are many dubious tales about the Besht, but it seems he was orphaned at the age of five and raised by the Jewish community. As a youth, he often skipped school to spend the day in the woods, showing little interest in academic study and none in asceticism. In his early twenties, the Besht had a spiritual awakening and became a popular healer using the divine name.

The Besht saw God in every person, event, and place, even in such mundane activities as cooking and smoking a pipe. Everything in the universe, both mind and matter, manifests God, he said, and nothing, not even evil, can be separated from God. All creation is therefore good and to be relished. Experiencing God in everyday things, the Besht said, brings an exalted delight.

The Besht launched a hugely successful Jewish renewal movement known as Hasidism (from the Hebrew word for steadfast love). He was the first in a line of *zaddikim* (holy men) who wrote little or nothing and whose teaching is preserved in collections of tales and sayings. By 1900, roughly half of eastern European Jewry was Hasidic. Although Adolf Hitler nearly wiped out the Hasidim, communities thrive today in Israel, America, Canada, Australia, and elsewhere (see #142).

When wood burns, the smoke alone rises upward, leaving the grosser elements below. So it is with prayer. The sincere intention alone ascends to heaven.
—The Baal Shem Tov

The world is new to us every morning. This is God's gift, and everyone should believe he is reborn each day. —The Baal Shem Tov

I have no time to study because I must serve my Maker. —The Baal Shem Tov

Is it possible to see God in everything, all the time, everywhere?

108
Nicholaus von Zinzendorf

Born 1700, in Dresden, Germany
Died 1760, in Herrnhut, Germany

By the seventeenth century, Lutheranism (see #95) had grown cerebral and rigid and a group of Lutherans known as Pietists were seeking to restore personal devotion and vitality to their church. Nicholaus von Zinzendorf, of a noble Austrian family and reared by a devout Pietist grandmother, was a key figure in this movement.

A small group of Protestants later called Moravians, spiritual descendants of the fourteenth-century Bohemian reformer Jan Hus, were seeking refuge from persecution. In 1722, Zinzendorf allowed them to found the village of Herrnhut on his family estate near Dresden. It soon became a refuge for other religious dissidents as well.

When conflict broke out in Herrnhut over doctrinal differences, Zinzendorf undertook personally to mediate the dispute. He went door to door, offering counsel and starting small groups for prayer and study.

Zinzendorf's efforts produced the "Brotherly Agreement" of 1727. Participants experienced this as an outpouring of the Holy Spirit. Known as the Moravian Pentecost, it led to a spiritual revitalization and harmonious social relations based on mutual respect and agreed upon behavioral norms rather than doctrinal consensus. Zinzendorf organized "little churches within the church," centered not around nuclear families, but on similarities such as age, sex, and marital status. He called them "choirs."

Zinzendorf was consecrated a bishop in the Moravian Church in 1737. His hope, however, was to foster renewal within the Lutheran and other churches rather than promote a separate denomination. He felt that each Christian denomination had a unique gift to offer the wider church. The world's nearly one million Moravians today continue to stress the religion of the heart over the religion of the mind and loving relationships over doctrinal correctness.

Although German Pietism eventually passed from the scene, Zinzendorf traveled the world and sent missionaries to North and South America, Greenland, Africa, Sri Lanka, and elsewhere. They made a lasting impact, most notably on the Wesley brothers (see #109, #111). The largest group of Moravians today is in Tanzania.

There can be no Christianity without community. —Nicholaus von Zinzendorf

Every heart with Christ is a missionary; every heart without Christ is a mission field. —Nicholaus von Zinzendorf

Do you agree that "there can be no Christianity without community"?

109
John Wesley

Born 1703, in Epworth, England
Died 1791, in London, England

The son of an Anglican vicar and a devout mother, John Wesley took his religion seriously even as an Oxford undergraduate. He joined a group of students called the "Holy Club" organized around a regular discipline of prayer, study, and good works. Others called the group by the derisive name "methodists." Wesley was ordained and began work as a priest, but felt little joy.

Then, while attending a small Moravian (see #108) meeting in London on May 24, 1738, Wesley felt his heart "strangely warmed" and came to a profound trust in Christ. The focus of his faith began to change. Although well-educated and in many ways a traditional thinker, Wesley began emphasizing the religion of the heart and preaching for conversion.

Invitations to preach in parish churches grew fewer until Wesley took to preaching in fields and on street corners to anyone who would listen. He sometimes drew crowds in the thousands, including many from the working classes who were abandoning the countryside to seek jobs in the new factories being built in the cities. For the next fifty-three years, Wesley rode up and down the length of Great Britain, traveling an estimated 250,000 miles on horseback, preaching as often as four times a day.

Wesley understood the Christian life as a series of stages, each defined by a form of divine grace. First is God's "prevenient" (or preceding) grace, leading the sinner to a sense of being lost and helpless. Then comes a moment of conversion or breakthrough, called "saving" or "justifying" grace, when the sinner experiences the embracing love of Christ. And finally, God's "sanctifying" grace brings the sinner to holiness of life and the assurance of divine favor.

Wesley was widely seen as intrusive and unsettling. The established Church of England was reluctant to ordain anyone influenced by Wesley's "enthusiasm." Although he never left the Church of England, toward the end of his life, Wesley authorized his preachers in America to form a new church and ordain ministers for it. It was called the Methodist Church.

I look on all the world as my parish; thus far I mean, that, in whatever part of it I am, I judge it meet, right, and my bounden duty, to declare unto all that are willing to hear, the glad tidings of salvation. —John Wesley

Can a "religion of the heart" be enough?

110
Muhammad ibn Abd al-Wahhab

Born 1703, in Uyayana, Saudi Arabia
Died 1792, in Al-Diriyah, Saudi Arabia

A small tribe swept out of Asia Minor in the fourteenth century to form what would become history's most enduring Muslim state. Within decades, the Ottoman Turks ruled large swaths of Europe, Asia, and Africa. Their empire survived until World War I. While Islam was the Ottomans' state religion, by the eighteenth century, some observant Muslims became alarmed at what they deemed the Ottomans' luxurious lifestyle and casual attitude toward morals and religion. They feared a slide back into the "Age of Ignorance" before Muhammad's day.

Muhammad ibn Abd al-Wahhab was born into a family of Hanbalite (see #55) scholars and, after a rebellious adolescence, followed in their footsteps and began preaching in his hometown, urging a return to moral purity and the Islam of Muhammad and his close associates. He was drawn to Ibn Taymiyyah's (see #87) conservative, unbending faith, especially Ibn Taymiyyah's total rejection of the veneration of saints and extreme forms of Sufism. Al-Wahhab soon attracted both a wide following and many detractors.

Although Al-Wahhab's followers are usually called Wahhabis, they prefer to be called Monotheists or Unitarians to emphasize Al-Wahhab's central tenet of the absolute oneness and indivisibility of God. His best known written work is *The Book of Monotheism*.

Al-Wahhab also insisted on strict obedience to the commandments of God found in the Quran. He was particularly appalled by the veneration of Muslim saints centering around their tombs and sacred sites, which he saw as a violation of the truth that only God could grant a blessing. He and his followers destroyed such shrines in his hometown of Uyayana and elsewhere. Al-Wahhab called for holy war against Muslims whom he deemed lax and who did not share his understandings.

The turning point for Al-Wahhab came in 1744 when, expelled from his hometown, he found refuge in the neighboring town of Al-Diriyah, ruled by a chieftain named Muhammad ibn Saud. The two formed an alliance and the Saudi family soon controlled much of the Arabian peninsula, previously under nominal Ottoman rule. That alliance survives among the descendants of both families to this day, with the Wahhabis providing religious endorsement of the Saudi Arabian monarchy and the Saudis, using their oil wealth, advancing the strict Wahhabi brand of Islam throughout the Muslim world.

When you perceive that your country is sliding into decadence, what are the possible responses, and what response would you recommend?

111
Charles Wesley

Born 1707, in Epworth, England
Died 1788, in London, England

When someone mentions Wesley, it is usually John who is meant (see #109). And while John Wesley was a powerful preacher and the founder of the Methodist movement, few people can quote anything he said. Millions of Christians the world over, however, can recite—or more likely, sing—something from his younger brother Charles.

Until around 1800, the only singing deemed suitable for English Protestant worship was of biblical and liturgical texts. Anything else was dismissed as profane and "of mere human composure." The use of the first person singular pronoun was especially frowned upon as directing attention away from God and to oneself. The Congregationalist preacher Isaac Watts (1674–1748) was the first to break out of this bind with his "When I Survey the Wondrous Cross," but the greatest writer of English hymns came a half-century later.

Charles Wesley shared with his brother John a fervent, joyful, evangelical Christian faith, and both wrote hymns. For John, hymn writing was a sideline, but for Charles it was his defining passion. He wrote hymns at all times of day, even while riding his horse. Upon dismounting, he was known to run inside shouting, "Pen and paper! Pen and paper!" It is estimated that Charles Wesley wrote nine thousand hymns, an average of three every week for sixty years. Many of them have twenty or more stanzas, and over four hundred are still sung somewhere in the world today. Charles Wesley's hymns are cherished by English-speaking Christians of all denominations.

Wesley's hymns broke new ground. His texts are infused with biblical phrases and imagery, but he did not hesitate to use the first person pronoun, sprinkling his verses with phrases like "enable *me* to stand," keep *me* ever thine," "*I* seek to touch *my* Lord," and "the joy prepared for *me*." This gives Wesley's hymns uncommon intimacy and power and enables worshipers to personalize the words they sing. Wesley invites worshipers not only to praise their Lord, but to experience their Lord.

O for a thousand tongues to sing my dear Redeemer's praise, the glories of my God and King, the triumphs of his grace! —Charles Wesley

Thee we would be always blessing, serve thee as thy hosts above, pray and praise thee without ceasing, glory in thy perfect love. —Charles Wesley

What keeps Charles Wesley's hymnody from becoming a mere celebration of the worshiper's feelings?

112
Moses Mendelssohn

Born 1729 in Dessau, Germany
Died 1786 in Berlin, Germany

More than anyone else, Moses Mendelssohn chart-ed the course of modern Jewish life. Born to pov-erty, he suffered from malnutrition, which made him a hunchback from boyhood. But his intellectual curiosity was undaunted. Even as a youngster, he relished the work of Moses Maimonides (see #76), and as a teenager, he went to Berlin to read Locke, Spinoza, and Leibnitz. As an adult, he was called "the German Socrates" and "the Jewish Luther."

As a leading philosopher of the German Enlightenment, Mendelssohn viewed sound religion as an expression of rational truth, seeing the Torah as a guide to rational living given by God to the Jews. When others veered off course, the Jews, with their faithfulness to Torah, could serve as instructors, recalling humanity to the path of reason.

Mendelssohn lived in two worlds, those of rabbinic Judaism and the emerging German state, and felt at home in both. He sought to bring Germany's Jews out of the ghetto and into the mainstream of modern German life, envisioning a day when Jews would be both faithful to their traditions and full, contributing citizens of the na-tion. To this end, he translated the Hebrew Bible into German, giving Jews a means of conversing with other Germans, and advocated the then novel notions of religious freedom for all and complete separation of church and state.

Mendelssohn saw a "plurality of truths." As nations require different forms of gov-ernment, he said, so individuals require different religions. The test of a religion is not its beliefs—these could be divisive, he observed—but whether it produces moral human beings. Perhaps taking him more seriously than he intended, within three generations all of Mendelssohn's descendants, including his grandson, composer Felix Mendelssohn, had abandoned Judaism.

> We send no missions to the Indies, East or West, or to Greenland to preach
> our religion to those distant peoples. The latter, in particular, according to
> descriptions of them, observe the law of nature better—alas!—than we do
> and are therefore, according to our religious teachings, an enviable people.
> —Moses Mendelssohn

> Let us not feign agreement where diversity is evidently the plan and purpose
> of Providence. —Moses Mendelssohn

> No nation can dispense with even the humblest and seemingly most useless
> of its inhabitants without seriously harming itself. —Moses Mendelssohn

Can there be "a plurality of truths"?

113
Ram Mohan Roy

Born 1772, in Radhanagore, India
Died 1833, in Bristol, England

Ram Mohan Roy has been called the "Father of modern India" and the "Father of modern Hinduism." Both titles are apt.

Roy was born to a noble Indian family. He took an interest in spirituality at an early age and then received a modern British education which taught him science, Western philosophy, and the Christian faith.

Roy attempted to bridge the gap between traditional Indian Hindu culture and the liberal Western culture he had learned in school. An extraordinary linguist, he knew Sanskrit, Bengali, English, Arabic, Persian, Latin, and Greek. He studied the New Testament in Greek and translated the Vedas (see #1) into English. He was the first scholar to write in English about classical Hinduism.

Politically, Roy sought to abolish or reform traditional Indian and Hindu practices, which he saw as holding India back from entering the modern world. He was particularly eager to see women attain equality with men, campaigning against child marriage, the denial to women of the right to inherit property, and the practice of requiring a widow to immolate herself on her husband's funeral pyre. He opposed the caste system and advocated freedom of the press.

Roy's religious views were no less progressive. He was a Hindu monotheist and in his writings blended a rational, ethical Advaita Hinduism (see #56) drawn from his reading of the Vedas with a Christian Unitarian understanding of God as supreme and unknowable. Islam provided him with ideas as well. Roy wrote a book endorsing the ethical teachings of Jesus, for which many Hindus condemned him. Some Christians also faulted him for his refusal to accept the divinity of Christ. His syncretistic views were not widely embraced during his lifetime.

In 1828, Roy formed a religious movement called the Brahmo Samaj in Kolkata, which founded several excellent schools for women. It was an inspiration in the forming of the modern Indian state following World War II.

Ram Mohan Roy died of meningitis in 1833, while in England on a diplomatic mission for the Mughal Emperor Akbar Shah II.

Superstitious practices which deform the Hindu religion have nothing to do with the pure spirit of its dictates. —Ram Mohan Roy

If Ram Mohan Roy were alive today, what causes do you think he would promote, and would you sign on with him?

114
Swaminarayan

Born 1781, in Chhapaiya, India
Died 1830, in Gujarat, India

Born into a noble Indian family, Swaminarayan is said to have mastered the Hindu scriptures by the age of seven. At eleven, he began a seven-year pilgrimage across India and Nepal searching for a hermitage where Hindu teachings were faithfully observed. He mastered yoga (see #16) and in 1802 was given leadership of a budding Hindu sect which blossomed under him and soon took his name. At Swaminarayan's death, his followers numbered 1.8 million.

The Swaminarayan faith accepts the Vedas (see #1) and adds additional scriptures written by Swaminarayan and others. Swaminarayan's most popular book is a transcript of extemporaneous debates, recorded by his disciples. It deals with the classic Hindu themes of morality, self-understanding, detachment, and devotion.

Swaminarayan and his disciples are noted for their purity of life. The sexes do not mix. Swaminarayan also forbade adultery, eating meat, animal sacrifice, the use of alcohol and drugs, and suicide. Human life is given by God, he said, and can be terminated only by God. Theologically, Swaminarayan was close to Ramanuja's qualified monism (see #70).

Swaminarayan drew disciples from all castes, especially the lower castes, to whom he often gave responsibilities in his movement. He organized food and water distribution to the poor and advocated for the education and rights of women, opposing the practice of widows immolating themselves on their husbands' funeral pyres.

Yet Swaminarayan refused to interact with women himself and barred them from leadership positions in his movement, causing critics to label him a hypocrite regarding the status of women. The belief of many Swaminarayans that their founder was the incarnation of the Supreme God has also drawn criticism.

Swaminarayan maintained good relations with the British and the first of nine temples built under his guidance was on land given by the British imperial government. He was cordial to Anglican bishops and adherents of other faiths. Muslims, Zoroastrians, and Parsis, as well as Hindus, expressed respect for him and his teachings.

Swaminarayan designated his nephews and their descendants to guide his movement following his death, setting up a hereditary succession of leaders. Later Swaminarayans have not always agreed on the succession. There are as many as twenty million Swaminarayans today, mostly in India.

Think twice before undertaking any work and ask whether it will benefit you.
—Swaminarayan

Can one be progressive and reactionary at the same time?

115
John Henry Newman

Born 1801, in London, England
Died 1890, in Edgbaston, England

Few people have so anticipated and influenced the modern world as John Henry Newman. In his teens, Newman was an evangelical Christian but soon became a leading High Church Anglican, then ended his life as a cardinal in the Roman Catholic Church.

Newman's best known published works suggest an intense, cerebral personality, unflinching in the pursuit of truth. But he also formed deep, lifelong friendships, and some of his lesser known works disclose a lighter, humorous streak.

Both Anglicans and Roman Catholics revere Newman. Until he was received into the Roman Catholic Church in 1845, Newman was the leader of the Oxford (or Tractarian) Movement, seeking to restore Anglicanism to its apostolic roots. This included a doctrine of the church as the body of Christ, undistracted by national and political concerns; an understanding of bishops as successors to the apostles; and catholic sacramental teaching. These views were forcefully expressed in Newman's "University Sermons" preached from the pulpit of the Church of St. Mary the Virgin in Oxford and in widely circulated tracts known as "Tracts for the Times." He promoted Anglicanism as the *via media* (Middle Way) between Roman Catholicism and Protestantism.

All the while, however, Newman was moving spiritually closer to Rome. His conversion shook the nation and for many years thereafter, neither Anglicans nor Roman Catholics were sure they could trust him. But Newman's integrity and intelligence eventually won him a cardinal's hat.

Newman's foremost contribution during the latter part of his life was his work in education. In *The Idea of a University*, he envisioned the university as championing free intellectual inquiry while also honoring revealed truth. With its expansive, liberal tone, it has become a foundational treatise for modern educational theory. Newman also wrote a powerful spiritual autobiography.

Fear not that thy life shall come to an end, but rather that it shall never have a beginning. —John Henry Newman

To live is to change, and to be perfect is to have changed often.
—John Henry Newman

Lead, Kindly Light, amidst th'encircling gloom, lead Thou me on! The night is dark, and I am far from home, lead Thou me on! Keep Thou my feet; I do not ask to see the distant scene; one step enough for me. —John Henry Newman

How could one's life "never have a beginning"?

116
Joseph Smith

Born 1805, in Sharon, Vermont
Died 1844, in Carthage, Illinois

Religious pioneers are often controversial and many have been martyred, but not usually in the United States. A major exception is Joseph Smith, founder of the Mormon Church. Born to a poor farming family that migrated from Vermont to upstate New York, in his teenage years Smith undertook to determine which of the various Christian denominations known to him taught the truth.

Smith's search began to diverge from those of other young seekers when, sometime around 1820, he experienced a vision while praying in the woods near his home. He was told that his sins were forgiven and that other churches had "turned aside from the gospel."

More visions would follow. In one of them Smith was told of a trove of golden plates buried in a nearby hillside and inscribed with the history of an ancient American civilization. Smith retrieved and translated the plates which became the Book of Mormon, published in 1830 and seen by Smith and his followers as a supplement to the Christian Bible. In the same year he organized a new church to restore the ancient Christian church, called the Church of Christ and later the Latter Day Saints, or Mormons.

The Book of Mormon tells of a group of Jews who migrated from Jerusalem to America around 600 BCE, the story of their subsequent conflicts, and an appearance to them by the resurrected Christ who repeats the Sermon on the Mount (Matthew 5–7).

Smith was a forceful preacher and energetic personality. His church soon attracted thousands of disciples. They followed Smith first to Ohio, then to Missouri, and then to Illinois, where they founded the town of Nauvoo. Smith and his brother Hyrum were arrested in nearby Carthage, Illinois, for treason and inciting a riot. While they were in jail awaiting trial, a mob stormed the jail and killed them. Smith is buried in Nauvoo. Mormons regard him as a prophet equal in rank to Moses and Elijah.

While much of Joseph Smith's theology and ethics is consistent with orthodox Christian teaching, his practice of polygamy was widely condemned. He is said to have married around thirty women. Following his death, his disciple Brigham Young led Smith's followers farther west, to Utah, where they founded Salt Lake City. The Mormon Church, which soon abandoned the practice of polygamy, today claims roughly fifteen million members worldwide.

How would you recognize a prophet today?

117
Phoebe Palmer

Born 1807, in New York, New York
Died 1874, in New York, New York

Phoebe Worall was born into a devout family and took her religion seriously from an early age. The family's Methodist church emphasized the need for an emotional conversion experience, but Phoebe could not recall having had such an experience. She felt she'd always been a Christian, yet lacked the assurance she'd been told came with a religious conversion.

Phoebe married Walter Palmer in 1827. Three of their four children died at an early age, one of them burning to death when curtains caught fire near her cradle. These tragedies induced a profound sense of guilt and remorse in Phoebe Palmer. Wondering whether her lack of Christian conviction had caused the tragedies, she began to probe her faith more deeply and the Palmers started hosting "Tuesday Meetings for the Promotion of Holiness" in their home.

Palmer came to a new understanding of the key Wesleyan doctrine of holiness, or sanctification (see #109). For her, holiness, traditionally seen as the goal of a lifelong Christian journey, was an act of divine grace at the beginning of a Christian life, delivering the believer from intentional or voluntary sin.

First comes the grace of regeneration through faith, Palmer said, freeing the believer from the effects of sin and without which no amount of human effort can attain holiness. This is followed by a "second blessing," delivering the believer from the inclination to sin. She referred to this second blessing as the "baptism of the Holy Spirit." It is given instantaneously and requires no conversion experience, Palmer taught, the biblical promise serving as sufficient assurance of its validity. Palmer said in 1837 that she was "entirely devoted to God" and "dead to sin."

Holiness of life was to be lived out in works of mercy. Palmer headed a Methodist mission in a slum area of New York, providing food, clothing, and shelter, on the grounds that this would enable the recipients better to come to a living faith. She opposed slavery and alcohol and sought to advance the role of women as Christian ministers.

Palmer wrote several books, most notably *The Way of Holiness* (1843). The Holiness movement which she launched impacted older Christian denominations and led to the founding of new ones. It also influenced the later Pentecostal movement (see #126, #128) and William and Catherine Booth, founders of the Salvation Army.

What does holiness look like and how is it attained?

118
Søren Kierkegaard

Born 1813, in Copenhagen, Denmark
Died 1855, in Copenhagen, Denmark

Copenhagen's gentry saw Søren Kierkegaard as an awkward, self-conscious literary dilettante. Having inherited a small fortune, he could write what he pleased without financial worries. He lived alone, having persuaded his one-time fiancée to terminate their relationship for reasons never disclosed. Few people took him seriously. But Kierkegaard had seen the future.

Kierkegaard wrote two kinds of books. The first were dense, obscure philosophical treatises. In his *Philosophical Fragments*, Kierkegaard compared Christ to Socrates, saying that Socrates asked questions enabling his students to discern the truth that was always within them, whereas with Christ, truth lay in the student's relationship to Christ himself, not in knowledge, either discerned from within or acquired from study. In *Concluding Unscientific Postscript*, Kierkegaard said that truth is not objective and changeless, but subjective and evolving.

It was faith, however, not philosophy, that was Kierkegaard's burning passion, and it was his overtly religious writings that meant the most to him. Faith, he said, is a groping toward a truth that is always present but never definable, a paradox full of uncertainties and ambiguities. He refers to the "leap of faith," a leap into the unknowable. Faith does not depend on and is not validated by outward experiences and authorities, but is inward and subjective. If this sounds absurd, such is the nature of faith, Kierkegaard said. Twentieth-century existentialists, many of them not religious believers, seized on this kind of talk as anticipating their own struggles with the nature of human existence. They saw Kierkegaard as the first of their number.

Kierkegaard wrote scathing criticisms of "Christendom," a term denoting the officially Christian nations of Europe. He saw Denmark as Christian in name only, wedded to an arid, lifeless shell of a church, and he rightly predicted that most Danes would abandon it within a couple of generations. Kierkegaard perceived himself as a lone voice, even a martyr, calling for a return to the vibrant, subjective, risk-taking faith of Europe's Christian past.

> *In ancient times, only a few people knew the truth, but now everyone knows it; but the conviction with which it is held is inversely proportional to the number of people holding it.* —Søren Kierkegaard

> *It does no good to convince millions of the truth if the way they accept it turns it into falsehood.* —Søren Kierkegaard

Does religious faith make sense, or is it paradoxical and absurd?

119
Bahaullah

Born 1817, in Tehran, Iran
Died 1892, in Acre, Israel

Reared in Tehran as a Shia Muslim, Bahaullah was twenty-seven years old when he first heard of "the Bab," an unorthodox Muslim claiming to be the redeemer of the faith. The Babist movement quickly gained a following in Persia, and the Qajar government moved to suppress it. When the Bab was executed in 1850, Bahaullah became the movement's leader. He was imprisoned in Tehran for four months in 1852, in a dank, gloomy, underground pit where he was forced to lie in his own excrement.

Incarceration changed Bahaullah. He had several mystical encounters while confined, including a vision of a maiden sent from God who told him he was a divine messenger, the coming one "whom God shall make manifest," prophesied by the Bab.

Upon his release, Bahaullah was exiled from Persia. He traveled to Baghdad, then to Kurdistan, and eventually to Constantinople, accompanied by a number of disciples. In 1866, Bahaullah first proclaimed that he was "him whom God shall make manifest." Bahaullah wrote to many world leaders urging them to accept his revelation, renounce material wealth, settle their differences, and seek a more just and equitable society.

Most Babists accepted Bahaullah's claim and began calling themselves "Bahais." The word derives from the Arabic for splendor or glory. Bahais see Bahaullah as the latest in a series of divine messengers, including Krishna, Moses, Buddha, Jesus, Muhammad, and the Bab, each messenger prophesying the appearance of the next. Bahaullah taught that all religions emanate from the same God and are one. The purpose of human life is to know and love God, he said, with prayer and worship the means to do it. Bahaism sees all persons as created equal and all races and cultures as valuable.

There are over five million Bahais in the world today, including a large community in Iran, Bahaism's country of origin, where they are persecuted as a deviant, apostate form of Islam.

It is no cause for pride to love one's country. Rather, someone who loves the whole world has reason to be proud. The earth is but one country, and humankind its citizens. —Bahaullah

A thankful person is thankful under all circumstances. A complaining soul complains even in paradise. — Bahaullah

Religion without science is superstition. Science without religion is materialism. — Bahaullah

Why would Muslims see Bahaism as apostasy?

120
Mary Baker Eddy

Born 1821, in Bow, New Hampshire
Died 1910, in Newton, Massachusetts

Mary Baker was a sickly child, given to nervous disorders. When her poor health continued into adulthood, she avoided nineteenth-century medicine (which she rightly noted was often ineffective) in favor of alternative treatments such as hypnotism, homeopathy, special diets, hydropathy, electrical charges, and morphine. Her first husband died after a few months of marriage, leaving her alone and expecting a child. Mary then returned to her parents' home. She would eventually marry again, be divorced, and marry a third time (to Asa Gilbert Eddy in 1877), only to be widowed again.

In 1866, Eddy fell on an icy sidewalk and broke several bones. Told she would probably not recover, she began reading the Bible and, to the amazement of her physicians, was healed. This, she later said, was the moment she discovered the science behind Christ's healings in the Bible, or Christian Science. Eddy then began nine years of intensive Bible study and concluded that the key factor in recovery from illness was the patient's belief system.

All reality is spiritual, Eddy taught, and the material world is illusory, including the human body, sickness, and death. Illness was for her a spiritual phenomenon, not a physical one, resulting from wrong thinking and curable by a clearer understanding of the spiritual nature of reality. Anyone, Eddy said, could experience the kingdom of heaven in this life.

When the older Christian churches rejected her teaching, Eddy formed her own church, First Church of Christ, Scientist, in Boston. It is the mother church of the world's roughly 1,100 Christian Science congregations today. Most Christian Scientists reject most medical treatments.

The similarity of Christian Science to Hinduism (see #56) and ancient Gnosticism (see #26) has often been noted. Eddy herself acknowledged the similarity to Hinduism.

Eddy published *Science and Health* (later renamed *Science and Health with Key to the Scriptures*) in 1875. Along with the Bible, it is the definitive text for Christian Scientists. She also founded *The Christian Science Monitor*, a daily (now weekly) newspaper as a means of keeping Christian Scientists informed of current events. It has long been known for its balance and objectivity.

All is infinite Mind and its infinite manifestation, for God is All-in-all.
Spirit is immortal Truth; matter is mortal error. —Mary Baker Eddy

How does Christian Science compare to orthodox Christianity? See Irenaeus (#26).

121

Ramakrishna

Born 1836, in Kamarpukur, India
Died 1886, in Kolkata, India

Ramakrishna told stories, cracked jokes, sang songs, and acted out spoofs. But that's not why throngs of visitors went to see him.

Worship was deeply personal and emotional for Ramakrishna. Even as a youth, he had intense mystical visions, sometimes losing consciousness of his surroundings. He sought to achieve complete union with God, whom he worshiped as the divine Mother, and served at a temple near Kolkata. He saw the divine Mother incarnated in his wife, whom he married after taking monastic vows (hence the marriage was not consummated) and whom he addressed as "Holy Mother."

Ramakrishna had become a popular Hindu priest when, in 1866, he shocked his disciples by converting to Islam. Turning his back on all things Hindu, he began dressing like an Arab, meticulously observed Muslim devotional practices, and had a mystical vision of the Prophet Muhammad. Then, in 1873, having heard the Bible read aloud, he converted to Christianity, immersed himself in Christian spirituality, and had a vision of Jesus and the Virgin Mary.

In the end, Ramakrishna returned to the monistic Hinduism of his youth (see #56), but he had changed. He continued to worship on occasion with Muslims and Christians and to affirm other faiths as pathways to God. The idea that many paths lead to God is an ancient Hindu belief (see #1), but Ramakrishna gave it new visibility and thrust.

God fashions various religions, Ramakrishna said, so that every culture, every time, and every person will have an access to God suited to its needs. Convert to another faith? No need for that, he said. Hold firm to your own faith and practice it diligently while also honoring the faiths of others. Ramakrishna used the analogy of the wind, which blows everywhere, but not all unfurl their sails and cross the sea.

If you desire to be pure, have firm faith, and slowly continue with your devotional practices without wasting your energy in useless scriptural discussions and arguments. Your little brain will otherwise be muddled. —Ramakrishna

All religions are true. The important thing is to reach the roof. You can reach it by stone stairs, by wooden stairs, by bamboo steps, or by climbing a rope or a pole. —Ramakrishna

If all faiths are true, would differences in teaching amount to nothing?

122
Shivananda

Born 1854, in Pattamadai, India
Died 1934, in Rishikesh, India

Shivananda met Ramakrishna (see #121) in 1880 and became his disciple. In 1886 he helped found a small monastic community in a run-down house near Kolkata, and then became an itinerant monk for several years. He traveled to Ceylon (now Sri Lanka) in 1897 to introduce Ramakrishna's monistic, inclusive Hindu philosophy there. In 1910 he was elected president of the Ramakrishna Mission (see #124) and guided its expansion.

Shivananda is best known, however, as the founder of the Divine Life Society. The society teaches its founder's distinctive type of yoga (see #16), known as "synthesis yoga," on a foundation of purity, integrity, nobility, and generosity. Synthesis yoga leads to the harmonious integration of the body, intellect, and emotions. Shivananda said this was possible for everyone, regardless of nationality, race, caste, or religion, and that to achieve it is to be fully human. He explained various yogic paths to this goal, all leading ultimately to liberation and the end of the long cycle of births and rebirths.

Shivananda was a prolific author, with over three hundred titles to his name, plus many letters and articles. His writing is plain and to the point, making his works readily accessible to millions of seekers. Today the Divine Life Society maintains centers throughout the world.

> Moral purity and spiritual aspiration are the first steps in the seeker's path. Without a strong conviction in moral values, there can surely be no spiritual life, or even a good life. . . . Stern self-discipline is absolutely essential. Self-discipline does not mean suppression, but taming the brute within. It means humanization of the animal and spiritualization of the human. . . . The spiritual path is rugged, thorny, and precipitous. The thorns must be weeded out with patience and perseverance. Some of the thorns are internal; some are external. . . . The spiritual path may, in the beginning, appear to be very hard, thorny, precipitous and slippery. . . . If you once make a strong determination and firm resolve, then it becomes very easy. You get interested and new joy. Your heart expands. . . . You have to plod on and scale many hills. You cannot climb Everest in one jump. There is no jumping on the spiritual path. —Shivananda

> Eating, drinking, sleeping! A little laughter! Much weeping! Is that all? Do not die here like a worm. Wake up! Attain immortal bliss. —Shivananda

Why is there "no jumping on the spiritual path"?

123
William Wadé Harris

Born ca. 1860, on Cape Palmas, Liberia
Died 1929, in Spring Hill, Liberia

In 1900, Africa's population was just under one hundred million. About nine million were Christians, mostly Europeans or members of the historic churches of Egypt and Ethiopia. Today the continent's population is over one billion, of whom half are Christian, most of them native Africans. Western missionary work contributed to this growth, but much of it resulted from African evangelists and the creation of indigenous African churches. The continent is home to ten thousand independent, indigenous churches.

These churches vary greatly. Many emerged from Protestant churches brought to the continent by European and American missionaries and retain the theology of those communions. Others express their faith in uniquely African ways. Some claim just a few hundred members; others number in the hundreds of thousands, span several countries, and send missionaries to other parts of the world. Healing is usually a major part of the ministry of African indigenous churches and Bible stories are taken at face value—life in much of the continent resembles life in the ancient Near East, making it easy for Africans to identify with biblical stories and characters.

William Wadé Harris was born into the Grebo tribe in Liberia (Wadé, pronounced "Waddy," was his Grebo name; William Harris, his baptismal name). Harris converted to Christianity around the age of twenty and worked in Methodist and Episcopal missions. But he chafed under the Liberian government, run by descendants of American slaves who discriminated against native tribes. He began agitating for Liberia to become a British colony and was imprisoned in 1910.

While incarcerated, Harris had a vision of the angel Gabriel who anointed him a prophet, and when released in 1913, he became an itinerant preacher. Emphasizing his African roots, he wore a white robe and turban and carried, along with his Bible, a bamboo cross, a gourd rattle, and a bowl for baptism. Two women disciples accompanied him, singing and shaking calabash rattles. Harris's preaching gained few converts at first, but when he crossed into nearby Côte d'Ivoire, a flood of conversions ensued. During an eighteen-month period in 1913–14, he baptized 120,000 people.

Harris preached orthodox Christianity with an emphasis on abandoning pagan fetishes and occult practices. Healings and other miracles often accompanied his conversions. Some of his converts established independent Harrist churches, but many, with Harris's encouragement, joined established denominations, both Protestant and Catholic.

What might account for the success of Harris's missionary efforts?

124
Vivekananda

Born 1863, in Kolkata, India
Died 1902, in Belur, India

On September 11, 1893, at the Art Institute of Chicago, an Indian Hindu monk addressed the World Parliament of Religions, the first gathering of its kind. Suddenly and for the first time, thousands of Westerners saw Hinduism not as a primitive superstition, but as a major world faith. The speaker, Vivekananda, received a rousing ovation.

Vivekananda then toured America, addressing enthusiastic audiences at every stop. Because of him, Westerners began to practice yoga, transcendental mediation, and other Hindu spiritual disciplines.

Vivekananda had dismissed his native faith after receiving a British education in India. That changed when he met Ramakrishna (see #121) in 1881. He embraced Ramakrishna's monistic, inclusive Hinduism, concluding that all things embody God and hence that service to God and service to humanity are the same.

Following Ramakrishna's death in 1886, Vivekananda traveled throughout India. He worked to end poverty, hunger, and illness, and advocated for women's rights. He founded the Ramakrishna Mission, which is today India's largest charitable organization ministering to the poor. Noting that his countrymen were denied self-respect under British rule, he also preached Indian nationalism.

> If there is ever to be a universal religion, it must be one which will have no location in time or place; which will be infinite, like the God it will preach, and whose sun will shine upon the followers of Krishna and Christ, on saints and sinners alike; which will not be Brahminical or Buddhist, Christian or Mohammedan, but the sum total of all of these, and still have infinite space for development; which in its catholicity will embrace in its infinite arms, and find a place for every human being. . . . It will be a religion which will have no place for persecution or intolerance in its polity, which will recognize divinity in every man and woman, and whose whole scope, whose whole force, will be centered in aiding humanity to realize its own true and divine nature. —Vivekananda

> I do not come to convert you to a new belief. I want you to keep your own belief. I want to make the Methodist a better Methodist, the Presbyterian a better Presbyterian, the Unitarian a better Unitarian. I want to teach you to live the truth, to reveal the light within your own soul. —Vivekananda

Is a "universal religion" possible?

125
Hehaka Sapa (Black Elk)

Born 1863, along the Little Powder River
in Wyoming (?)
Died 1950, on the Pine Ridge Indian Reservation,
South Dakota

When a tradition is superseded or absorbed into another tradition, its spirituality survives, if at all, only in isolated places and in truncated expressions. Moreover, many traditional cultures communicated orally and through music and dance. Lacking written records, much of their wisdom has been lost to history.

Native American spirituality varied from place to place, but an Oglala Lakota (Sioux) holy man and healer named Hehaka Sapa (Black Elk) embodied elements of Native American spirituality found throughout North America. Interviews conducted in the 1930s have preserved his insights for later generations.

A cousin of the warrior Crazy Horse, Black Elk was wounded at the Battle of Little Bighorn in 1876. But the determinative event of his life occurred at age nine when he had a vision in which he lapsed into an apparent coma for several days. In the vision, Black Elk was taken up into a white cloud, introduced to the Powers of the World, and "saw that the sacred hoop of my people was one of many hoops that made one circle, wide as daylight and as starlight, and in the center grew one mighty flowering tree to shelter all the children of one mother and one father. And I saw that it was holy."

The Lakotas, like most Native American nations, revered the natural world and saw themselves as part of it, understood human life in communal rather than individualistic terms, experienced the transcendent as intimately involved with daily life, and approached the holy intuitively rather than cerebrally. Black Elk became a Roman Catholic and saw his native spirituality and Christian faith as complementary.

Black Elk traveled Europe for two years as part of Buffalo Bill's Wild West Show. He perceived white Americans and Europeans as selfish, materialistic, dishonest, and superficial.

No good thing can be done by any man alone. —Black Elk

Sometimes dreams are wiser than waking. —Black Elk

I knew the real was yonder and the darkened dream of it was here. —Black Elk

Everything the Power of the World does is done in a circle. —Black Elk

Nothing can live well except in a manner that is suited to the way the sacred Power of the World lives and moves. —Black Elk

What might modern Americans learn from Black Elk?

126
C. H. Mason

Born 1866, near Memphis, Tennessee
Died 1961, in Detroit, Michigan

The son of devout former slaves, C. H. Mason was a sharecropper with no formal education. But he learned to read and write and, in 1893, began preaching at a Missionary Baptist church in Arkansas. Mason soon learned of the Holiness movement (see #117) and became a convert.

Mason and several other Baptist pastors began preaching the Holiness doctrine and were expelled from their local Baptist association. They formed a new church, initially called the Church of God, but later renamed the Church of God in Christ.

The real turning point in Mason's life came in 1907 when he was sent to Los Angeles to investigate the Azusa Street Revival (see #128). Mason was initially put off by the preaching of William Seymour, but soon the "Spirit came upon the saints and upon me. . . . Then I gave up for the Lord to have His way within me. So there came a wave of Glory into me and all of my being was filled with the Glory of the Lord." Mason received the baptism of the Holy Spirit and began speaking in tongues.

Holiness preachers often spoke of the baptism of the Holy Spirit but understood it as another name for sanctification. Tongue-speaking was not part of Holiness spirituality, but Mason understood tongue-speaking as the identifiable mark of Spirit baptism. When he returned home, his former Holiness associates refused to have fellowship with him, but a court gave Mason the rights to the church's name.

At a time when women were usually seen but not heard and interracial gatherings were virtually unknown, Mason encouraged female evangelists, preached to interracial audiences, and ordained hundreds of white pastors. He was also a pacifist who encouraged African-American men not to serve in World Wars I and II because they were denied the liberties enjoyed by white Americans. For this he was arrested and probed by the Federal Bureau of Investigation.

Mason also embraced his African-American religious heritage, encouraging shouting, dancing, gospel singing, and personal testimonies in his worship services. The Church of God in Christ is now the largest Pentecostal denomination in the United States, with five million U.S. members. Mason also preached in 1914 at the founding of the Assemblies of God, a largely white offshoot of the Church of God in Christ and today the world's largest Pentecostal church, with sixty-five million members.

What question would you like to ask C. H. Mason?

127
Mohandas Gandhi

Born 1869, in Porbandar, India
Died 1948, in New Delhi, India

Though not a conventionally religious man, everything the twentieth century's leading apostle of nonviolence did reflected his immersion in his native Hinduism and other faiths.

After studying law in London, Mohandas Gandhi
served for twenty-one years in South Africa where discrimination against nonwhites
galvanized his social conscience. When he returned to India in 1915, Gandhi began
working for the rights of women and the poor and for the nation's independence from
British rule. A reviled nemesis to the British, he became a folk hero to his countrymen. The British imprisoned Gandhi four times over three decades.

Gandhi lived simply and was unfailingly consistent in refusing to use or advocate
force. He patiently endured oppression while using long fasts and civil disobedience
to build support for Indian independence.

India gained its independence in 1947. Envisioning an India where different faiths
would live peaceably together, Gandhi opposed the partition of the nation into separate Hindu and Muslim states. He was assassinated in 1948 by a radical Hindu na-
tionalist who accused him of favoring the Muslims. Gandhi's accomplishments and
martyrdom have inspired later nonviolent protesters the world over.

An eye for an eye only ends up making the whole world blind. —Mohandas Gandhi

*Happiness is when what you think, what you say, and what you do are in
harmony.* —Mohandas Gandhi

*Humanity is an ocean; if a few drops of the ocean are dirty, the ocean does not
become dirty.* —Mohandas Gandhi

*Prayer is not asking. It is a longing of the soul. It is daily admission of one's
weakness. It is better in prayer to have a heart without words than words without
a heart.* —Mohandas Gandhi

You must be the change you wish to see in the world. —Mohandas Gandhi

*I like your Christ, I do not like your Christians. Your Christians are so unlike
your Christ.* —Mohandas Gandhi

*There are many causes that I am prepared to die for but no causes that I am
prepared to kill for.* —Mohandas Gandhi

**Does subsequent history validate or invalidate Gandhi's pacifism? Would you
have voted for him as president of the United States?**

128
William J. Seymour

Born 1870, in Centerville, Louisiana
Died 1922, in Los Angeles, California

The first stirrings of Pentecostalism occurred in 1901 in Topeka, Kansas, where Charles Fox Parham, a Holiness preacher (see #117), was conducting evangelistic services. Parham was the first to speak of the baptism of the Holy Spirit as an identifiable experience marked by speaking in tongues. After Parham relocated to Houston, Texas, a young black Holiness preacher named William J. Seymour, blind in one eye from smallpox, began attending his services and embraced Parham's ideas.

In 1906, Seymour was invited to become pastor of a small Holiness church in Los Angeles. In his first sermon, on Acts 2:4, Seymour said that someone not speaking in tongues had not received Spirit baptism. Later that day, he found the church padlocked so that he could not enter. Seymour began preaching in a private home and attracting large crowds. A larger facility was needed, and one was found at 312 Azusa Street in a run-down section of Los Angeles.

The Azusa Street Revival is usually seen as the beginning of the Pentecostal movement. People traveled to Azusa Street from the world over. Crowds often numbered in the thousands, spilling into the surrounding streets. Worshipers received the gift of tongues and often the gifts of healing and prophecy as well. Services ran nonstop, day and night, and missionaries were sent from Azusa Street all over the world. Seymour founded a newspaper, *The Apostolic Faith*, which attracted fifty thousand subscribers.

The revival ended in acrimony after three years, in 1909, but the Pentecostal witness would not be contained. Today one in five Christians worldwide is a member of a Pentecostal church—roughly 6 percent of the world's population—and the Roman Catholic, Anglican, and other older communions have gained new energy from those in their ranks, usually called "charismatics," who have also received Spirit baptism.

> *There are many wells today, but they are dry. There are many hungry souls today that are empty. But let us come to Jesus and take Him at His Word and we will find wells of salvation, and be able to draw waters out of the well of salvation, for Jesus is that well.* —William J. Seymour

> *The Pentecostal power, when you sum it all up, is just more of God's love. If it does not bring more love, it is simply a counterfeit.* —William J. Seymour

Must an authentic spiritual experience have an outward sign?

129
Aurobindo

Born 1872, in Kolkata, India
Died 1950, in Pondicherry, India

At the age of seven, Aurobindo was taken from his native India to England to be educated. He was tutored in Western science, philosophy, and history. Indian thought and culture were not part of his curriculum. But Aurobindo learned of the American Revolution and other colonialized people's efforts to throw off British rule, and when he returned home at twenty-one, to become a teacher and civil servant, he was drawn into the leadership of the Indian independence movement. The British imprisoned him for his insurrectionist writings.

But politics was not to be Aurobindo's life vocation. While incarcerated, he had mystical visions and upon his release renounced politics and moved to India's east coast, where he wrote extensively, developed a new expression of yoga (see #16), and remained for the rest of his life.

Aurobindo felt that earlier forms of yoga denied the sanctity of human life by urging the spiritual seeker to turn from the physical world and the human body and rise through meditation to the immaterial realm of Spirit. Aurobindo, however, affirmed material reality. This world, he said, is the scene of spiritual evolution or self-discovery in which the dulled human mind is transformed into the mind of God. For him, yogic meditation was meant to enable one to rise to the realm of Spirit and then return, bringing the Supermind down, to enlighten and transform life on earth, eventually uniting all people. He called this "integral yoga."

Aurobindo saw this as a three-step process. First is psychic transformation, the discovery of one's evolving soul and of the unity of all created things. Then comes spiritual transformation, the infusion of light from above through intuition and revelation. And finally there is supramental transformation in which the whole self—body, mind, and soul—is recreated.

The New Age and human potential movements in the West look to Aurobindo as one of their early inspirations.

To listen to some devout people, one would imagine that God never laughs.
—Aurobindo

[India sees] that man has the power of exceeding himself, of becoming himself more entirely and profoundly than he is, truths which have only recently begun to be seen in Europe and seem even now too great for its common intelligence.
—Aurobindo

Does the solution to the world's problems lie in knowledge and enlightenment?

130
Carl Jung

Born 1875, in Kesswil, Switzerland
Died 1961, in Küsnacht, Switzerland

The son of a Swiss Protestant pastor and a moody, eccentric mother, Carl Jung was a private child most comfortable when left alone with his own thoughts. He became a physician but was strongly drawn to the new discipline of psychoanalysis, becoming a disciple and close friend of its founder, Sigmund Freud, twenty years Jung's senior.

Freud had discovered the unconscious mind with its hidden but powerful motivations, which he saw as primarily sexual. Freud regarded spirituality as illusory, but after six years as Freud's protégé, Jung came to see the unconscious mind as spiritual in nature. He broke with Freud in 1913 and began to develop his own approach, called analytical psychology.

The key concept in analytical psychology Jung called "individuation," the formation of a "true self" in healthy relation to other selves. The individuated person is aware of his motives and drives, even those once hidden in the unconscious, and integrates them with his conscious desires and values so as to become a mature, whole, responsible person. Freed from the unhealthy influences of unacknowledged subconscious drives, the individuated person realizes the potentiality that is within him.

Jung saw individuation as a spiritual quest. He studied Christianity and other faith traditions and discovered in them a common mystical core leading to the discovery of both the true self and the divine. Religious stories, myths, dreams, and art were points of contact with the divine, Jung felt. Faith for him was not believing a set of static doctrines, but a lifelong act of trusting exploration of the world within.

Jung's influence on the modern world has been enormous. Many of his concepts, such as the introverted and extraverted personalities and the psychological complex, have entered the vocabulary of everyday speech, and twelve-step recovery programs are partly based on his insights.

Whether summoned or not, God will be present. —Carl Jung

God speaks chiefly through dreams and visions. —Carl Jung

Who looks outside, dreams; who looks inside, awakens. —Carl Jung

Eternal truth needs a human language which alters with the spirit of the times. The primordial images undergo ceaseless transformation and yet remain ever the same, but only in new form can they be understood anew. —Carl Jung

If God speaks through dreams and visions, how does one know what God is saying?

131
Albert Schweitzer

Born 1875, in Kaysersberg, France
Died 1965, in Lambaréné, Gabon

Albert Schweitzer was a brilliant concert organist, authoritative interpreter of the works of J. S. Bach (see #106), and renowned New Testament scholar. His *The Quest for the Historical Jesus* (1906) claimed that historical understandings of Jesus are always conditioned by the time and culture of the interpreter and that the New Testament showed that Jesus had expected the imminent end of the world. Studies of the four Gospels would never be the same again. A life of adulation and further accomplishments seemed assured.

But in 1912, having completed a medical degree, Schweitzer and his wife set out for Africa as medical missionaries, building a small hospital in Lambaréné, in what is today Gabon. Financing their work through concerts, lecture fees, and sales of Schweitzer's books, they treated over two thousand patients the first year for malaria, dysentery, sleeping sickness, leprosy, sandflea, and other illnesses unknown in Europe. They rarely left Africa again.

Schweitzer was responding to Jesus's call to his disciples to become "fishers of men," but he also sought to make a small act of recompense to the African people for the cruelty of European colonialism. A book containing a full account of colonialism would contain many pages, he said, "which the reader would have to turn over unread because their contents would be too horrible."

Schweitzer received the 1952 Nobel Peace Prize for his philosophy of "Reverence for Life," expressed both in his medical work and in published works such as *Civilization and Ethics* (1923). He valued all conscious life and honored its "will to live." Human beings, Schweitzer said, are not superior to other living things or the capstone of creation, but part of a wider network of living things. He said humanity is "in a personal spiritual relationship to the universe."

> *Success is not the key to happiness. Happiness is the key to success. If you love what you are doing, you will be successful.* —Albert Schweitzer

> *Compassion, in which all ethics must take root, can only attain its full breadth and depth if it embraces all living creatures and does not limit itself to mankind.*
> —Albert Schweitzer

> *Do something for somebody every day for which you do not get paid.*
> —Albert Schweitzer

What is the key to success for you?

132
Martin Buber

Born 1878, in Vienna, Austria
Died 1965, in Jerusalem

Reared by his paternal grandparents in Ukraine, the young Martin Buber was a private, cerebral boy whose best friends, as he once said, were found in books. He studied Kant, Kierkegaard, Nietzsche, and other philosophers, then taught philosophy at the University of Frankfurt am Main until he resigned in protest in 1933 when Adolf Hitler came to power. Later that year the Nazis forbade Buber to lecture. He left Germany in 1938 and settled in Jerusalem.

Buber had joined a Zionist organization in 1898, advocating a two-nation federation based on reconciliation and mutual respect. In Buber's utopian vision, Jews and Arabs would govern jointly and neither would dominate. This alienated many other Zionists. Buber also edited collections of Hasidic tales (see #107), seeing the Hasidim as a source of Jewish renewal—open, communitarian, apolitical, and embracing God in everyday experience—what he had hoped to see in the Zionist movement.

Buber compiled a volume entitled *Tales of the Hasidim*, giving a vivid picture of Hasidic life and thought, but it is for his little book *I and Thou* that Buber is chiefly remembered. Published in 1923, it is an essay on relationship as the essential characteristic of human life. People are always engaged in one of two kinds of relationship and move between the two, he said. An I-It relationship is one-dimensional and static, treating the other as an object, and is useful when examining and analyzing facts. An I-Thou relationship is two-dimensional, fluid, mutual, holistic, and unpredictable. Authentic living is opening ourselves to the Thou of other people and of God. For Buber, God is not a being whose existence is to be proved—that would be to relate to God as an It—but the ultimate and eternal Thou.

> *When two people relate to each other authentically and humanly, God is the electricity that surges between them.* —Martin Buber

> *The world is not comprehensible, but it is embraceable: through the embracing of one of its beings.* —Martin Buber

> *You can rake the muck this way, rake the muck that way—it will always be muck. Have I sinned or have I not sinned? In the time I am brooding over it, I could be stringing pearls for the delight of heaven.* —Martin Buber

When have you experienced an I-Thou relationship?

133
Ramana Maharshi

Born 1879, in Tiruchuli, India
Died 1950, at Mount Arunachala, India

Many Westerners regard the conscious self as a product of the central nervous system. Easterners, however, see the conscious self as independent of the human body. Out-of-body experiences and memories of earlier lives are therefore not deemed extraordinary occurrences. Bodies come and go; the self remains.

Born to a Brahmin family, Ramana Maharshi showed no spiritual inclinations as a youth. At age seventeen, a terrifying fear of death suddenly overtook him. His mind retreated inwards. Convinced death was at hand, Ramana lay still and held his breath, as if experiencing *rigor mortis*. But while his body was silent and inert, Ramana still felt the force of his personality and mind. He concluded that the self transcended the body and could not die. Ramana never feared death again.

Transformed by this gripping experience, Ramana spent the rest of his life focusing on his interior self. He traveled to the holy mountain of Arunachala and found an underground vault in a temple where he practiced round-the-clock silent meditation on the self. Weeks later, he was discovered, in poor health and covered with insect bites that had not fazed him. Ramana was removed from the vault, bathed, and given food. He remained at Arunachala (though not in the underground vault) for the rest of his life, mostly in silent meditation.

Ramana's sole desire was to journey inward to answer the question "Who am I?" He sought no disciples and wrote nothing, teaching largely by example. Nonetheless, by the 1940s pilgrims from around the world were arriving to sit at his feet. He usually said nothing to them and is reported to have radiated tranquility.

Many Hindus worship Ramana as a divine incarnation. His teaching has been called neo-Advaita (see #56) and claims several million adherents today, including many in the West.

The Self, one's real nature, alone exists and is real. The world, the soul, and God are superimposed on it like [the illusion of] silver in mother-of-pearl. . . . Self itself is the world; Self itself is the "I"; Self itself is God; all is Siva, the Self.
—Ramana Maharshi

The degree of freedom from unwanted thoughts and the degree of concentration on a single thought are the measures to gauge spiritual progress. —Ramana Maharshi

How does Ramana's focus on the self differ from spiritual pride?

134
William Temple

Born 1881, in Exeter, England
Died 1944, in Westgate-on-Sea, England

When William Temple became archbishop of Canterbury in 1942, it was hard to imagine what he might do that he had not already done.

Born into a deeply Christian home, Temple became president of the Workers' Educational Association in 1908, seeking economic reform on behalf of the working classes. He then traveled throughout England for eighteen months promoting a greater voice for the laity in church governance. This resulted in Parliament's passing the Enabling Act of 1919.

In 1929, Temple gained the trust of Christians of many denominations as he addressed differences of doctrine and polity among the world's Protestant churches as chair of the Faith and Order Continuation Committee. This was a precursor of the World Council of Churches, formed four years after Temple's death.

As archbishop of York in the 1930s, Temple not only continued working for social reform, but also visited college and university campuses, preaching to standing-room-only crowds, challenging the prevailing intellectual skepticism of the day, injecting new energy into the church on campuses, and resulting in hundreds of conversions.

As archbishop of Canterbury during World War II, Temple often addressed the nation, defending the war as a tragic but necessary fight against evil, advocating humane treatment of German prisoners of war, and seeking to prepare England for reconciliation and forgiveness when the war ended.

Temple was also a noted author. In *Nature, Man and God,* he envisioned science and religion as partners in the pursuit of truth, and his *Readings in St. John's Gospel* is a popular devotional commentary on the Fourth Gospel. *Christianity and Social Order* expounds the principles of Christian engagement in social, economic, and political decisions.

> *Christianity is the most materialistic of all great religions. . . . Christianity, based as it is on the Incarnation, regards matter as destined to be the vehicle and instrument of spirit, and spirit as fully actual so far as it controls and directs matter.* —William Temple

> *It is a great mistake to suppose that God is only, or even chiefly, concerned with religion.* —William Temple

> *The art of government in fact is the art of so ordering life that self-interest prompts what justice demands.* —William Temple

Is Christianity a "materialistic" religion in your view?

135
John XXIII

Born 1881, in Sotto il Monte, Italy
Died 1963, in Vatican City

The son of northern Italian peasants, Angelo Giuseppe Roncalli always remembered his humble origins, once remarking that he often awoke in the middle of the night thinking that he must ask the pope about some pressing problem. "Then I wake up completely and remember that I *am* the pope."

Roncalli was ordained in 1903 and entered the Third Order of Franciscans (see #80). He carried wounded Italian troops on a stretcher during World War I and later served as a papal diplomat in Bulgaria, Turkey, and France. During World War II, he negotiated to save thousands of Bulgarian Jews and others from Nazi persecution, and later, as Pope John XXIII, prayed on behalf of his church, "Forgive us for the curse we falsely attached to their name as Jews. Forgive us for crucifying Thee a second time in their flesh. For we knew not what we did."

When Roncalli was elected pope in 1958, at the age of seventy-seven, most observers expected his pontificate to be brief and inconsequential. They were half right. Although it lasted only five years, John ushered in a new day for the Roman church. He visited prisoners and children with polio, often slipped out of the Vatican at night to walk the streets of Rome (earning him the nickname "Johnny Walker"), and instructed the Vatican newspaper to stop writing, "These are the words of the Holy Father, as we were able to gather them from his august lips," telling them instead to write, "The pope said."

Apart from his disarming humility, John is chiefly remembered for convening the Second Vatican Council in 1963. He died before its conclusion, but that council threw open the long closed shutters of the Roman Catholic Church, embracing liturgical, social, and theological ideas it had long dismissed, while also strengthening the church's commitment to its core teachings. Unlike previous such gatherings, it issued no new dogmas and condemned no heretics, but launched a wide-ranging ecumenical dialogue and fellowship, authorized worship in languages spoken by the people, and reaffirmed the church's commitment to the sacredness of human life, including the life of the unborn.

See everything, overlook a great deal, correct a little. —John XXIII

A peaceful man does more good than a learned one. —John XXIII

What distinguishes true humility from false humility?

136
B. R. Ambedkar

Born 1891, in Mhow, India
Died 1956, in Delhi, India

The fourteenth child in a family of India's lowest, "untouchable" class, B. R. Ambedkar learned early the meaning of social ostracism. He studied and accepted the Hindu scriptures as a boy, but was made to sit outside the classroom when lessons were given. Water was poured from a pitcher directly into his mouth lest his lips touch a glass or fountain. He was required to sit on a gunnysack so that his skin would not contaminate upholstery.

But Ambedkar was determined to overcome every obstacle and eventually earned graduate degrees from Columbia University and the London School of Economics. Back in India, he began to advocate for political reform, attracting a wide following.

The caste system was deeply rooted in Indian culture. Abolish it, Ambedkar urged. But others, including Mohandas Gandhi (see #127) favored a more deliberate approach, gradual reform rather than outright abolition. Ambedkar organized protests, leading marches to open public facilities and Hindu temples to all.

Ambedkar won the respect of more than the untouchables. When India won its independence in 1947, he was named chair of the team that drafted the nation's first constitution, setting India on a democratic path. But all the while, his efforts to abolish the caste system continued.

Finally Ambedkar had enough. In 1950, he publicly abandoned Hinduism and converted to Buddhism. Six years later, shortly before his death, he presided over a mass conversion ceremony in which half a million Indians, most from the untouchable class, also embraced Buddhism. This sparked a small revival of Buddhism in the land of its origin, where it had largely died out. His *The Buddha and His Dhamma* (1957) is an important text. The "Ambedkar Buddhists" today comprise the largest Buddhist sect in India.

> *Life should be great rather than long.* —B. R. Ambedkar

> *The sovereignty of scriptures of all religions must come to an end if we want to have a united integrated modern India.* —B. R. Ambedkar

> *Religion must mainly be a matter of principles only. It cannot be a matter of rules. The moment it degenerates into rules, it ceases to be a religion, as it kills responsibility which is an essence of the true religious act.*
> —B. R. Ambedkar

What would make a life "great rather than long"?

137
Reinhold Niebuhr

Born 1892, Wright City, Missouri
Died 1971, in Stockbridge, Massachusetts

The son of an immigrant Evangelical German pastor, Reinhold Niebuhr began his career espousing the prevailing Protestant theology of his day, which assumed continual progress through education and scientific advance. Niebuhr's first parish was in Detroit, where he saw income inequality and the dehumanization of mass production and embraced socialism and pacifism as the means to progress.

After Niebuhr became a professor at New York's Union Theological Seminary in 1928 (where he remained for the rest of his life), the Great Depression and the rise of Nazism shattered his optimistic theology. He became the chief exponent of "Christian realism," reviving the long neglected doctrine of original sin and viewing evil not as eradicable through progress, but as profoundly rooted in the human heart. He greatly impacted the thinking of Dietrich Bonhoeffer (see #144) and Martin Luther King Jr. (see #156).

Insecurity feeds pride and egoism, Niebuhr said, which leads to extreme nationalism and absolutism. In *Moral Man and Immoral Society* (1932), he said that people behave morally as individuals, but evil emerges in the actions and hypocrisy of nations and social classes. Niebuhr's *The Irony of American History* (1952) applied this view to America, endorsing U.S. opposition to Communism while criticizing American self-righteousness and claims to a special status among nations.

During World War II, Niebuhr abandoned his pacifist views and supported the Allied effort against Germany and Japan, winning him the praise of political conservatives. But he later opposed the U.S. involvement in Vietnam, which allied him with liberals of the day. He saw liberals as naïvely optimistic and conservatives as idolatrously equating their views with the divine will. To this day, American politicians across the spectrum claim Niebuhr as a formative influence on their thinking.

Original sin . . . makes [man] capable of conceiving of his own perfection and incapable of achieving it. —Reinhold Niebuhr

Goodness, armed with power, is corrupted; and pure love without power is destroyed. —Reinhold Niebuhr

True religion is a profound uneasiness about our highest social values. —Reinhold Niebuhr

God grant me the serenity to accept the things I cannot change, the courage to change the things I can, and the wisdom to know the difference. —Reinhold Niebuhr

How would Niebuhr advise today's political leaders?

138
A. C. Bhaktivedanta

Born 1896, in Kolkata, India
Died 1977, in Vrindavan, India

The name "Hare Krishna" will suggest to older Americans saffron-clad youths distributing literature in airline terminals in the 1970s. But today the roughly 100,000 Hare Krishnas in America (the worldwide number is about one million) are indistinguishable in attire and behavior from anyone else. The movement remains, however, the rare expression of Hinduism that seeks converts.

Hare Krishnas are part of the International Society of Krishna Consciousness (ISKCON) founded in New York City in 1966 by A. C. Bhaktivedanta. In 1922, Bhaktivedanta's spiritual mentor asked him to spread the practice of yoga (see #16) to the West. He first sought to do this while also maintaining a family and a small drugstore in Kolkata and, from 1950, by producing commentaries and translations of the Hindu scriptures. While his literary work has been widely influential, not until 1965, at the age of sixty-nine, did Bhaktivedanta begin the work for which he is best known: he sailed for New York with seven dollars in his pocket and several crates of books.

Knowing no one, Bhaktivedanta began offering yoga classes in a small loft in the Bowery. At first, only a few down-and-outs took notice, but soon others arrived at his door as word spread of Bhaktivedanta's goodwill and serenity. During the next twelve years, until his death, he visited six continents, lectured at prominent universities, wrote dozens more books, saw ISKCON grow into a fellowship of over a hundred temples and communities the world over, and became a popular figure in the American counterculture.

Bhaktivedanta's message was simple: to find true happiness, live simply, dedicate yourself to serving God and other living things, preach the glory of God, and chant the divine name of Krishna. Krishna is a youthful incarnation of the god Vishnu (see #38). Bhaktivedanta declined to use the Western term "God" because he felt the name "Krishna" included all other divine names.

Hare Krishnas are vegetarians and, like other Hindus, believe in reincarnation. Many of the teachings of Bhaktivedanta have entered Western culture and are embraced by people who know little or nothing of their origin.

First-class religion teaches one how to love God without any motive. If I serve God for some profit, that is business—not love. —A. C. Bhaktivedanta

What in modern Western culture might account for the appeal of Bhaktivedanta's message?

139

Dorothy Day

Born 1897, in Brooklyn, New York
Died 1980, in New York, New York

Dorothy Day and her friends scorned the Christian church as hypocritical and worldly. But Day noted that the masses of poor immigrants arriving in New York found comfort and strength in it. How could that be? Despite her many friends, Day also felt lonely—but for what? When she finally realized she was lonely for God and joined the Roman Catholic Church, she came to understand that choosing God also meant choosing compassion, justice, and peace. But how was she to live that out?

Day was a journalist, so she founded a newspaper. The first edition of *The Catholic Worker* in 1933 had a press run of just 2,500 copies. Within a year, 100,000 copies were being printed and churches were ordering bulk subscriptions. Day's column, called "On Pilgrimage," contained news, devotional material, travelogues, editorials, personal comments, and quotations from other sources. It had a tone of immediacy, for Day didn't edit her prose, preferring to spend that time serving the poor. She edited *The Catholic Worker* for forty-seven years, until her death.

The homeless and needy often dropped by the paper's offices in the Bowery. So Day began feeding them. "We do not feel we can talk in the paper about something we are not practicing," she said. Readers began sending money, resulting in the founding of "houses of hospitality," first in New York, then across the world. Day lived in one of these houses and traveled to visit others. No one was turned away, no questions were asked, and no sermons preached. Any hungry or homeless person could find a meal and a bed at one of Day's houses, and people could remain as long as they wished.

Believing that Christian love extended to everyone, Day became an absolute pacifist—she opposed killing anyone, ever, for any reason. This cost her many subscriptions and supporters during World War II and the paper's circulation did not fully recover for twenty years.

It is not a duty to help Christ; it is a privilege. —Dorothy Day

Don't call me a saint. I don't want to be dismissed that easily. —Dorothy Day

I feel that I have done nothing well. But I have done what I could.
—Dorothy Day

Why do so many Christians regard helping Christ as a duty rather than a privilege?

140
C. S. Lewis

Born 1898, in Belfast, Northern Ireland
Died 1963, in Oxford, England

C. S. Lewis was the twentieth century's most popular Christian author and his popularity is undiminished today. Lewis's life was orderly; he rarely varied from his daily routine. He taught English literature at Oxford and later at Cambridge and remained a bachelor most of his life. "I like monotony," Lewis once said.

In his imagination, however, Lewis traveled to fantastic new worlds, wrestled with perplexing religious dilemmas, and encountered the holy. He had not expected such an encounter, having embraced atheism as a young man. Lewis tells of his initially reluctant conversion to Christianity in his autobiographical *Surprised by Joy*.

Soon after that surprise, Lewis began writing works of theology and devotion. In a series of radio addresses later published as *Mere Christianity*, Lewis seeks to demonstrate the reasonableness of Christian faith by means of logic, homespun images, and lucid analogies. It remains a classic work of Christian apologetics. His *The Screwtape Letters* purports to be the correspondence of Satan to one of his lieutenants on earth.

Lewis is perhaps best known for his children's books, *The Chronicles of Narnia*, in which a group of children visit a mythical world where they encounter talking animals, dwarfs, dragons, witches, surrealistic creatures, and a powerful lion named Aslan who mysteriously appears at critical moments. Lewis also wrote three science-fiction novels for adults, known as his space trilogy, and a charming novella about heaven and hell entitled *The Great Divorce*. The Christian content in these stories is clear but never blatant.

Although he had little formal theological training, Lewis also wrote two major studies of thorny theological issues, *The Problem of Pain* and *Miracles*. His most emotive work, *A Grief Observed*, tells of his searing grief and encounter with doubt at the death of his wife, Joy, whom he had married in 1956.

Lewis's theology was solidly orthodox. He sought no new perspectives, but to elucidate traditional Christian teachings. Throughout his diverse body of work, the reader encounters again and again Lewis's gripping sense of the transcendent. Lewis was convinced that this world, this universe, this life, are not all there is, but stand in relation to an unseen reality, what is usually called the supernatural. This is true whether one acknowledges it or not, and everything that matters hangs on one's response to that reality.

What would bring an atheist to acknowledge the supernatural?

141
Ruhollah Khomeini

Born 1902, in Khomeyn, Iran
Died 1989, in Tehran, Iran

In 1953, to protect their nations' oil interests, the American and British governments engineered a coup d'état, overthrowing the democratically elected government of Iran. For the next twenty-six years, Mohammad-Reza Pahlavi, installed as monarch, ruled autocratically, advanced Western interests, promoted secularism, and suppressed dissent. Rage seethed beneath the surface until, in February of 1979, a grassroots revolution deposed Pahlavi. Throngs celebrated throughout the country.

The revolution's leader was Ruhollah Khomeini, a Shia (see #46, #47, #61) cleric and scholar. Khomeini had stirred opposition to the Pahlavi regime in Iran until his arrest and exile in 1964, after which he corresponded with dissidents inside the country who circulated videotapes of his fiery sermons and his books promoting his vision of a godly Iran.

That vision harked back to the earliest days of Islam when Muhammad had exercised both political and religious authority in Medina (see #45). Shia Muslims—a minority elsewhere but a majority in Iran—had never entirely lost sight of this ideal. Khomeini saw Islamic law as the norm for every aspect of day-to-day living. Government leaders should be clergymen versed in Islamic law, he said, and the nation's supreme leader should be a cleric renowned for his knowledge of it. Government by the clergy would provide justice for all, prevent corruption, and guard against anti-Islamic forces from abroad. A new constitution based on these principles was adopted by referendum and Khomeini himself was named "Supreme Leader." Opposition to the government, he said, was opposition to God.

Minority religions were subject to discriminatory laws. Jews and Bahais (see #119), the latter seen as apostate Muslims, were sometimes tortured.

Outside Iran, Khomeini is remembered as an authoritarian firebrand who denounced America as the "Great Satan;" approved the takeover of the American embassy on November 4, 1979, which led to a diplomatic crisis lasting 444 days; and issued a death sentence for British novelist Salman Rushdie.

Within Iran, however, Khomeini was—and is—revered as a courageous, saintly, otherworldly national hero. Even his occasional critics praise his character. Faithfulness to God, not economics, was Khomeini's guiding passion, and when the new government's economic policies led to food shortages, he said, "I cannot believe that the purpose of all these sacrifices was to have less expensive melons."

Where and by whom should the line be drawn between freedom of expression and the suppression of harmful ideas?

142
Menachem Mendel Schneerson

Born 1902 in Nikolaev, Russia
Died 1994 in Brooklyn, New York

A new expression of Hasidism (see #107) arose in the Lithuanian town of Lyubavichi in the late eighteenth century. Called Habad, it moved beyond early Hasidism by emphasizing academic study and deemphasizing the role of the *zaddik* as divine spokesman. But it was only after the Nazi invasion caused Habad to move its headquarters in 1940 to Brooklyn, New York, that the movement began to revitalize Jewry around the world. The force behind Habad's new vitality was its new leader Rabbi Menachem Mendel Schneerson, the most charismatic and gifted Jewish leader of the modern era. He led Habad for forty-four years until his death.

Besides immersing himself in Torah and Talmud, Schneerson had studied mathematics, philosophy, physics, electronics, and engineering. He was among the last Jews out of Europe in 1941 before German U-boats blockaded the continent. During the next four years, a third of the world's Jews would be murdered. Many who survived the Holocaust were confused, demoralized, and exhausted. After assuming leadership of Habad from his father-in-law in 1950, Schneerson sought to instill new pride in the Jewish people and reconvert lapsed and discouraged Jews to the study of Torah. He oversaw a huge expansion of Habad, building schools, youth camps, community centers, synagogues, and "Habad houses" around the world, all promoting Orthodox Judaism.

Unusual for an Orthodox Jew, Schneerson was cordial to other Jews, seeing in Habad a means of bringing them into the Orthodox fold. He also felt that God had given each human being, of whatever faith, the potential to live a moral and productive life and urged everyone to achieve that potential. The Jews, however, had been chosen by God to serve as divine agents and, through godly living, to usher in the Messianic age of universal peace (see #5).

Critics faulted Schneerson for failing to defuse the "personality cult" that grew around him. So captivating was his person and so pervasive his influence that some of his followers regarded him as the long-awaited Messiah. A few do even today.

> *When you waste a moment, you have killed it in a sense, squandering an irreplaceable opportunity. But when you use the moment properly, filling it with purpose and productivity, it lives on forever.* —Menachem Mendel Schneerson

What about Schneerson gave hope to demoralized Jews?

143
David du Plessis

Born 1905, in Twenty-Four Rivers, South Africa
Died 1987, in Pasadena, California

The early Pentecostals (see #126, #128) had no dealings with other Christians, often dismissing them as heretics who denied the plain meaning of the Bible, while the historic Christian churches scorned the early Pentecostals as uneducated and disreputable. Among the first to bridge this chasm was David du Plessis.

Born to missionary parents, at age thirteen, du Plessis took a Friday off from school so that he, his father, and a few others could pray with him. They prayed all night and into Saturday until du Plessis received the baptism of the Holy Spirit, experienced holy laughter, and began speaking in tongues. He was later ordained an Assemblies of God minister.

Like most early Pentecostals, du Plessis expected throngs of Christians to leave the theologically bankrupt historic churches for the new Pentecostal fellowships. But a further conversion awaited du Plessis. Recognizing his earlier attitude as harsh and critical, he began accepting other Christians with love and humility.

After moving with his family to the United States after World War II, du Plessis approached the World Council of Churches headquarters in New York in 1952. An open-hearted Pentecostal fascinated the council's leadership. They quickly embraced du Plessis and began referring to him as "Mr. Pentecost." He attended every major meeting of the council from that time until age forced his retirement. Du Plessis was also an official observer at the Second Vatican Council (see #135). When Roman Catholics, Anglicans, and others began experiencing the baptism of the Holy Spirit, he encouraged them to remain in their churches and interpreted the Pentecostal witness to church leaders. The result was a spiritual revitalization of the historic churches usually known as "charismatic renewal." The Assemblies of God revoked du Plessis's ordination in 1962, but restored it in 1979.

Du Plessis spent his final years teaching at the Fuller Theological Seminary in California, a major Protestant evangelical institution. As a key figure in both the growth of Pentecostalism and ecumenical dialogues, he participated in the two most significant Christian movements of the twentieth century.

"Lord, they're enemies." Then love them. "How can I love people that I don't agree with?" Forgive them. "I can't justify them." I never gave any child of mine authority to justify anyone. I gave you full authority to forgive them. That's all you have. —David Du Plessis

What changes must occur for someone to forgive those who have rejected him?

144
Dietrich Bonhoeffer

Born 1906, in Wroclaw, Poland
Died 1945, in Flossenbürg, Germany

Dietrich Bonhoeffer was a gifted theologian, seemingly destined for a distinguished academic career. But for Bonhoeffer, knowing the truth was not enough; one must also live the truth.

When Adolf Hitler came to power in 1933 and the German church fell under state control, Bonhoeffer helped found the Confessing Church, which staunchly opposed the Nazi regime, and headed its underground seminary. In 1937 he published *The Cost of Discipleship*, an extended meditation on the Sermon on the Mount that attacked "cheap grace," the dispensing of divine favor without moral commitment.

Bonhoeffer declined opportunities to flee Germany for an academic post abroad, remaining home to work in the resistance movement. In his *Ethics*, written during this time, he rejected passivity and advocated taking the risk to confront evil directly.

In 1940, Bonhoeffer took part in a plot to assassinate Hitler. When this was discovered, he was arrested and imprisoned. Letters and papers written during his confinement were smuggled out of the prison and later published. They contain tantalizing hints of a future "religionless Christianity," an idea Bonhoeffer could not develop because the Nazis hung him on April 8, 1945, two weeks before the U.S. Army liberated his concentration camp.

Cheap grace is the deadly enemy of our church. We are fighting today for costly grace. Cheap grace is the grace we bestow on ourselves. Cheap grace is the preaching of forgiveness without requiring repentance, baptism without church discipline, Communion without confession, absolution without personal confession. Cheap grace is grace without discipleship, grace without the cross, grace without Jesus Christ, living and incarnate. —Dietrich Bonhoeffer

Silence in the face of evil is itself evil: God will not hold us guiltless. Not to speak is to speak. Not to act is to act. —Dietrich Bonhoeffer

Only he who believes is obedient and only he who is obedient believes. —Dietrich Bonhoeffer

To endure the cross is not tragedy; it is the suffering which is the fruit of an exclusive allegiance to Jesus Christ. —Dietrich Bonhoeffer

Who am I? They mock me, these lonely questions of mine. Whoever I am, thou knowest, O God, I am thine. —Dietrich Bonhoeffer

Where today is "cheap grace" offered?

145
Hasan al-Banna

Born 1906, in Mahmoudiyah, Egypt
Died 1949, in Cairo, Egypt

The election of Muhammad Morsi as president of Egypt in 2012 brought to power, albeit briefly, a Sunni Muslim reform movement suppressed for most of its eighty-four-year history.

The Muslim Brotherhood was founded in 1928 by a school teacher and preacher named Hasan al-Banna and six friends. The British had administered Egypt since 1882. Grieved over the poverty of his fellow countrymen when nearby British nationals lived comfortably, Al-Banna sought to restore Egyptian independence and prosperity through a renewed commitment to a strict, conservative Islam.

Al-Banna felt Muslims had abandoned their spiritual roots. He was a gifted organizer, promoter, and communicator, forging a united organization out of scattered malcontents. Within a decade the Brotherhood claimed half a million members, from all levels of Egyptian society, with branches in every Egyptian province, and hundreds of thousands of sympathizers extending far beyond Egypt. It built and ran schools, clinics, hospitals, and factories paying good wages.

At first the Muslim Brotherhood promoted Islam peacefully, against Christian missionaries and Western secularism. But in the 1930s Al-Banna led the movement into violent protest, supporting the Nazis in World War II. After the war, the partition of Palestine forcibly removed two-thirds of Palestinians from land that had been theirs for 1,300 years. This was felt as a lacerating injustice. The Brotherhood provided thousands of soldiers in the 1948 Arab-Israeli War, which the Arabs lost decisively.

Al-Banna and the Brotherhood saw the Egyptian government as complicit with the West in perpetuating these atrocities, and after Cairo's chief of police was assassinated in 1948, the Brotherhood was banned, its assets seized, and its leaders jailed. "When words are banned, hands make their move," Al-Banna said. A Brotherhood member assassinated Egyptian prime minister Noqrashi Pasha later that year. Two months later, Al-Banna himself was gunned down in the street.

Islam performs two tasks: First, it molds individuals into a new shape based on the faith and noble human qualities; then, using these people as building blocks, it establishes righteous, God-focused communities. —Hasan al-Banna

Islam is a faith and a nation. Unlike nations based on land, the nation of Islam is based on brotherhood in faith and is therefore far stronger and more meaningful than the former. —Hasan al-Banna

Under what circumstances, if any, would you resort to violence to promote ethical, spiritual, or religious goals?

146
Mother Teresa

Born 1910, in Skopje, Macedonia
Died 1997, in Kolkata, India

Agnes Gonxha Bojaxhiu's father died when she was eight. She was reared by her mother, a devout Roman Catholic who welcomed the destitute of Skopje to dine at her table, explaining to her daughter, "Some of them are our relatives, but all of them are our people." Agnes joined the Sisters of Loretto at eighteen, taking the name Teresa, and taught for seventeen years at the order's school in Kolkata.

Mother Teresa felt drawn to the destitute outside the school's walls. In 1948, with no funds, she started an open-air school for their children and a home for the dying in a run-down building. Two years later, she founded her own order, the Missionaries of Charity, with twelve other women. They ministered to Kolkata's poorest, giving them medical care and a dignity most had never known. When they died, Christians, Muslims, and Hindus were each afforded the burial rite prescribed by their faith. "A beautiful death is for people who lived like animals to die like angels—loved and wanted," Mother Teresa said. In 1955, she opened a home for orphans.

Mother Teresa was awarded the 1979 Nobel Peace Prize. At her death, the Missionaries of Charity had grown to over 4,000 nuns in 610 locations in 123 countries on every continent. Some criticized her for opposing contraception and disregarding Western medical practices.

When Mother Teresa's private letters were published in 2003, the world learned that for nearly fifty years she had struggled with profound doubt, sensing no divine presence either in her heart or in worship. "Where is my faith?" she wrote. "I feel nothing but emptiness and darkness." These revelations made some people feel closer to Mother Teresa than ever before.

Loneliness and the feeling of being unwanted is the most terrible poverty.
—Mother Teresa

We ourselves feel that what we are doing is just a drop in the ocean. But the ocean would be less because of that missing drop. —Mother Teresa

When we die and it comes time for God to judge us, he will not ask, "How many good things have you done in your life?" Rather he will ask, "How much love did you put into what you did?" —Mother Teresa

Compare Mother Teresa's way of expressing love to yours.

147
Thomas Merton

Born 1915, in Prades, France
Died 1968, in Bangkok, Thailand

Thomas Merton spent the first twenty-six years of his life being shuffled from one relative to another and then wandering and searching for he knew not what. When he arrived at a Trappist monastery in central Kentucky in 1941, he knew he was where he belonged.

Although Merton joined the Trappist order, he was hardly the typical Trappist. Trappists value silence, and that's what Merton sought. But his 1948 autobiography *The Seven Storey Mountain* was such a sensation that a steady parade of admirers sought him out. Moreover, Merton continued to write books and articles, led retreats, delivered lectures, and carried on correspondence with hundreds of people. He fell out with his superior at the monastery and eventually took up residence in a hermitage located on the grounds but removed from the monastery itself.

For all that, however, Merton craved solitude. For him solitude was not silence or merely being alone. He sought relief from "that inner dialogue with self that is a jumble of frivolous thoughts, worrisome cares, and negative feelings" that leave no room in the soul for God. Solitude was detachment from worldly concerns, leading to true humility and compassion.

Merton distinguished between the "false self" and the "true self." The false self is the self we fancy ourselves to be and that we show to the world. It is addicted to the ways of the world and driven to succeed. The true self is the self God calls us to become, unique to each person but always in union with God, one another, and the creation. We are unable to abandon our false self—only God can deliver us from it through an act of grace, "the sanctifying energy of God acting dynamically in our life."

As he grew older, Merton became increasingly engaged with the struggle for justice and peace in the world, living out his solitude in the midst of the world rather than in isolation from it. At fifty-three, he was accidentally electrocuted in Bangkok where he had traveled to learn of Eastern spirituality and enter into conversation with Buddhist monks.

My life is a listening. His is a speaking. My salvation is to hear and respond. For this, my life must be silent. Hence, my silence is my salvation.
—Thomas Merton

What is the noise that afflicts your soul? How do you seek relief from it?

148
Maharishi Mahesh Yogi

Born 1917 (?), in Jabalpur, India (?)
Died 2008, in Vlodrop, Netherlands

Maharishi Mahesh Yogi developed Transcendental Meditation and introduced it to the world. He became wealthy, entertained the Beatles and other celebrities who looked to him for spiritual guidance, and was often shown on television giggling while seated on a deerskin, cross-legged in a lotus position. He became known as the "Giggling Guru." Skeptics have dismissed him as a fake, a cultist, or a joke.

But millions of people worldwide have found serenity and a happier life in Transcendental Meditation (or TM, a trademarked designation for the practice). TM seeks to put one in touch with absolute reality, leading to happiness or bliss. Happiness, the Maharishi said, is everyone's birthright and the purpose of life is to find happiness. This can be done, he said, without retreating from everyday relationships and duties.

After earning a degree in physics in 1942, the Maharishi served as administrative assistant and secretary to a prominent Hindu master. In 1955 he began touring India to teach what he said was a traditional version of yoga (see #16). He began calling it Transcendental Meditation. The technique was simple: go into seclusion and meditate while repeating a mantra with eyes closed for twenty minutes twice each day. This brings relaxation, relief from stress, clear thinking, and inner happiness. The Maharishi said there was no need to issue moral directives because TM produced a state of mind leading to harmonious living without codes of conduct.

The Maharishi's influence sky-rocketed when he visited America in 1959. In 1971, he established the Maharishi University of Management in Fairfield, Iowa, an accredited university offering degrees in traditional subjects with an emphasis on developing knowledge of oneself. The Maharishi was a gifted promoter and businessman. He toured the world thirteen times and conducted training sessions in fifty countries.

The Maharishi wrote over twenty books. The best known is *Science of Being and Art of Living*, a philosophical treatise promoting ancient Hindu devotional practices, especially TM, in terms readily understood by educated Westerners.

> *Like the air, God's grace is available to us. It is permeating every fiber of Being and . . . the entire universe. When we take our attention to that Being . . . we establish ourselves on the level of God's grace. Immediately we just enjoy. Life is Bliss!* —Maharishi Mahesh Yogi

Is attaining happiness life's highest purpose?

149
Ajahn Chah

Born 1918, in Ubon Rajathani, Thailand
Died 1992, in Ubon Rajathani, Thailand

Buddhism may have reached Thailand in the third century BCE, brought by missionaries commissioned by the Emperor Ashoka (see #17). The conservative, monastic Theravada tradition quickly took root in the country.

Thai monks developed a rigorous form of meditation known as the Thai Forest Tradition. Practitioners spend extended periods in the forest, often alone, ignoring cobras and wild animals, seeking liberation by concentrating on the impermanence of ordinary things. The most renowned of these monks is Chah Subhaddo, everywhere known by the honorific title Ajahn (Thai for teacher).

Ajahn Chah took monastic vows at the age of twenty-one. He learned Pali in order to read classic Theravada texts (See #28, #39) but failed to find the insight he sought. Searching elsewhere, he met Ajahn Mun, a monk seeking to revive the Thai Forest Tradition. Ajahn Mun recommended that Ajahn Chah practice a simple form of mindfulness by concentrating on his breathing.

Ajahn Chah then began spending weeks meditating alone in the jungle, which eventually led to an awakening and his return to his native town. There he founded a monastery and began to attract disciples. Buddhist seekers from the United States eventually sought him out, learned his meditation techniques, and founded monasteries in the United States. Ajahn Chah began to travel the globe, leading retreats and seminars. His teachings were known for their humor and lack of technical jargon. He spent the last ten years of his life bedridden and unable to speak, accepting his condition as testimony to the impermanence of material things.

The breathing meditation practiced by Ajahn Chah involves sitting in the lotus position—legs folded beneath the body, hands resting in the lap—and concentrating on the rhythm of one's breath. Calm, regular breathing indicates calmness of mind. Other thoughts, distractions, and feelings are not fought, but acknowledged and then quietly let go. Many people today, including Christians and New Age seekers, are drawn to this form of meditation.

When we see beyond self, we no longer cling to happiness. And when we stop clinging, we can begin to be happy. —Ajahn Chah

Letting go a little brings a little peace. Letting go a lot brings a lot of peace. Letting go completely brings complete peace. —Ajahn Chah

Imagine meditating alone for a week in the woods. What kinds of insights would you expect?

150
Billy Graham

Born 1918, in Charlotte, North Carolina

"Someone here tonight is carrying a great burden that needs to be lifted. Somewhere in this stadium is a soul struggling to be free. You know who you are. I'm going to ask you now to come. . . ."

Evangelist Billy Graham has repeated those or similar words for over half a century, thousands of times, in stadiums and amphitheaters all over the world. Countless streams of people have walked forward in response to such an invitation to give their lives to Christ. Graham's method is a version of the altar call that has been part of the American holiness and evangelical tradition since the eighteenth century. Conversion to Christ is the goal. Graham's own conversion occurred at the age of sixteen, in response to an evangelist named Mordecai Hamm.

Graham understands conversion to have three components: repentance, faith, and new birth. While distinguishable, these three usually occur instantaneously and simultaneously, Graham says. Repentance is the negative realization that the sinner has rebelled against God and cut herself off from God; faith is the positive turning to Christ as Savior. Both are active, requiring that one accept the truth and make a decision. The third component of conversion, new birth, is passive—it is the work of the Holy Spirit.

Like John Calvin (see #100), Graham affirms the absolute sovereignty of God and that salvation is the work of God alone. But in his preaching, he emphasizes the moment of individual decision. When questioned about this, Graham says the relationship between divine sovereignty and human free will must forever remain a mystery.

Aware that many evangelists have committed sexual or financial improprieties, Graham has never allowed himself to be alone with a woman other than his wife, Ruth, and has insisted on open financial accountability. His salary has never been keyed to offerings received in response to his preaching.

Some conservatives have faulted Graham for associating with liberal Christians, while some liberals have accused him of ignoring the great social issues of his day. But hundreds of thousands of Christians, of many theological persuasions, can point to a Billy Graham crusade as the beginning of their intentional commitment to Christ.

Conversion can take many forms. The way it is accomplished depends largely upon the individual—his temperament, his emotional balance, his environment, and his previous conditioning and way of life. —Billy Graham

Is a religious conversion necessary for everyone?

151
Malcolm X

Born 1925, in Omaha, Nebraska
Died 1965, in New York, New York

Malcolm Little was raised by his widowed mother, along with ten siblings, in Lansing, Michigan. At fifteen, he moved to Massachusetts to live with his half-sister Ella. There Malcolm worked as a shoeshine boy at the Roseland State Ballroom, where he was introduced to big band music and the criminal underworld. Two years later, in New York City, he held odd jobs during the day and spent his nights dealing drugs, gambling, racketeering, robbing, and pimping. At twenty, Malcolm was apprehended and imprisoned.

While incarcerated, Malcolm taught himself to read and write. He transcribed the entire dictionary by hand and read widely. Through the influence of his siblings, Malcolm also embraced the Nation of Islam, an unorthodox expression of the faith, while in prison. Paroled in 1952, he turned his back on his former life and adopted an uncompromising moral code. He changed his last name to X since his true last name had been lost when his ancestors were forcibly removed from Africa.

The Nation of Islam teaches that white people are a genetically altered, satanic race inferior to blacks and that the repressive white culture will soon collapse. It seeks justice for blacks through a separate, independent state for black people. Malcolm X began preaching this doctrine and was named head of the Nation of Islam's tiny Harlem temple. A captivating orator, he addressed huge rallies in Harlem and throughout America, quickly becoming his faith's most renowned spokesman. The movement's rapid expansion in the 1950s and 1960s was largely due to him.

But a second conversion awaited Malcolm. In 1964 he made a pilgrimage to Mecca where he was stunned to see Muslims of every color, rank, and nationality worshiping together. Upon his return, he broke with the Nation of Islam, embraced orthodox Sunni Islam, and, while continuing to attack the racism of white America, began preaching a message of inclusiveness and reconciliation.

Agents of the Nation of Islam assassinated Malcolm as he addressed a rally in Harlem on February 21, 1965. Since then, the Nation of Islam has drawn somewhat closer to orthodox Islam, though it still seeks a separate, racially based state.

The Autobiography of Malcolm X, written with Alex Haley and completed weeks before Malcolm's death, is a classic text.

Why would a member of an oppressed minority race endorse racial segregation rather than racial integration?

152
Thich Nhat Hanh
Born 1926, in Tha Tien, Vietnam

During the past century Buddhism has produced several major figures who combine the faith's traditional emphasis on meditation and mindfulness with an activism in worldly affairs. Prominent among them is the Vietnamese Zen master Thich Nhat Hanh, who coined the term "Engaged Buddhism," seeking through inner transformation to effect change in individuals and society at large.

Nhat Hanh was ordained a monk in 1942. In 1960 he spent two years studying and teaching world religions in the United States. Upon his return to Vietnam, while faithfully practicing the discipline of mindfulness, he also began working to meet the needs of war victims and to challenge unjust social structures. His School of Youth for Social Service, founded in 1964, trained and deployed over ten thousand young people to rebuild villages bombed by American warplanes. They created schools, hospitals, resettlement programs, and agricultural cooperatives, all the while upholding a strict code of nonviolence.

In 1966, Nhat Hanh traveled to the United States again, to ask President Lyndon Johnson for a cease-fire. While there, he met with Dr. Martin Luther King Jr. (see #156), who became the first American civil rights leader publicly to oppose the Vietnamese War. In 1969, Nhat Hanh led a group of Buddhists who participated in the Paris peace talks.

Also in 1966, Nhat Hanh established the Order of Interbeing to teach detachment and the interconnectedness and impermanence of all things. A printed page, for example, depends on a tree, which depended on rain and the sun—everything is interdependent. The order now has approximately 1,500 members, mostly laypeople, in Vietnam, Europe, and the United States.

Forbidden by Vietnam's Communist government from reentering the country after the Paris Peace Accords were signed in 1973, Nhat Hanh relocated to Bordeaux in France, where he founded what is today Europe's largest Buddhist community and where he leads retreats. Fluent in seven languages, Nhat Hanh has written a hundred books. He was permitted to return to his native land in 2005.

The seed of suffering in you may be strong, but don't wait until you have no more suffering before allowing yourself to be happy. —Thich Nhat Hanh

For things to reveal themselves to us, we need to be ready to abandon our views about them. —Thich Nhat Hanh

What is the key to finding happiness amidst suffering?

153
Sivaya Subramuniya

Born 1927, in Oakland, California
Died 2001, in Kapaa, Hawaii

A tall, stately man with snow-white hair, Sivaya Subramuniya brought Hinduism into the modern age by founding the magazine *Hinduism Today*, posting on the web a free daily summary of news pertinent to Hindus, urging friends and followers to learn to use Apple computers, and suggesting that tithes be payable by credit card.

But modern technology wasn't Subramuniya's only interest. He was thoroughly grounded in traditional Hindu values and devotion and saw modern technology as a tool to promote spirituality.

Although a renowned dancer in San Francisco at age nineteen, Subramuniya longed to go to India. Arriving on a freighter just before his twenty-first birthday, he spent three years searching for a spiritual mentor, mainly in Ceylon (now Sri Lanka), staying at times in Buddhist temples. After a time of meditation and fasting in a cave, Subramuniya had a powerful mystical encounter which he experienced as his enlightenment. Only then did he find the mentor he sought, who told him to return to America, which he did in 1949.

Upon his return, Subramuniya spent seven more years in yogic meditation. In 1957 he began teaching in San Francisco and founded there what is thought to be the first Hindu temple in America, the first of some three dozen temples and missions he founded around the world. Subramuniya lauched the Himalayan Academy in San Francisco in 1965, offering classes, lectures, retreats, and home study courses. In 1970, he relocated to the Hawaiian island of Kauai, founding a monastery on 458 acres. It remained his home until his death.

Subramuniya's Hinduism was of the Shaivite variety (see #48), but like all Hindus, he recognized the validity of other expressions of the faith and sought, through the pages of *Hinduism Today* and his thirty books, to give voice to Hindus and urge unified efforts to promote the faith in the West. During the Sri Lankan civil war in the 1980s, he spearheaded relief efforts for the island's Hindu minority and helped many to relocate.

> [The] great strength [of one practicing disciplined meditation] is humility,
> a shock absorber for the malicious experiences in life. Humility makes one
> immune to resentment and places everything in proportion and balance
> within the mind. —Sivaya Subramuniya

What is the connection between humility and the ability to absorb "the malicious experiences of life"?

154
Elie Wiesel

Born 1928, in Sighetu Marmatiei, Romania

Born to a devout Jewish family, the young Elie Wiesel had a genuine if conventional faith, assuming God would protect his chosen people, the ominous rumors from central Europe notwithstanding. But in May 1944, the German army deported Elie and his family to the Auschwitz concentration camp. His mother and younger sister perished in captivity and Elie watched as his beloved father, already weak from dysentery and malnutrition, entered the crematorium. Elie Wiesel himself would survive the death camps (he spent time in three over a period of eleven months), but neither he nor his faith in God would ever be the same.

For ten years after the war, Wiesel worked as a journalist in France, writing not one word about the death camps. But a Roman Catholic priest urged him to write about them, and when he finally began to do so, the words flowed and have not stopped flowing. Wiesel has written several dozen books, fiction and nonfiction, reflecting on his experiences, probing the Bible, and peering into philosophical enigmas. He has received dozens of awards and honorary degrees, including the 1986 Nobel Peace Prize.

Wiesel's best known book is his first, called *Night*. Graphic in detail, it is a narrative of terrifying inhumanity and torture. The incarcerated teenager accuses God of cruelty. Had God turned his back on his people? Should Wiesel turn his back on God? Could he forgive God? No painful question is unasked and no easy answers are received. Wiesel's has been the leading voice among post-war Jews seeking to come to terms with the Holocaust.

> *Never shall I forget that night, the first night in camp, which has turned my life into one long night. . . . Never shall I forget those moments which murdered my God and my soul and turned my dreams to dust. Never shall I forget these things, even if I am condemned to live as long as God Himself. Never.* —Elie Wiesel

> *The opposite of love is not hate, it's indifference. The opposite of art is not ugliness, it's indifference. The opposite of faith is not heresy, it's indifference. And the opposite of life is not death, it's indifference.* —Elie Wiesel

> *Because of indifference, one dies before one actually dies.* —Elie Wiesel

Is indifference the chief obstacle to faithful living?

155
Hans Küng

Born 1928, in Sursee, Switzerland

Mutual respect among different faiths was rare in the West until the World Parliament of Religions in Chicago in 1893 (see #124). Marking the centennial of that event, over eight thousand spiritual and religious leaders from across the world gathered again in Chicago in 1993, seeking to understand one another, celebrate what they had in common, and work together for shared goals.

The tone for the meeting was set by Swiss Roman Catholic theologian Hans Küng, principal author of *Towards a Global Ethic: An Initial Declaration*, a document signed at the parliament by over two hundred leaders representing over forty traditions. It commits its signers to nonviolence and respect for life, a just economic order, respect for differing viewpoints, truthfulness, and equality of the sexes.

Küng had already earned a reputation for questioning his own tradition and seriously engaging other traditions. He had publicly rejected papal infallibility in 1971, for which his license to teach as a Roman Catholic theologian was revoked (though he was not excommunicated). He had served as a theological advisor at Vatican II (see #135) and has since deplored his church's retreat from the reforms endorsed there.

Küng sees himself as both a Christian and a humanist and has a pluralistic understanding of truth. "We all may continue along our own proven way to salvation, but should grant that others can likewise attain salvation through their religions," he has said.

In recent years, Küng has explored the spiritual implications of quantum physics and neuroscience and advocated assisted suicide for those with irreversible terminal illnesses. At eighty-seven, Küng suffers from Parkinson's disease and has said, "I do not want to live on as a shadow of myself."

I believe in God, origin and primal meaning of all things. I understand faith here in the full and radical sense. I do not just believe that God exists; I do not just believe God, believe his words, but I believe in God, put my whole unconditional and irrevocable trust in him. —Hans Küng

The essence of Christianity is not something abstract and dogmatic, some general teaching, but has always been a living historical figure: Jesus of Nazareth. . . . A Christian is rather someone who . . . makes an effort to orientate himself or herself practically on this Jesus Christ. No more is required. —Hans Küng

Can more than one religion be true?

156
Martin Luther King Jr.

Born 1929, in Atlanta, Georgia
Died 1968, in Memphis, Tennessee

Martin Luther King Jr. enjoyed a loving, secure up-bringing. His father was a Baptist pastor and his mother the daughter of one. When King also entered seminary, he proved to be an outstanding scholar and student leader.

In 1954, at the age of twenty-five, King became pastor of Dexter Avenue Baptist Church in Montgomery, Alabama, and although new to the community, was asked to lead a boycott of the city's racially segregated bus system. He agreed, and after 382 days, the buses were integrated and the boycott ended.

King and others organized the Southern Christian Leadership Conference in 1957 to galvanize black Southern churches to work for racial justice. Dozens of sit-ins and marches followed. King was beaten and jailed. Intimidation, harassment, and threats on King's life were almost daily events. On August 28, 1963, 250,000 support-ers marched on Washington and King delivered his famous "I have a dream" speech envisioning a day when all people would live as brothers and sisters. He was awarded the Nobel Peace Prize that year.

As the nation reeled with news of beatings, bombings, and assassinations, public opinion turned. The U. S. Congress passed the Civil Rights Act in 1964 and the Vot-ing Rights Act in 1965, effectively ending legalized racial discrimination in America.

Through it all, King insisted that the best and most Christian tactic against injus-tice was nonviolent opposition. He was guided by Jesus's Sermon on the Mount and what he had learned of Mohandas Gandhi (see #127) on a 1959 trip to India.

In the mid-1960s, an increasingly wearied King expanded his concerns to include poverty and the Vietnam War, which he saw as integrally related to racial inequality. He was killed on April 4, 1968, by an assassin's bullet while seeking to organize city sanitation workers in Memphis, Tennessee.

Faith is taking the first step even when you don't see the whole staircase.
—Martin Luther King Jr.

Nothing in the world is more dangerous than sincere ignorance and conscientious stupidity. —Martin Luther King Jr.

I have a dream that my four little children will one day live in a nation where they will not be judged by the color of their skin, but by the content of their character. —Martin Luther King Jr.

Is violence ever useful in the struggle for justice?

157
Anne Frank

Born 1929, in Frankfurt am Main, Germany
Died 1945, in the Bergen-Belsen Concentration
Camp, Germany

Anne Frank was not a religious leader. She died too young to have been a leader of anything. But she possessed a deep spiritual sensibility, and as a well-known victim of the Holocaust, she represents the six million Jews, religious and otherwise, who perished in the Nazi death camps.

After Adolf Hitler's party won control of the Frankfurt municipal council in 1933, Anne Frank's father, Otto, a prosperous businessman, took his family to Amsterdam, where they enjoyed a few years of relative peace until the German army overran the Netherlands in 1940. Two years later, with Jews disappearing by the day, the Frank family of four went into hiding in a small "secret annex" behind Otto Frank's place of business. Friends secretly cared for the Franks for two years until an unknown person betrayed them. They were arrested and sent to Auschwitz and then to Bergen-Belsen. Anne Frank spent nine months in captivity, growing bald and emaciated, until she died in a cold, rat-infested infirmary, a few weeks before British troops liberated the camp. She was fifteen years old.

Anne had kept a diary during the family's time in hiding. Found and published after the war, it has become a popular classic. In fluent prose and with disarming candor, Anne tells of hiding in cramped, dark quarters, including strained family relationships and her alternating moods of despair, resignation, and hope. The diary reveals a teenage girl of courage and grace, clinging to faith in a good God. The act of writing seemed to console her.

Anne's arrest ended her diary, so no one knows how incarceration affected her and her budding faith, but survivors of Bergen-Belsen recalled that though lonely and often tearful, she was a strong and courageous presence.

It's God who has caused us to be as we are, but it's also God who will lift us up again. In the eyes of the world, we're doomed, but if, after all this suffering, there are still Jews left, the Jewish people will be held up as an example. Who knows, maybe our religion will teach the world and all the people in it about goodness. That's the reason, the only reason, we have to suffer. —Anne Frank

Despite everything, I believe that people are really good at heart. —Anne Frank

Are people "really good at heart"?

158
Desmond Tutu

Born 1931, in Klerksdorp, South Africa

The white supremacist government in South Africa began imposing apartheid (apartness) on the nation's black natives—80 percent of the population—in 1948. Natives were herded into "reserves" comprising just 13 percent of the country and were forbidden to travel elsewhere without a government permit. Their homes were bulldozed and homes for whites were built on their land. Black men were forced to work apart from their families for eleven months out of the year. Potentially fatal diseases were intentionally introduced into native neighborhoods.

Desmond Tutu had been a school teacher, but when teaching native children to read was forbidden, he turned to the church as an arena where he could work for justice. Tutu was ordained in 1960. At first he was not politically active, but eventually he began openly agitating for the end of apartheid.

In 1978 Tutu was named General Secretary of the South African Council of Churches. Testifying in 1982 before a government commission investigating the alleged Communist infiltration of the council, he said it was not the council that was on trial, but Christian faith, and that the God of the Bible was subversive to every system of injustice.

Tutu was awarded the Nobel Peace Prize in 1984 and became Anglican archbishop of Cape Town in 1985. The South African government forbade him to travel abroad and sought to silence him, but given his prominent position, they dared not arrest him.

The government announced the end of apartheid in 1990. Newly elected president Nelson Mandela named Tutu chair of the country's Truth and Reconciliation Commission. Under Tutu's guidance, the commission neither pretended that apartheid had not happened nor sought to punish its perpetrators, but created forums where victim and perpetrator alike could tell their stories—provided they told the truth. The telling and listening to these human stories had a cathartic, healing effect on the entire country.

Tutu sees all people as interconnected and interdependent. In recent years, he has sharply criticized the native-led South African government for corruption and failing to address the poverty of its citizens. His continuing efforts for peace and reconciliation have spanned the world. Tutu has worked with and spoken out for Palestinian refugees, AIDS victims, gays, Tibetans, women, and many other marginalized people.

A self-sufficient human being is subhuman. . . . God has made us so that we will need each other. —Desmond Tutu

Is striving for self-sufficiency a subhuman pursuit?

159
The Dalai Lama

Born 1935, in Taktser, Tibet (China)

Tibet's spiritual leader bears the title Dalai Lama (Ocean of Wisdom). The current Dalai Lama, whose actual name is Tenzin Gyatso, is only the four-teenth in a line going back seven centuries. He is one of the world's best known, and certainly its longest serving, spiritual leader.

When a Dalai Lama dies, his successor is not elected or appointed, but discovered in infancy through prayerful discernment by other Buddhist scholars. He is then reared in a monastery and educated in Buddhist teachings until he is of age to assume his responsibilities.

Since the fifth Dalai Lama in the seventeenth century, the Dalai Lama has often exercised both spiritual and political authority in Tibet. That is not true today. The current Dalai Lama does not even live in Tibet. He became Tibet's head of state in 1950, at the age of fifteen, following the Chinese invasion of the country. When efforts to preserve Tibetan autonomy failed, Tibetans rebelled in 1959. China suppressed the rebellion and the Dalai Lama fled the country. Granted asylum in neighboring India, he set up a government-in-exile and founded schools to teach Tibetan Buddhism, language, and culture to Tibetan expatriates. The Dalai Lama continues to embody the hope of Tibetans worldwide for the restoration of a free Tibet.

The Dalai Lama has engaged people in many fields around the world. He has consulted other religious and spiritual leaders, seeking common ground with their faiths. One need not convert to Buddhism to gain from Buddhist teachings, he says. He discourages conversions until one has thoroughly explored one's own tradition.

The interface between science and faith is another of the Dalai Lama's interests. He has met with physicists and biologists to explore how modern science and Buddhist meditation methods shed light on each other.

And then there is world peace. The Dalai Lama won the 1989 Nobel Peace Prize for his nonviolent resistance to Chinese rule in Tibet and is known the world over for his gentle humor and winning smile. "My religion is kindness," he says.

If you want others to be happy, practice compassion. If you want to be happy, practice compassion. —the Dalai Lama

I do not judge the universe. —the Dalai Lama

In the practice of tolerance, one's enemy is the best teacher. —the Dalai Lama

Is compassion alone enough?

160

Rosemary Radford Ruether

Born 1936, in Saint Paul, Minnesota

Until modern times, virtually every spiritual tradition on earth has largely overlooked the experience and insights of women and forbidden or discouraged women from exercising leadership. Rosemary Radford Ruether is not only a notable exception to this (she is a theological scholar of the first rank), but she has challenged in her writing the rationale for male dominance in spiritual and religious life.

Ruether identifies with the Hebrew prophets, Jesus, the Protestant reformers, and figures often dismissed as heretics, who challenged the established religious practices of their day, seeking to reclaim forgotten or marginalized parts of the tradition. She speaks of an oppressive "patriarchy" that denies the full humanity not only of women, but of men as well. Women's experience, she says, is typically less fractious and competitive, more unifying and conciliatory than that of men. Unlike secular feminists who reject institutional religion, Ruether sees the Christian church as possibly the "avant-garde of liberated humanity."

Ruether's Jesus is an earthy, this-worldly figure far removed from the metaphysical Christ of the Christian creeds. She sees Jesus as a countercultural iconoclast who rebukes the secular and religious authorities of his day. He is a social revolutionary who would make the last first and the first last. Ruether also rejects exclusively male images of God, preferring the admittedly awkward term "God-ess" which combines masculine and feminine terminology while retaining the idea that God is One.

Ruether seeks more than to advance the cause of women. She rejects other forms of chauvinism as well, including making white Westerners the norm of humanity and human beings the center of creation. She sides with marginalized people of all sorts—the poor, African-Americans, Jews, Palestinians, gays, and laypeople in her Roman Catholic Church.

Ruether begins her search for truth with human experience, not with sacred texts or church dogma. Nor is she averse to incorporating into her thought insights from long-rejected traditions like ancient Canaanite religion and Christian heresies (which she calls "dissenting voices"). Anything that liberates the human spirit, she affirms; anything that suppresses it, she rejects.

It is blasphemous to use the image and name of the Holy to justify patriarchal domination. —Rosemary Radford Ruether

How would things be different if Ruether's ideas were fully implemented?

161
Aung San Suu Kyi

Born 1945, in Yangon, Myanmar

Aung San Suu Kyi's story has all the features of a blockbuster movie—true love, sacrifice, an ordinary woman given an extraordinary mission, and—possibly—a stirring triumph in the end.

Reared by her mother in Burma (now Myanmar) and then educated abroad, Suu Kyi was happily married to an Oxford professor and rearing their two sons in 1988 when she returned to Burma to care for her critically ill mother. She expected to return shortly to her family—but she would never see her husband again.

The military had ruled Myanmar with an iron fist for twenty-six years, reducing it from Asia's wealthiest country to one of its poorest. Finally, in 1988, a student-led uprising ensued. Visiting her mother in the hospital, Suu Kyi found hundreds of wounded, dying students shot by the military. The rebels appealed to Suu Kyi, whose father had been a hero of Burmese independence in 1947. Despite her devotion to her family, she agreed to remain in Burma and be their spokesperson.

Suu Kyi was arrested in 1989 and spent fifteen of the next twenty-one years under house arrest, unable to communicate with the outside world. The military would release her if she left Myanmar, but she knew they would never permit her to return. With her husband's strong support until his death in 1999, she remained under house arrest in Myanmar, a symbol of hope for millions of her fellow-countrymen. She was awarded the Nobel Peace Prize in 1991.

Suu Kyi embraces Engaged Buddhism (see #152) and once stood down a group of soldiers aiming loaded rifles at her. She says that Buddhist meditation strengthens her and calms her spirit. Compassion is the Buddhist principle she most admires and she is open to learning from other faiths as well. Suu Kyi's political strategy is nonviolent, modeled after Mohandas Gandhi (see #127) and Nelson Mandela.

In 2010, the military loosened its grip on Myanmar and freed Suu Kyi. In 2012, her party won forty-three of forty-five contested seats in parliamentary elections. If she is allowed to run, she will be a leading candidate for the presidency of Myanmar in 2015.

It is not power that corrupts, but fear. Fear of losing power corrupts those who wield it and fear of the scourge of power corrupts those who are subject to it.
—Aung San Suu Kyi

What corrupts? Power, fear, or something else?

162
Mata Amritanandamayi

Born 1953, in Parayakadavu, India

Mata Amritanandamayi has personally hugged over thirty million people. She travels the world, sitting for days as tens of thousands of people line up to receive an embrace and a few words of affection from her. After days of such activity, without a break, she still radiates serenity and seems energetic and rested. Mata Amritanandamayi is known as the "hugging saint" and is usually called simply Amma (Mother). Amma's touch conveys love and a sense of worth. She teaches and exemplifies divine qualities like compassion, patience, forgiveness, and self-control.

Even as a toddler, Amma adored and sang to the god Krishna (see #138). Her schooling ended at age nine when she began gathering scraps of food to feed her younger siblings. Amma began her ministry of hugging during those years and shared what little she scavenged with those even less fortunate.

Devotees often give her money. With these funds, Amma has built a university with several campuses and nearly twenty thousand students, hospitals providing free medical care to the destitute, homes for the homeless, schools to teach job skills and meditation, youth programs, homes for the elderly, and orphanages. No hint of impropriety has touched her, and the gifts continue to flow in.

Stymied by politics and red tape, the Indian government sometimes asks Amma for assistance. With a mere word, she mobilizes thousands of volunteers who organize and accomplish tasks like disaster relief and cleaning polluted sites. The reason, volunteers say, is that they trust Amma totally and that working with her affords them a satisfaction they find nowhere else.

> *I don't see if it is a man or a woman. I don't see anyone different from my own self. A continuous stream of love flows from me to all of creation. This is my inborn nature. The duty of a doctor is to treat patients. In the same way, my duty is to console those who are suffering.* —Mata Amritanandamayi

> *Attempting to change the world [completely] is like trying to straighten the curly tail of a dog. But society takes birth from people. So by affecting individuals, you can make changes in the society and, through it, in the world. You cannot change it, but you can make changes. . . . If you can touch people, you can touch the world.* — Mata Amritanandamayi

What's so special about a hug?

163
Tariq Ramadan

Born 1962, in Geneva, Switzerland

Born and reared in Switzerland after his parents had been exiled from Egypt, Tariq Ramadan is perhaps Islam's foremost spokesman for dialogue with the West. He is the grandson of Hasan al-Banna (see #145), and although he sounds like his grandfather at times, he can also sound light-years removed from him.

With degrees in philosophy, French literature, and Islamic studies, Ramadan now teaches at Oxford University. Like his grandfather, he rejects much of Western culture. Representative democracy, secular values, and confusing the roles of the sexes are dangerous, he says, and it is Western arrogance that assumes the rest of the world will someday fall in line behind the West in such matters. Western powers gave up their colonial empires only to engage in "ideological imperialism," he says.

He is also a harsh critic of American foreign policy, which he sees as driven by hubris, greed, naïveté, and the desire for power. He was particularly critical of the 2003 invasion of Iraq. From 2004 to 2010, the U.S. State Department denied Ramadan a visa to enter the country.

But Ramadan is not a theological or political absolutist—he has also been denied entry to Arab countires because of his opposition to autocratic governments. Ramadan advocates interreligious dialogue, theological humility, and the development of a distinctive "Western Islam" adapted to Western life. He refuses to divide the world into Muslim and non-Muslim communities because the Quran mentions no such division and says Muslims must adapt universal values and work for the good of non-Muslims.

Although Western culture can be unduly permissive, Ramadan says, it is not Islam's enemy because Muslims are not compelled to act contrary to their faith. The Quran, though authoritative, is to be interpreted in the light of the cultural norms of its time.

Tariq Ramadan has been called "the Muslim Martin Luther."

Humility is my table, respect is my garment, empathy is my food, and curiosity is my drink. As for love, it has a thousand names and is by my side at every window. —Tariq Ramadan

When you don't know who you are, you are scared of who you are not.
—Tariq Ramadan

Acknowledged differences may create mutual respect, but hazy misunderstandings bring forth nothing but prejudice and rejection.
—Tariq Ramadan

Compare and contrast Tariq Ramadan to Martin Luther (see #95).

Appendix

Hindus: 1, 16, 48, 56, 64, 70, 73, 75, 81, 113, 114, 121, 122, 124, 127, 129, 133, 136, 138, 148, 153, 162

Jews: 2, 4, 5, 6, 14, 19, 25, 27, 36, 62, 68, 76, 86, 107, 112, 132, 142, 154, 157

Buddhists: 11, 12, 13, 17, 28, 39, 41, 49, 54, 58, 67, 74, 77, 79, 82, 92, 136, 149, 152, 159, 161

Christians: 20, 21, 22, 23, 24, 26, 29, 31, 32, 33, 34, 35, 37, 38, 40, 42, 43, 63, 66, 71, 80, 84, 85, 88, 89, 91, 95, 96, 97, 98, 99, 100, 101, 103, 104, 105, 106, 108, 109, 111, 115, 116, 117, 118, 120, 123, 126, 128, 131, 134, 135, 137, 139, 140, 143, 144, 146, 147, 150, 155, 156, 158, 160

Muslims: 2, 4, 20, 44, 45, 46, 47, 50, 51, 52, 53, 55, 57, 59, 60, 61, 65, 69, 72, 78, 83, 87, 90, 102, 110, 141, 145, 151, 163

Others: 3, 7, 8, 9, 10, 15, 18, 30, 93, 94, 119, 125, 130